The Frontier of National Sovereignty

The Frontier of National Sovereignty

History and theory 1945–1992

Alan S. Milward, Frances M. B. Lynch,
Ruggero Ranieri, Federico Romero
and Vibeke Sørensen

London and New York

First published in 1993
by Routledge
11 New Fetter Lane, London EC4P 4EE

Simultaneously published in the USA and Canada
by Routledge
29 West 35th Street, New York, NY 10001

© 1993 Alan S. Milward, Frances M. B. Lynch, Ruggero
Ranieri, Federico Romero and Vibeke Sørensen

Typeset in 10/12 Times by Megaron, Cardiff, Wales
Printed in Great Britain by T. J. (Padstow) Press Ltd, Padstow,
Cornwall

British Library Cataloguing in Publication Data
Milward, Alan S.
　The Frontier of National Sovereignty : History
　and Theory, 1945–1992
　I. Title
320.15

Library of Congress Cataloging in Publication Data
The Frontier of National Sovereignty: history and theory,
1945–1992/ Alan S. Milward . . . [*et al.*].
　　p.　　cm.
Includes bibliographical references and index.
1.　Europe–Politics and government – 1945–.
2.　European Economic Community.
3.　Europe–Economic integration.
I. Milward, Alan S.
D843.F77　1993
940.55–dc20　　92–36702

ISBN 0-415-08892-5

Contents

Tables

Notes on the authors

Frances M. B. Lynch is lecturer in Economic History at the University of Manchester. She is currently completing a book on *The French Economy from National Recovery to European Integration*. She has published articles in *The Economic History Review, Revue Historique* and elsewhere.

Alan S. Milward is Professor of Economic History at the London School of Economics and Political Science. He is the author of several books on modern and contemporary history including *The Reconstruction of Western Europe* (1984) and *The European Rescue of the Nation State* (1992).

Ruggero Ranieri teaches European Studies and History at the University of Essex. He is completing a book on the post-war British and Italian steel industries and is the author of articles in *Passato e presente* and other journals.

Federico Romero is Associate Professor of History at the University of Bologna. He is the author of *Gli Stati Uniti e il sindacalismo europeo 1944–1951* (1989) and *Emigrazione e integrazione europea 1945–1973* (1991).

Vibeke Sørensen teaches international relations in the Department for the Interdisciplinary Study of International Organizations in the University of Groningen. She is currently completing a book on Danish foreign economic policies after 1947. She has published articles in *Co-operation and Conflict* and elsewhere.

Preface

This is a genuine book, planned and written as one coherent volume by several people. It is not a collection of conference papers. It is not a collection of articles rejected by journals. It is not a set of miscellaneous half-finished essays which never even made it to a journal editor. If Milward's name appears first in the list, that is only because he did all the secretarial work and copy-editing; intellectually everyone played an equal part in the book's genesis and writing and we have all commented freely on one another's work.

We set out to use history to answer questions which repeatedly recur in current political debate. What is the future of the nation? Will it be merged in a European federation? Will there be a common European government and currency? And if so, how many countries will it embrace? Or will the idea of European union and the Maastricht Treaty prove a failure? Would the European Community survive the failure of the European Union Treaty? Or will the whole structure collapse carrying Eurocrats and European Parliament alike into oblivion? We think history offers clearer, although not always decisive, answers to these questions than other subjects, such as economics or political science, which are usually used to answer them.

We have used history to derive a consistent theory of European integration. How did the European Community come about and why does it survive? These are questions which all sorts of people must from time to time ask themselves. Although there are well-founded histories of the negotiations which led to the early agreements on European integration, the answers to these questions are typically provided not from them but from theories of political behaviour, which aim also to predict what will happen. It seemed to us that these theories failed the crucial test; they did not correspond to the historical facts. We are not surprised therefore that their predictive force has been weak. We have used the historical evidence to construct a theory in accordance with historical reality, so that if people ask themselves what the future of national organization and of the European Community is they can turn to our book for what is at least a consistent way of working out the answers.

We derived our theory from existing historical accounts of the process of European integration, including our own. Out of the period in which a reasonably accurate history of the processes of integration and inter-dependence can be written we then selected certain topics as tests of the theory. They are taken from the history of France, usually thought of as the country which has been the driving force behind the formation of the European Community; of Denmark, which in 1992 suddenly, although as our study shows not surprisingly, brought the issue to a head; of the United Kingdom; and of Italy. At the end we have considered the questions arising from the standpoint of the dominant country in the international system, the United States. Discussion about the European Community is particularly ill informed and tendentious, on both sides of the argument, in the United Kingdom and we hope that this short book may lead to a better understanding there of what is involved. There is no member state however where, in our view, serious misconceptions are not prevalent, as they are within the Community's own administration too. We hope our work will remove them.

It might be interesting to know how we came to write it. The idea came to us about eight years ago. All were temporarily attached in different ways to the Department of History and Civilization of the European University Institute in Florence. The centre of social life there was a stuffy windowless attic whose two attractions were cheap alcohol and conversation. While outside the pitilessly cheerful Italian sunlight cut into profile the shadowless edges of the buildings, inside the force of some incipient idea kept us long in that dark corner. A simple progressivist discourse about European integration was in those days surprisingly often heard in the Institute; we were developing another speech. Since then we have moved to other places, and it has been in those other atmospheres that we have found the perspective to write about the ideas we were then developing.

To be surrounded by aspiring lawyers, politicians and civil servants was to understand how widespread was the contempt for history as a serious method of interpreting the world. That the Institute had been equipped with a Department of History (and Civilization) by its founders was a source of irritation to many, because in their judgement history could have no bearing on the real task, the formulation of European policies and advancing the cause of integration. It was seen, rather, as a self-indulgent hobby, a waste of money which they could

have spent on better purposes. We would not for one moment wish to
deny that much of the history which is taught and practised in our
educational institutions is indeed the uncritical, self-indulgent hobby of
a comfortable middle class. We refrain here from comment on other
subjects, except to say that in that small Institute where so many scholars
from so many countries delivered so many seminars on those other
subjects, it was not their discourse but hard historical research which
first led us to what we thought was a clearer understanding of the path of
political developments in western Europe over the last fifty years. No
one listened to us, but we were handsomely funded for the work we did
and we gave one direction and purpose to the Department of History
which offered others a way of explaining why it was there.

Three of us were also social scientists and another one of us has since
moved in that direction. As history, following the conservative trend of
the times, turned like the middle class which writes and reads it towards
semantic parlour games and called the outcome 'social history', we
found ourselves left behind in the belief we had maintained in the
Institute that there was no history of society which was not also a history
of the economy and of political response. It was from that standpoint
that we began to explain fifty years of European integration. In
retrospect we can see why we were already hiding in a dark corner; the
mounting rejection of the idea that history should be based on a
theoretical understanding of economic and social trends was part of the
present movement towards bringing back public executions. It is a way
of denying the need for accurate enquiry or measurement, and
substituting for it mere anecdote. It is true that economic history and
other social-science-based histories rarely explain as much as they
pretend to. But to abandon them, worse still to denounce them, is to
abandon hope of attaining anything more than occasional accidental
flashes of insight into society. For us, it was in the history of the systemic
connections between the economy on the one hand and politics on the
other that we saw the real explanation of the European Community, and
that was why we eventually sat down to write.

At the time when our ideas began to develop we were already criticized
on the grounds that the true origins of European integration were
'cultural', to be found in the history of ideas, as though such a history
were devoid of any connections to the pattern of economic change, and
that our work was materialistic, ignoring the grand sweep of European
idealism. Others insisted that the causes of European integration were
primarily political, as though there were some division between politics
and the economy. Yet others criticized us from the opposite point of
view, that in putting the emphasis on the history of relations between

states, even if it was not the history of diplomacy, we were overlooking the true history of European integration, which was one of societal change. The underlying concept of our book however is that changes in the economy, society and political organizations which are closely interlinked in the post-war state have been the motivation for the choice of integration, and that it should be possible therefore to design a theoretical approach to identifying those very changes in society which do lead to integration. We could add that our own explanation of the European Community does not seem to exclude any of the historical approaches which we were accused of ignoring. It merely denies them the primacy which they claim and forces them to widen the scope of their enquiry.

History is, we contend, of urgent, close relevance to an understanding of the future of the nation and the Community, the best guide to it in fact. It would please us if among those who read our book were theorists who despise history, historians who despise theory, and all who cannot see the point of history. And as for the place where it all started, that long day's journey into night the Bar Fiasco. . . turn down an empty glass.

June 1992

Acknowledgements

The contribution of Alan S. Milward and Federico Romero to this volume was financed by a grant from the Leverhulme Trust (F4 AB) and from the Economic and Social Research Council (grant no. E0023 2270). Both authors express their sincere gratitude.

Frances M. B. Lynch would like to thank the Nuffield Foundation for the grant which financed the research on which her chapter was based.

1 Interdependence or integration? A national choice

Alan S. Milward and Vibeke Sørensen

Since the 1950s American cold war thinking has dominated our conceptual understanding of European integration. The Cold War was first and foremost a war of propaganda. Once the unity of western Europe became a goal of US foreign policy, political theories which predicted the likelihood of that goal's being achieved proliferated. Founded as they were on implicit celebrations of what were thought of as the best aspects of American society, their role in strengthening the nation's will may have been at least as important as their practical value as a basis for foreign policy formulation. Nevertheless they had an important function in supporting the mission of US foreign policy abroad. A comparison can be made with W. W. Rostow's more famous stage theory of economic growth. Theories which predicted the 'integration' of western Europe, like Rostow's 'Non-Communist Manifesto', were essentially models of social engineering for the containment of communism and the promotion of economic growth. They were progressive and predicted the ultimate dilution of political ideologies based on redistribution by the growth of wider markets, higher levels of consumption for all, and the diminution of separate national sovereignties.[1]

Most of these cold war theories of European integration have been abandoned, partly because they proved to have little predictive value, but mainly because historical research over the last decade has demonstrated the inaccuracy of their factual underpinning. Such has been the case for example with the attempts by Deutsch to explain the growth of a North Atlantic community through the increasing permeability of the frontiers of North American and West European countries to people, goods, capital and ideas and to relate the process of European integration to the particularly rapid increase in the incidence of such phenomena in western Europe itself.[2] Such also has been the case with the attempts to explain European integration as the inevitable outcome of the increasing range of functions of the nation-state. The force of long-run economic development, so it was argued, meant that to continue to carry out its functions adequately the nation-state inescapably had to enter into a network of international functional institutions, whose activities, although they were essentially problem-solving ones of a relatively low level of political importance, would continue to expand and so would increasingly restrict the state's capacity for unilateral exercise of its power.[3] One cold war theory of integration alone survives and has indeed undergone a recent revival as a way of explaining recent trends in Europe. That is the concept of neo-functionalism.

Whereas for early versions of functional theory the creation of integrationist international institutions was seen as an acknowledgement of the inescapable historical forces driving the state towards surrenders of sovereignty, neo-functionalists moderated this view and confined their argument to the premiss that once such institutions were created they would increasingly tend to seek integrationist solutions even if integration had not been the original purpose of creating them. The mechanism by which they were alleged to do so was the concept of 'spillover', which demonstrated how a cumulative integration process could acquire sufficient momentum eventually to erode the nation-state and build a new supranational state. National bureaucracies, like the rest of national government, were conceived as coalitions of divergent interests and this divergence would lead to the use of integrationist institutions like those of the European Community to claim the support of one element in these pluralist coalitions against another. This announcement in the 1950s of the operation of a self-sustained momentum in the European integration process lent intellectual credibility to the State Department's claim that US support of European piecemeal economic integration would eventually result in the re-creation of Europe in the image of the United States.[4] During the 1960s, neo-functionalism's interest in regional integration in Latin America, Africa and South-East Asia reflected the political preoccupation in the State Department with the growth of nationalism after decolonialization and the belief that regional integration could provide a non-interventionist model for the containment of communism in the Third World.[5]

Unlike the other theories of European integration, neo-functionalism was developed by a relative small and self-conscious circle of American scholars concerned not so much with European integration as with the construction of a systematic predictive theory of international political integration.[6] Within a short span of years they came to dominate studies in the field of European integration as well as that of international relations in general; an academic success which owed much to the fact that neo-functionalism in the 1950s and 1960s became the intellectual foundation for a hegemonic foreign policy architecture.[7]

In Europe too some policy-makers were strongly attracted by the theory's great simplicity: its strong predictive element not only promised an uncomplicated future for European integration but also gave precise policy prescriptions for how to bring about integration. The theory's technocratic elitism appealed strongly to European Community officials who naturally saw the extensive theorizing about the workings of the Community as a confirmation of their historical role as guardians of the European integration process.

The fact that no other theory appeared to explain the historical events associated with the foundation of the European Community probably explains why neo-functionalism, even after failing the crucial test of the historical laboratory in the late 1960s, was taken up by Europeans from Americans and spared the critical exposure of its ideological bias which other cold war theories were to suffer at the hands of revisionist critics in the 1970s. In the United States, regional integration theory was eventually pronounced obsolete in the aftermath of Vietnam. However, while American theorists quickly moved on to interdependence theory, Europeans were understandably more reluctant to accept the non-existence of a theoretical framework for the Community they were living in. Hence the tortuous inspection during the last twenty years of Community policies to detect functional linkages that can help rehabilitate the most ideologically attractive element of neo-functionalism – the self-sustaining momentum of Community development.

Seen in this perspective it is not surprising that the excitement created by the renewed political activity about European integration in the second half of the 1980s has led some scholars to suggest a partial rehabilitation of neo-functionalism.[8] As historians of European integration we are concerned with this new development. It would be ironic indeed if the Community resurrected neo-functionalism, albeit in a modified form, as its official credo at a time when the Cold War has finally been done away with. According to our view the only purpose neo-functionalism serves today is as a reminder of how easily theorists can end up promoting the values of their political masters – a warning which seems of particular relevance in the present climate of Euro-optimism.

Neo-functionalism failed the test of history because it did not ask the crucial question about where the locus of power lay in the post-war period and, in its enthusiasm for a theory with predictive value, practically did away with the nation-state as the central unit of political organization. Drawing on system theorists like Talcott Parsons and David Easton, neo-functionalism defined the state as a political system driven by interest group pressures within a framework of over-arching consensus.[9] Not only was the common interest a given thing, it was also best served by the pursuit of conflicting individual and group interests within an accepted set of norms. Neo-functionalism expected political and ideological conflicts to be resolved by the upgrading of the common interest and the replacement of the monolithic concept of 'national interest' with a complex of group and individual interest at the international level where the state, no longer a unified actor in the international system, competed with other non-state actors for the loyalties of its citizens.[10] With this definition, neo-functionalism had effectively assumed away the nation-state from the very start.

The reality, as historians have subsequently shown, was that not only did virtually all power remain with the nation-state and its bureaucracy, with only limited surrenders of national sovereignty being made to integrationist institutions and only for narrowly defined purposes, but that states were also able to assert the priority of a national interest within the integrationist framework even against the wishes of large minorities of their populations or seemingly powerful interest groups.[11] There is in fact much to be said for the argument that the nation-state became more powerful after 1945 in western Europe than it had been before. It was oddly contradictory that theorists should have predicted the replacement of the nation-state at the exact time when European states were embarking on unprecedented programmes of intervention in economic and social life with the express purpose of shaping and controlling their national destinies. Concepts like 'the mixed economy' and 'the welfare state' reflect the recognition of this historical reality by other academic disciplines. Seen in this perspective it is difficult to escape the impression that the generous funding of American political science during the Cold War by private foundations and US government agencies to some extent explains theorists' reluctance to ask more penetrating questions about the sources and distribution of power.[12]

There is, in spite of this historical evidence, a marked reluctance to give up the idea that some kind of spillover has been and still is at play in European integration. This reluctance is to a certain degree under-standable because without the concept of spillover it is becoming increasingly difficult to maintain that the Community's institutions have a life of their own independent from bargains between national governments. This predicament causes considerable confusion in the present debate.[13] Rather than returning to American cold war theories to explain the present dynamics of European integration, the time has surely come to base any attempt at theory on the accumulating empirical evidence of the history of the European Community. Surely the first step towards eliminating the present confusion about European integration must be to get the historical facts right. In this book we set out to look at the history of European integration from the European viewpoint and to test an alternative theory. The hypothesis we test is based on the last ten years' detailed empirical research into member countries' national archives as well as on our deep dissatisfaction with the normative values inherent in American cold war theories.

Our hypothesis begins with the assumption that most western European states were so weakened by their experiences over the period 1929–45 that they more or less had to re-create themselves as functioning units in the immediate post-war period. Of course, when they did so they drew heavily on pre-war policy trends and discussions. But the Great Depression of 1929–32 had shattered the frail political consensuses in many of them, especially by the fall in agricultural incomes relative to those elsewhere. The claims of ideologies and competing political systems outside their borders on the allegiance of their citizens had in many cases weakened the capacity to rule effectively. Invasion, defeat and occupation left many of their governments eventually clinging in exile to the assertion of a dubious legitimacy. In this situation their objective once they returned was to reassert the nation-state as the fundamental organizational unit of political life as vigorously and securely as possible.

To do this all states selected a bundle of policies which would achieve that goal. We hypothesize that some of these policies could only be successfully advanced, or could be better advanced, through the international framework. It depended, of course, on the chosen policies. Increases in social welfare, an almost universal policy choice, had for example only indirect, and for some countries perhaps not very strong, repercussions on a country's international relations, although, as the study of French reconstruction in chapter 3 shows, they could become identified as a crucial determinant. Agricultural protection, another virtually universal policy choice, had, in contrast, such strong political implications for a country's external relations as to be obviously more satisfactory from the moment it became a domestic policy choice, if it could be pursued in a framework of international agreement. Employment policies, pursued in different guises in many countries, presented few international difficulties when high levels of employment prevailed over most of western Europe. At the opposite end of the spectrum industrialization policies which depended on protection in a world where the general trend was towards a lowering of protection insistently demanded an agreed international framework for their success.

The inherited international framework through which domestic policy choices could be advanced had developed since the mid-nineteenth century as one of general agreement to uphold certain principles of economic interdependence in the general interest. This agreement however had been eroded, and by some important countries renounced, in the 1930s. One of the reasons for this retreat from acceptance of the principles of interdependence had been the increasing priority given to certain aspects of domestic policy, work-creation schemes for example, or the defence of weak industrial sectors, which, in a world where not everyone could agree to do the same thing, required a greater degree of insulation of the national economy from international economic movements. Some of the new post-war national policy choices could, we hypothesize, be advanced through this altered and less liberal framework of interdependence. Others, we hypothesize, could not and required something new – integration.

To put some historical flesh on these hypothetical bones, let us take one example, some detailed knowledge of which is now emerging from empirical research. It relates to a particularly noticeable policy concern of the post-1945 state, its concern to promote industrialization and modernization, which was eventually incorporated into the search for economic growth. Most European states became much more actively involved than before the war in promoting the development of particular industrial sectors in which it was thought a comparative or competitive advantage in international competition could be obtained, or which, it was thought, were necessary for the further development of the economy.[14] Thus, French plans directed investment towards increases in the production of tractors, cement and energy and relied on high tariffs to shelter these sectors. The Netherlands protected with quotas infant industries such as chemicals, glass and electrical engineering. Norway protected with high tariffs some rapidly expanding non-ferrous metal industries. And almost all countries tried by various means to develop a larger steel industry. The different ways in which these industrial developments were attempted showed great variety, but the goal was similar. Industrialization was thought of as the basis of an increase in output, industrial modernization as the basis of an improvement in overall productivity, increases in output and improvements in productivity as the basis of economic growth, and eventually the concept of economic growth was defined as the quickest way towards consensual politics within a stronger nation.

In a country like Austria, France or Norway, where such policies were more systematically pursued, it had to be accepted that prolonged international deficits on commodity trade would be a likely outcome until the newly implanted and developed industrial technologies could themselves contribute a regular stream of exports. This looked to be extremely difficult in the more open framework of interdependence for the post-war world whose principles the United States and the United Kingdom had laid down at the Bretton Woods conference in July 1944. The system of fixed exchange rates with only infrequent alterations which Bretton Woods foresaw would be difficult to adhere to in a country where imports and investment had so high a priority as to make devaluation an acceptable choice for coping with persistent deficits in the foreign balance. The International Monetary Fund (IMF) was not designed to provide international credit on the scale on which France was to need it, and in fact France was excluded from access to it for a period because of its exchange rate policies. As chapter 3 shows, French governments sought one solution to this problem as early as 1948 by trying to develop agricultural exports to ease the balance of payments difficulties, but this only posed even more insistently the need to find an international framework in which those exports could be sold. As chapter 5 shows, the task of developing a larger and more modern steel industry faced both Italy and the United Kingdom, and France too, with crucial choices about the nature of the international order as early as 1950, to which they came up with different answers.

The European Payments Union (EPU) substituted in 1950 a European framework of multilateral interdependence for the worldwide one originally envisaged at Bretton Woods. It substituted, too, a much more generous provision of international credit for deficits on intra-western European trade and payments than anything envisaged at Bretton Woods. Long-term debtors in the EPU, such as Austria, Denmark, France, Greece or Iceland, were able to continue to run import surpluses on their trade with the other members because of the generous settlement terms in force before 1956, which required only partial payment of deficits in gold or hard currency. Those, like Austria, Greece or Iceland, who could not meet even these generous settlement terms were treated as 'structural debtors' and received American aid to allow them to stay in the union.[15]

When the EPU was first proposed some American bureaucrats saw it as an integrationist device, the first step on the road to a common West European currency, a common central bank and a common monetary policy. Every suggestion that these aspirations might be forwarded by the agreement to create the union was rejected by the European states. A condition of the union was that all hint of any such radical change in the nature of the international framework should be banished. All that the members of EPU would accept in the face of strong US pressure was the insignificant gesture of calling the unit of account in which the settlements were made the écu – while their central banks guarded carefully against any possibility that the écu could actually become a currency. To a certain extent therefore national industrial and development policies could be advanced, and imaginatively so, through the translation of the inherited and modified principles of interdependence into the post-war world, for the EPU was far more appropriate to the precise needs of western European countries in the post-war world than the abstractions of Bretton Woods. However even with this context the protection needed to ensure the success of industrialization and modernization policies proved inadequate when it had to be combined with the overall objective which all western European countries pursued of encouraging the growth of foreign trade as a stimulus to higher rates of economic growth.

Two accepted methods of protection on the frontier were handed down from the pre-war world, tariffs and quantitative restrictions. National tariffs had been the main instrument of control of imports on the frontier from the mid-nineteenth century to 1931. They were a cumbersome device and in many countries subject to close parliamentary scrutiny, which limited the capacity of governments to adjust them quickly or rationally. The tendency had been for tariff bargaining to relapse in all periods of difficulty into bilateral bargains, and the general evidence from their use was that they accelerated the tendency for the value and volume of foreign trade to fall in times of economic recession. The experience of the great slump of 1929–32 had, furthermore, demonstrated that the protective effect of tariffs was also inadequate, unless they were so high as to discourage any increase in trade. They were a singularly unsuitable device for the post-war policies of western European states.

The western European economies consisted, with few exceptions, of a contiguous group of territorially small, highly developed economies, whose foreign trade was dominated by their interchange of manufactured products. An increase in the value and volume of this interchange was seen by all of them, exaggeratedly so, as a necessity for the stimulation and continuation of economic growth. Trade in manufactures between western European economies, especially their interchange of manufactures with the German Federal Republic, soon asserted itself in the post-war world as the main force for the growth in world trade. The policies of national development sustained this pattern and required it to endure. At the same time, the same policies also demanded an increasingly selective and sophisticated form of protection for newly developing industrial sectors as well as, on occasions, for sectors becoming uncompetitive. The outcome was a search for a new form of neo-mercantilist commercial policy which could combine a more rapid trade expansion with more selective and more easily adjustable forms of protection.

Tariffs could not provide this, especially when tariff bargaining in the General Agreement on Tariffs and Trade (GATT) had to be of a worldwide multilateral nature. GATT proved in fact after 1951 to be too protectionist a body in which to forge such new commercial policies. It gave ample representation to Third World protectionists, to governments of major countries such as Australia, Brazil or South Africa whose first priority was import-substitution policies, and its most powerful member, the United States, was also forced to side with this protectionist stance because of the pressure of vested interests in Congress on the administration. The inability of US governments set on liberalizing commercial policy to do so, because of the parliamentary pressures on them in the 1950s, was the clearest example of the inadequacy of national tariffs as a device for regulating trade according to governments' own assessment of the national interest, and an example which the western European countries were repeatedly brought up against between 1951 and 1957.

The alternative inheritance was the quota restrictions imposed from 1931 onwards, linked in many cases to currency controls. By 1945 there was universal agreement that they had been one of the principal causes, perhaps *the* principal cause, for the failure of international trade to expand in the 1930s, a judgement which has subsequently been confirmed by historians. There was little or no disagreement, once the European Payments Union had established a functioning system for making international settlements, that most existing quotas should be widened and then removed.

But there was also general agreement that not all quotas could be removed, because of their centrality in domestic development policies, and particularly not if they had to be replaced by high tariffs. Out of the long arguments over the ways in which tariffs and quantitative restrictions could be mutually and co-operatively adapted to the perceived common interest of sets of western European countries with similar industrial and commercial objectives, there emerged a rejection of the inherited framework of interdependence by six of them – Belgium, France, the German Federal Republic, Italy, Luxemburg and the Netherlands – 'the Six' as they became known and as we now call them here. They chose a new form of international framework – integration. Between them the outmoded tariffs were progressively removed, the remaining quotas removed somewhat more cautiously, and both replaced by the regulation of trade within the new customs union by mutually agreed sets of non-tariff barriers. Behind the protection of a common tariff, still required for bargaining with older-fashioned systems like the United States, they forged an instrument both protectionist and expansionist which gave all of them part of an increasing share of the trade within the common market until the 1970s.[16]

Because there was such a variety of industrial development policies in western European states, because the links between these policies and commercial policies were also so different in different states, and because of the central importance of both industrial modernization and the growth of foreign trade to the reassertive policies of the post-war European states, it is understandable that the advancement of such policies through the international framework should have eventually led to different choices, for some the older framework of interdependence, for others the newer one of integration.

For other elements in the post-war bundles of policy choices the issues of choice could be simpler, not least because they were determined by others. Our book contains a telling example in chapter 2. For Italian governments before 1957 success in economic development, or even perhaps the preservation of social stability, was seen as depending on emigration. When the first steps towards European integration were taken in the Treaty of Paris in 1952 the attitude of the other five countries towards permitting the free movement of labour between them was very restrictive. Under narrowly defined conditions they would permit the free movement of skilled labour in the industries in question, coal, iron and steel, in which only a very small number of Italians was employed. Their attitude in the negotiations for the Treaty of Rome was equally cautious. Italians continued to emigrate, as they always had done, over the whole world. It was only therefore within the traditional framework of interdependence that such a policy could be advanced. Even within the common market migration policies remained under the firm hand of national control, albeit that internal migrations were partially liberalized.

The argument could be exemplified from two other post-war policy choices, preservation of employment and welfare in threatened industrial sectors, and income protection in the agricultural sector. The post-war history of the Belgian coal industry was typical of that of many declining industrial sectors in western European economies.[17] It is singled out here only for its weight in the economy as a whole, 12 per cent of total industrial output and, with its ancillary industries, 10 per cent of industrial employment in 1950. It had been uncompetitive internationally since 1929 but had been preserved in more or less its existing size until the outbreak of war by protection and cartelization. To accept the principles of interdependence would have been increasingly to expose the coal industry after 1945 to international competition, at first from the German Federal Republic and then from the United States, which it could not meet. Yet it was only with the worldwide collapse of the coal market in 1958 that a serious start was made with the managed decline of this large industry. In the bargaining for the formation of the Coal Iron and Steel Community (commonly called the European Coal and Steel Community) the Belgian government was able to use the device of integration to protect its coal industry not only from competition external to the Community but from competition within the common market as well. The cost was high. Without counting the opportunity costs of using high-price domestic coal instead of cheaper imports, the cost of preservation of so much employment in coal-mining in subsidies alone was $141.42 million between 1953, when the common market in coal opened, and 1958. But $50.08 million of this sum was contributed by other Community members, mainly by the German Federal Republic. The integrationist solution was used to sustain levels of welfare and employment in Belgium which would have been much less easily sustainable within a system of interdependence. The example is the more striking because coal-mining, a low-wage employment in the 1930s, was the highest-paid industrial labour in Belgium throughout the period 1945–58.

The second example is better known, because we are still struggling with its consequences. The protection of incomes in agriculture quickly led to overpriced agricultural surpluses, the result of subsidized inputs, excluded imports and guaranteed domestic markets.[18] If there were any chance of marketing these surpluses, it could only be within a European framework, unless their export attracted a permanent subsidy. Once the Six had agreed on a new framework for regulating the much more important trade between themselves in manufactures, they resolved the issue of trade in agricultural products, where it was generally agreed that quotas and state-supported cartels would have to remain, by a bold proclamation of a 'common agricultural policy', which was certain to be far from a liberal uncontrolled trading system. The birth-pangs, twists, turns and idiosyncrasies of that policy have dominated much of the European Community's financial and administrative history since that decision, while to explain the number of ways in which it distorts the market has taxed the ingenuity of economists ever since. Even though the Common Agricultural Policy was essentially national policies elevated to the European level, it seems improbable that the long decline of employment in the agricultural sector could have been so gradual without this internationalization of policy. The inevitable decline of the influence of agricultural pressure groups within a purely national framework, as their relative weight in the economy and in the electoral system relentlessly diminished, would surely have forced western European agriculture more rapidly into a world of interdependence and thus into a more rapid shrinkage. As with Belgian coal-mining, integration safeguarded national policy choices for a high priority for welfare and employment in that particular sector for longer than any other arrangement that was not merely unilaterally protectionist and thus open to more immediate international criticism, and also less effective.

The historical evidence, we hypothesize, suggests, as far as it has been discovered, that the choice between interdependence and integration as international frameworks for advancing national policy choices depended on the nature of national policies. The implication of this is that without a theory which can predict the future nature of national policy choice it is not possible to predict whether integration will continue in Europe, or even whether it will remain at its present level. The only predictive value of a theory derived from historical research would be that once national policies were specified, their international consequences for the nation-state could be specified. There would seem therefore, at least in a world of theory, in stark contrast to the conclusions drawn by neo-functionalists, to be no inherent momentum within the nation-state towards the increasing surrender of its national sovereignty to supranational government.

But in the real world a further historical question arises. Because integration is a concession of state power to international bodies, whereas the limitations on sovereign actions imposed by interdependence remain a matter for adjustment purely within the national political system, why should a state ever choose integration and pay such penalties? There are perhaps some general advantages, in addition to the specific single policy-related advantages so far considered, in an integrationist framework which are lacking in a world of mere interdependence.

One such possible advantage which immediately suggests itself is what we here call irreversibility: the certitude that once a fundamental bargain has been agreed to among governments it is not likely to be lightly reversed. Uncertainty about the long-term viability of international agreements is the penalty which governments must pay in a world of interdependence. Depending on the nature of the issues involved and the priority which governments attach to them, the costs of this uncertainty can in some cases be relatively insignificant while in others of such crucial importance as to undercut, if not actually prevent, international agreement. International trade, involving important national long-term investments, is clearly an example of the latter. As we have argued above, expansion of trade was one of the most notable concerns of the post-war state. In pursuing this goal European states were diverting a substantial share of their long-term investment to the development of manufactured exports. At first they did so without any guarantee that trade barriers would be lowered and markets opened for their exports, but the pressures on them not to continue running that risk were great indeed.

Marshall Aid in 1948 and the debtor-biased provisions of the European Payments Union after 1950 provided a temporary safety net. But the trade liberalization programme of the Organization for European Economic Co-operation (OEEC), which was launched by the United Kingdom with American encouragement in 1949 and based on a mutual systematic easing of quota restrictions on trade between member states, cut both ways. It encouraged an initial expansion of intra trade, but also brought under threat some of the quantitative protection which countries wished to retain in order to protect their investments. Once the growth of defence spending and the control of inflation became overriding priorities of the USA's European policy after the outbreak of the Korean War in 1950, the initial progress made in freeing trade from quota restrictions quickly collapsed as European states, under the pressure of growing defence budgets and large balance of payments deficits, retreated from earlier commitments. By the end of 1951 the OEEC trade liberalization programme had come to a virtual halt; an event which in itself demonstrated the acute need for a more durable arrangement for trade that would discourage defection from existing inter-governmental bargains.

The need for this was made even more evident by the vital and ever-growing importance of the German Federal Republic to the trade of the other western European countries. Within three years of the creation of the Federal Republic it had become the biggest, and also the most rapidly expanding, market for the manufactured exports of all the OEEC member states except the United Kingdom, Ireland and Portugal. Furthermore, the German market was growing particularly rapidly in most of those modern manufacturing sectors which governments were especially seeking to develop. The Federal Republic was important to the development of more modern manufacturing industries, not only as a market but also as a supplier. In a period when dollars were in such short international supply that importing from the dollar zone was discouraged by currency and trade controls, German exports of machinery, machine tools and chemicals were in high demand throughout western Europe. In most categories of capital goods Germany had been since the late nineteenth century the only exporter of equal importance to the United States and the active pursuit of policies of industrialization and modernization by western European governments after 1945 could only enhance that importance, particularly in a period of dollar shortage. It followed that fundamental areas of national economic policy in western Europe were dependent on a guarantee that the trade with the German Federal Republic would endure.

Given the equivocal status of the Federal Republic, and given the experience of great uncertainty and bad faith which had characterized trade with Germany in the 1930s, it was all the more understandable that some western European countries should seek guarantees that the existing commercial links with the Federal Republic and the liberal nature of commercial policy there should not be reversed. Although not absolutely irreversible, the Treaties of Rome signed in 1957 (one referring to the common market and one to Euratom) constituted a much more long-term guarantee of the continuity of commercial policy than any earlier form of commercial agreement or treaty. The negotiations made specific links to the earlier integrationist Treaty of Paris, emphasized in the text in the commitment to 'an ever closer union'.

It was not until this fundamental bargain was struck, which also tied the need for continued protection of agriculture to the freeing of trade in industrial products, that the clash of national interests which had lain at the heart of the OEEC trade liberalization programme could be resolved. Although the programme was revived in 1953, France (see chapter 3) had effectively not participated. And the nearer resumed trade liberalization came to the removal of quotas and other non-tariff barriers on agricultural trade, the more apparent was the need for some alternative policy unless one universal element in the post-war policy bundle, agricultural income protection, were to be abandoned. Through the surrender of national sovereignty over trade in manufactures between themselves the signatories acquired an exclusive access to one another's markets on a more permanent basis than either the OEEC or GATT could provide, a framework for mutually regulating the terms of that access, and opened the door to different arrangements for agriculture.

The advantages of integration in this case were many, as were the disadvantages of rejecting it. And, of course, the decision was taken by France with specific reference to a choice of foreign policy made in 1950 in which the 'integration', vaguely conceived, of the French and West German economies offered also one road to security in the future, a road which appeared safer than mere interdependence with the new German country. We are not implying that integration, once entered into, is absolutely irreversible. Even less are we implying that it is necessarily progressive. On the contrary, a change in policy bundles across the Community could lead theoretically, as we insisted, to the reversal of these fundamental bargains and the disintegration of the European Community. However, because the choice of integration was so much more momentous a step, and yet worth making for the advantages which it brought, it is far more likely, we hypothesize, that changes in member states' domestic policies would be confined in their consequences to limiting further integration rather than reversing existing bargains. The structure of the Treaty of Rome points also to that conclusion. As well as an actual law for the customs union, the EEC treaty was also a framework for the future: it set out the detailed steps to completion of the customs union and beyond that a statement of objectives and principles left to the institutions to work out in concrete measures.[19] The Rome treaties thereby allotted a comprehensive future policy-making task to the institutions, in the first instance to the Council of Ministers acting on proposals from the European Commission. It was this policy-making function that neo-functionalists believed would become the driving force of the integration process once the requirement of unanimity was replaced by a qualified majority vote. De Gaulle's intervention in 1965 proved neo-functional theory to be wrong.

To interpret that event as a reversal of the process of European integration, as most theorists and contemporary observers did, is, however, equally wrong. De Gaulle's action was not an attempt to revise the fundamental bargain underlying the Treaties of Rome – the customs union. Although we still have to await a detailed historical analysis of the events leading up to the 1965 crisis, we know that it was not prompted by French dissatisfaction with the developing common market. Most analysis points to the French discontent with the Community's agricultural policy triggered by a growing apprehension over the double prospect of the Commission's acquiring an independent source of revenue for its activities and the strengthening of the power of the European Parliament.[20] The wish to maintain national control over the future development of the European Community, not the wish to reverse what was already there, motivated de Gaulle's action.

Elusive notion though it is, the pragmatic delineation of irreversibility as a new system of international relations can be discerned in the Treaties of Rome as well as in Community law. Unlike most international treaties, the Rome treaties have no time limit and contain no specific procedures either for unilateral withdrawal or for their cancellation. The preamble's commitment to 'an ever closer union among the European peoples' – an ideal which is constantly reconfirmed in the public speeches of heads of state and national politicians – is repeated in the Single European Act and, with the claim that it is a reinforcement, in the European Union Treaty.[21] However, it is the concept of *acquis communautaire* which more than any of the treaty provisions expresses the importance attached to the notion of irreversibility within the European Community. The rage which Margaret Thatcher provoked in the Community arose more from her questioning of the *acquis communautaire* and her belief that new members could recast old bargains, a belief still close to the heart of the present British government, than from her reluctant attitude towards the Community's deepening. It does not follow from our argument that all later signatories of the Treaties of Rome valued irreversibility so highly. Indeed the United Kingdom may well have regarded the commercial benefits as not requiring irreversibility.

There are other advantages of integration which suggest that once chosen it may be retained even if the dissimilarities between national policy bundles become wide. One is that it better justifies discrimination against outsiders to the bargain and more easily allows a limitation of the number of participants because the price of entry in terms of national sovereignty is higher. Integration in fact substituted for the traditional multilateral pattern of international co-operation, one based on exclusion. This has been the main critique of it by the United Kingdom even when that country was part of the bargain. But exclusion offered a more realistic basis for resolving the issues at stake in 1952 and 1957 and the United Kingdom's attitude arose from eventually having to accept the *acquis communautaire* because it could not find, much less impose, a better solution to its own difficulties. The history of OEEC in the 1950s provides the best illustration of how impossible it would have been to resolve the issues then at stake had they had to have been resolved by sixteen countries with quite different political and economic structures. Even if we exclude such particular cases as Greece and Turkey, the OEEC remained a forum where domestic policy objectives which were in fact basically irreconcilable were supposed to be resolved. They were of course merely discussed and reported in an increasingly sanitized form. An obvious way to simplify agendas, increase efficiency and reduce potential conflicts was to restrict problem resolution to a few selected states.

Maintaining the rapid growth of trade in manufactures with the German Federal Republic as its centre provided, in the case of the Rome treaties, the basic guideline for this process, but other motivations were present too. Although divisions of opinion on the question were strong, France openly expressed its preference to exclude the United Kingdom from some areas of economic influence on the continent. The Netherlands, as chapter 4 shows, was clearly advantaged by a treaty which favoured its own agricultural exports against those of Denmark on the German market. This limitation of participants, justified by the original political bargain of the Coal and Steel Community, represented the hard political realities of the situation in western Europe in the early 1950s and was therefore more effective in binding states together than the multilateral framework provided by the OEEC and other post-war international institutions.

Exclusivity however had further advantages than just improving effectiveness. Once created, the European Community profoundly changed power relations within western Europe. Because the establishment of the customs union and the simultaneous commitment to 'an ever closer union', indicated the Six's intention to stay an exclusive group unless others accepted their terms, it strengthened the Community's bargaining power with respect to non-members, not least through the ability to exclude states in the long term from important markets. In marked difference to the multilateral negotiations of the OEEC, Community members could now set the conditions for their mutual relations with non-members: some could be allowed in while others could be kept out; some could be allowed specific exemptions and privileges on entry, others not. This is particularly well illustrated by the Community's relations with the United Kingdom. Earlier, the United Kingdom had been able to redefine agendas and impose not only its preference for interdependence in European negotiations but also the terms of that interdependence, because it was much the strongest western European power. After 1957 it either accepted the nature of the Community bargain or incurred discrimination. Greater commercial power and greater military force alike could not alter the terms of a treaty signed between members who would individually have been entirely unable to assert the primacy of their national interests over those of the United Kingdom.

Insistence on acceptance of the *acquis communautaire* permits a strictly controlled process of Community enlargement. Rather than operating by the shifting of loyalties from nation-states to European institutions, as postulated by neo-functionalists, the driving force behind the expansion of the Community has been discrimination and the exclusive power to define agendas. Completing the internal market will inevitably mean new discrimination against outsiders and the increased economic and political power this confers on the Community is reflected in the number of membership applications as well as in the recent negotiations to create a European Economic Area (EEA). In the latter, the Community's insistence on the so-called Interlaken principles, establishing that the EEA agreement must not interfere with Community priorities, actually means that European Free Trade Association (EFTA) countries have had to surrender important parts of their national sovereignty to reach the agreement without acquiring the compensation of influencing Community decision-making that follows from membership, a serious drawback which played a major role in Sweden's decision to apply for Community membership.[22]

Another advantage integration has over interdependence is that it provides a central system of law. The theory of international relations has always assumed that all domestic policies that have international repercussions could be more efficiently and peacefully advanced in a world system that recognizes one universal law. This proposition, however, rests on two idealistic assumptions. One is that the chaos and conflict which otherwise prevail in the international system can be eliminated if nation-states learn to recognize a higher law than that flowing from their own consent. Another is that if this recognition did exist, policies would be reconcilable. In fact, compliance with international obligations can on occasions be achieved without a central system of law. As we argued above, the European Payments Union was an example of this. For compliance to be enforced within the framework of interdependence however the penalties need to be severe and the advantages of not incurring them strong, and for this balance to be struck the advantages of continued adherence to the agreement have to be evident for an overwhelming majority of parties. When the United Kingdom tried to break up the EPU every other one of its members preferred to keep the union together. The EPU allowed them to finance large balance of payments deficits, but the penalties of having to make gold payments once the drawing rights were exceeded were the harder to bear because of dependency on the latitude which the system offered. But only few inter-governmental arrangements could have such efficient instruments of compliance at their disposal or could claim so wide a measure of self-interested loyalty. In most cases supervision of implementation and settlement of disputes could, theoretically speaking, be achieved more efficiently within a framework of integration whose law enjoys a certain supremacy over the law of the member states.

The historical evidence suggests however that within the process of integration it was the overriding nature of national concerns which necessitated a central system of law, essentially the vital need to guarantee a certain national control within the integrationist framework after its creation. Assuming, as we have done, that nation-states, in order to advance important domestic policy objectives, choose to transfer sovereignty over certain policy areas to common institutions, then their principal national interest will be not only to define and limit that transfer of sovereignty very carefully but also meticulously to structure the central institutions so as to preserve a balance of power within the integrationist framework in favour of the nation-states themselves.

This can only be done by a constitution, in the form of treaties that call into being a new distinctive legal order to regulate the powers, rights and obligations residing in the integrationist framework and their relationship with the member states. The Treaties of Paris and Rome state the powers of the institutions as well as the precise relationship between them. Important in this respect was the allotment of the task of policy-making to the Council of Ministers composed of members of national governments, which ensures that control over the future development of the Community remains with the member states. That such control was considered crucial can be seen from the reluctance to include a more detailed goal for the Community than the rather vague commitment to the 'ever closer union'. It can be seen too in the elimination of the word 'supranational' from provisional drafts of the Treaties of Rome. That member states are still on their guard against any encroachment on their powers within the Community was confirmed in 1991 by the storm of government protest which followed the Dutch attempt to include the word 'federal' in the draft for the European Union Treaty. The states themselves, provided there is some concord in policy goals between them, can, as historical events have shown, create an effective, en-forceable international law which remains securely under their joint control. It is effective because it is based on reconcilable policies, within whose reconciliation national advantage is achieved. It is, in that respect, in stark contrast to the more optimistic and idealized assumptions of universal international law.

From this analysis therefore we tentatively assume that, although its costs are higher, integration has certain advantages over interdependence. It is less easily reversed, more exclusive and more law-abiding. All are important advantages in the pursuit of national policy and may in some bargains compensate for the partial loss of sovereignty. But this conclusion does not change our reservations about the predictive value of a theory of European integration based on historical evidence, because predicting whether integration will be preferred to inter-dependence is dependent on the ability not only to predict policy choice within any one nation-state, but also to predict the likelihood that similar and reconcilable sets of policy choices will be made in sets of nation-states, particularly in those which now form the European Community.

The historical evidence seems to suggest that until now integration has been chosen only in cases where interdependence has been inadequate as a framework to advance important national policy objectives. This may be a reasonable basis for predicting that, if European integration is to continue, it most probably will take place only after the extension of inter-governmental co-operation to new areas as an initial measure has proved itself unsatisfactory for the advancement of domestic policy objectives for a majority of those co-operating. But for a further carefully negotiated and defined transfer of sovereignty to take place, the similarity and reconcilability of national policy choices would, perhaps, have to be greater than is necessary in a merely interdependent world.[23] It is beyond the scope of a historically based theory to say anything about such a likelihood.

In our opening remarks we warned against the temptation to resurrect American cold war theories of European integration and argued that the only valid theory of integration would be one derived from empirical research into Europe's own history. Obviously, we are open to the reproach that the empirical evidence is still insufficient. In the following chapters we are concerned with adding to that evidence, with seeing whether it does in fact bear out the hypotheses we have derived here from earlier research, and with trying to add to the understanding of both interdependence and integration as systems of international relations. While we start from the realist position that the modern nation-state is still the ultimate arbiter of its own destiny, our hypotheses are open-ended about the implications of such a statement for European integration. We do not, unlike Aron and Hoffmann, conclude from this realist position that European integration therefore necessarily will be for ever confined to 'low policy' areas.[24] They, like neo-functionalists, posit a fundamental antagonism between European integration and the nation-state which, on the basis of the present state of historical research, appears false. We, in contrast, assume the European Community to be an international framework constructed by the nation-state for the completion of its own domestic policy objectives – a hypothesis that allows for an episodic development of European integration reflecting changes in domestic politics rather than the incremental progression postulated by other integration theories.

To resume, our argument runs like this. Nation-states have a certain portfolio of policy objectives which they will try to realize in the face of economic and political internationalization. These policy objectives are almost entirely shaped by domestic political pressures and economic resources and will therefore vary from country to country and over time. In order to advance these objectives nation-states will attempt to use what international framework there is at hand. Many of these objectives can and will be pursued by expanding what we have here called the inherited framework of interdependence, traditional inter-governmental co-operation among states. However, as we have argued, some fundamental objectives after 1945 could not be achieved through such a framework and were therefore advanced through integration. While historical research cannot predict the nature of future policy choice it is not beyond the bounds of possibility that it might enable us to specify more exactly in what policy areas the interdependent framework is more likely to be perceived as inadequate and the costs of integration as worthwhile. Because the integration which has occurred was linked to sets of policy choices, one of whose dominant characteristics was the pursuit of economic growth, that should not be interpreted as a modern 'end of ideology' thesis, in the sense that pursuit of economic growth, or any other objective, automatically will lead to a similar mix of national politics over time. On the contrary, we maintain that national diversity is reproduced even in a framework of integration and is of crucial importance in understanding why the history of European integration has been one of fits and starts rather than of linear progression.

Even in a period like that between 1945 and 1967, when there was a sufficient convergence of policy objectives to make integration a possible choice, diversity was still very evident. Agreement on the role of foreign trade in the economy permitted a treaty which freed markets for industrial products, and guaranteed that loss of domestic market shares would be compensated by a growing share of the common market. Included in this bargain was an agreement to create common policies for agriculture to prevent a too rapid decline in agricultural incomes. But this was as far as agreement went among governments in the 1950s. Conspicuously absent from the Treaty of Rome was any mention of industrial policies, apart from those which might interfere with the realization of the customs union. This reflected the very different approaches to industrial policy and the importance attached to these different policies by the signatories. Particularly difficult to bridge was the clash of interests between France and the German Federal Republic over the role of the state in the economy: whether *dirigisme* or free market forces should govern the development of a European industrial policy. A common ground for these different industrial policies in the 1950s could be found only in the form of a minimalist agreement to create a common market in which these policies could be protected and developed. This observation can only emphasize the complexity of the historical circumstances that we have to interpret. Given a restricted number of strong policy priorities held in common, a marked diversity of policy methods or even objectives in other areas may not impede integration.

We have so far confined the historical examples on which we have drawn to that period, more than thirty years ago, for which documentary historical research is possible. But what of very recent history, which has shown a renewed interest in integration on the part of European states? Can we maintain our historically based hypotheses in the face of recent events such as the Maastricht summit and the European Union Treaty? Do those events provide historical evidence, even if it is not yet susceptible to a full analysis, which might modify our hypotheses?

We will start by assuming, in accordance with our hypothesis, that the rapid progress of the timetable for the customs union in the 1960s owed more to the fundamental agreement between national governments on this basic issue than to the independent powers of the European Commission to sustain the momentum of integration. This conclusion allows us to take a less normative view of the 1970s. We do not, as do most students of European integration, see the 1970s as a period characterized by the reassertion of national political priorities over the process of European integration. The single most important change in the 1970s was the dramatic alteration in the Community's external environment which had a deep and lasting impact on domestic consensus patterns within the member states: the collapse of international monetary stability, sluggish growth, high inflation and, from the end of the decade, the gradual loss of market shares within the common market to the United States and Japan in high-technology products. Together these provided a formidable challenge for national governments which had used integrative institutions for national purposes.

As could be expected from our hypothesis, there was no concerted attempt through the European Community to harmonize a response to the crisis. The initial responses were purely national; governments attempted to deal with international change on an individual basis. Policies turned to protection of employment in declining industries like steel and shipbuilding and the encouragement of mergers on a national basis to create 'national champions' which could take up the competition with American and Japanese high-technology giants now became the overriding concern of national economic policy. In the latter case, some attempts were made within the Community framework to encourage the development of high-technology industries based on inter-governmental programmes, such as RACE or EUREKA, some incorporating both Community and non-Community members, but these various initiatives never rose beyond the co-operative level and were not particularly striking examples even of co-operation.

Monetary policy demanded at least a greater degree of commitment to interdependence and was seen by champions of the political goal of federation as the area of policy which they must ultimately transfer from national hands. Until 1969 the international monetary system had been an important stabilizing factor behind the development of the common market, a stability which disappeared after the collapse of the system of fixed exchange rates in 1971. The readjustment difficulties this occasioned within some European countries quickly led to the construction of a temporary alternative system of fixed but more flexible exchange rates, the 'snake', based on traditional inter-governmental co-operation in managing the exchanges. However, in some countries, notably the German Federal Republic, the Netherlands and, to some extent, Italy, an integrationist solution based on the harmonization of economic policies continued to be advocated in some circles as more effective in dealing with monetary instability. The policy clash between the priority of controlling inflation and the equally important one of preserving adequate growth rates which lay at the heart of these discussions still today haunts the negotiations for the proposed European Monetary Union. Throughout the 1970s and 1980s this clash of policies prevented agreement on a coherent integrationist response in the form of a monetary union, as it had been sketched out on the eve of the collapse of the Bretton Woods system of fixed exchange rates in the Werner Report of 1970. Yet the inter-governmental arrangement of the 'snake' was not working either. The difficulties experienced by the 'snake' during the 1970s were a clear indication of member states' reluctance to undertake national adjustment and to sacrifice growth for control over inflation. The common agreement that the 'snake' was thought to be too rigid a framework for its purpose speaks for itself and it was therefore not surprising that the outcome was another inter-governmental arrangement with even wider margins for swing between Community exchange rates, the European Monetary System (EMS).

The main reason however why scholars of European integration have condemned the 1970s as a partial reversal of the progress of European integration was the growing impact of inter-governmentalism on the institutional developments within the Community, in particular the creation of the European Council in 1974.[25] The Council is clearly a traditional inter-governmental arrangement. It stands outside the Community treaties and therefore cannot be directly subjected to the influence of either the Commission or the European Parliament. We do not ourselves see this as any reversal of the trends in international relations between Community member states since 1950. The creation of the Council was a natural response to the fundamental changes of the 1970s which demanded more determined action by the Community on the old policy areas which it had been created to deal with, as well as in new areas, and for neither of which the integrationist treaties now provided much help.

After the end of the timetable for the customs union provided by the Treaties of Rome, decision-making in the Community became more difficult. Any policy initiatives with respect to the future arrangements for intra-Community trade had to be taken without the guideline of the treaties except in so far as the EEC treaty willed an 'ever closer union'. This situation was made more difficult by the entry of the United Kingdom. Second, as a consequence of the changes in the Community's external environment a whole range of new policy issues now had to be dealt with. The Council of Ministers, based on the rotation of ministers according to the agenda, had always been, despite the co-ordinating function of the Foreign Ministers, highly ill suited to take decisions other than those pertaining to the management of the common market and the Common Agricultural Policy. With the new problems facing the Community in the 1970s, it became increasingly necessary to strengthen the Council's ability to take decisions involving the more overall national interests of its members by the regular meeting of heads of states rather than of government ministers. The practice of summitry not only reflected the international problems of the decade, in particular the desire for a common foreign policy stand on issues like the Middle East and the Conference on Security and Co-operation in Europe (CSCE), but also the wish to use the integrationist framework both to further national policy advancement for the future and to resolve fundamental disputes within it, like that with the United Kingdom over the size of member states' contributions to the Community.

Seen in this perspective, the European Council, rather than reversing the process of European integration, actually signifies a wish to extend Community decision-making to new areas in response to changes in national policy objectives arising from the fundamental change in the economic circumstances of the western European countries after 1974. The similar sets of policies which had allowed the choice of integration were no longer so appropriate to the new conditions. As conditions changed, the nation-states left open, exactly as before, the choice of interdependence or integration to advance whatever new policies might emerge.

For most of the 1970s national governments seemed to operate without direction. As traditional policy instruments produced unexpected and often adverse results, and as unemployment increased, the post-war consensus model in each country was challenged from within. Initially many governments responded by relying more heavily on corporatist arrangements and state management of industry, policies whose subsequent failure served to focus political attention on the rigidities created by such systems and their allegedly harmful impact on industrial efficiency and technological development. The relatively much lower rates of national income growth than in the first three post-war decades seemed to justify many of these allegations and paved the way for a gradual coalescence of national policies around a neo-conservative call for privatization and deregulation in the beginning of the 1980s. In northern Europe conservative governments replaced social democratic ones, while in southern Europe the weakening of the communists allowed socialist governments in France and Spain to embrace a more market-orientated approach to economic policy. President Mitterrand's choice to keep France in the European Monetary System and change the priorities of economic policy in 1983 from the earlier attempt to pursue full employment, income redistribution and industrial development in relative isolation from other European economies seemed to mark the final abandonment of the belief that the post-war model of the western European state could be made to generate the same results as it had done before.

The weakness of the European Community seemed to be reflected by the fact that for the first time since its foundation its share of the trade within the common market not only ceased to grow but actually began to fall, while that of Japan and the United States increased. Community programmes to pool resources in research and development were not more effective than state programmes of technological development or protective state procurement rules in stimulating greater European competitiveness in advanced technologies. It was against this background that the Commission in alliance with the Round Table of European Industrialists took the crucial step of proposing a timetable for the further development of the common market which quickly caught the imagination not only of governments but of some national electorates as well. Whereas in 1957 the common market by eliminating internal tariff barriers had allowed for a more sensitive regulation of the market by non-tariff devices, this regulation was now seen as being in restraint of trade. A freer commercial policy was needed inside the market to match the reduction in government intervention. The powers of the European Commission were to be used to make firms as well as governments dismantle the many arrangements which had made the common market so strong a support to earlier national policies.

This was celebrated by neo-functionalist theorists as the long-awaited confirmation of their views.[26] For the first time in the Community's history a strong president of the Commission in alliance with transnational business interests appeared to be providing leadership outside the national setting for an integrationist advance, a development which, coming after years of bitter struggle inside the Community over the British contribution to the budget, seemed the more impressive.

However, a more thorough analysis immediately places a question mark after such an interpretation.[27] As we argued, the creation of the European Council signified a wish to use the Community to advance national policy objectives with respect to new policy areas, but until 1984 there was no consensus among national governments that such co-operation should take place in an integrationist framework. Enlargement of the Community was followed by increased disagreement over the agricultural policy and the budget. It was only with the emergence of a gradual agreement on the need for internal market liberalization, at first within the states themselves, that there actually were any national policies which could more effectively be advanced through the integrationist framework. The 1983 'Solemn Declaration on European Union' which is often cited as confirmation of the new integrationist mood in the Community, was in fact little more than a confirmation of member states' commitment to the Luxemburg compromise, and if we look at the diversity of national policy objectives it is not difficult to see why. The United Kingdom was against both monetary union and institutional reform, but was eager to deregulate services within the Community. The German Federal Republic refused to consider monetary union before a liberalization of European capital markets had taken place, but was in favour of institutional reform and in particular of an increased role for the European Parliament. France was in favour of the creation of a central European bank and a monetary union, but unenthusiastic about liberalization of markets either for goods or capital.

The decisive step towards agreement came with the French government's wish to advance its new post-1983 economic policy through the Community framework. This led to a series of French concessions both on agricultural policy and on the British demand for *juste retour*. At the Fontainebleau summit in 1984 the outline of a compromise between three of the large Community states slowly emerged. Both the German Federal Republic and the United Kingdom favoured the issue of internal market liberalization, while France and the Federal Republic agreed on the need for institutional reform. It was within this framework of gradual consensus that the Council requested the Commission to draw up a timetable for the creation of a single market by 1992. In comparison to the initial expectations of institutional reform however, the white paper was a very restricted document. It proposed majority voting only for the policies pertaining to the 'completion' of the internal market and strictly limited the augmentation of the powers of the Parliament to the same policy areas. The original idea of a broad institutional reform within the Community had been sacrificed for a programme so minimalist that it at first failed to elicit any public excitement. Only after a concentrated publicity campaign by the Commission did the potential for accelerated economic growth inherent in the programme for completing the market begin to catch the imagination of public opinion in general.[28]

Rather than seeing the emergence of the Single European Act as a confirmation of neo-functionalist theories of integration, we see the new treaty as confirmation that the integrationist framework would still be chosen, where it was more appropriate, by governments for the advancement of new national policy objectives after the changes of the 1970s. The customs union was originally entered into in order to secure a more permanent guarantee of the beneficially rapid growth in the value and volume of intra-western European foreign trade after 1945. The programme of 'completing' the internal market was motivated by the loss of market shares both inside and outside the common market, demonstrating the inability of national non-tariff barriers and the Community tariff to continue to provide an adequate commercial policy within the changing framework of global competition during the 1980s. In both cases integration was undertaken in order to safeguard member states' future economic performance. In both cases we see that national diversity of policy objectives need not prevent integration as long as some strong policy priority is held in common. Even so, the Single European Act, in particular, underlines that there is nothing automatic about this realignment of common policies; the election of a Labour government in the United Kingdom at that time or a continuation of the

Socialist Party's earlier economic policies in France could have created a very different situation.

The Single European Act avoided the controversial issue of monetary integration except for a symbolic reference in the preamble. Within the Commission however, monetary integration was naturally seen as the next move in another 'relaunching' of Europe, akin to that which in the federalist mythology had taken place with the Treaties of Rome, and President Delors began a vigorous campaign for a reform of the EMS to support the 'completion' of the internal market. Many officials could be found to argue that the perfect market would require common monetary and fiscal policies which in turn would make a single currency a logical development. However it was the growing dissatisfaction among the member states with the dominant role of the Bundesbank, rather than concerns about the future inadequacy of the EMS, which eventually led to a new discussion of monetary reform. France in particular wished to reassert its role within the EMS and its call in 1987 for the creation of a European central bank and a single European currency was an attempt to claw back some of the influence lost to the Bundesbank. This was opposed by the German Federal Republic, which insisted on greater convergence of economic policies as a precondition for monetary union, and by the United Kingdom, which still refused to join the exchange rate mechanism and saw a single European currency as a rival to sterling and a surrender of national independence. Underlying these struggles for political pre-eminence in Europe was still the older issue, whether the purpose of a common monetary policy should be primarily to control inflation or primarily to restore higher growth rates.

The Delors Committee was set up by the European Council in 1988 with the specific brief to investigate ways of bridging these differences. The Delors Report which it produced suggested a move towards economic and monetary union in three stages but sensibly avoided the highly controversial issue of when to end the second stage of the process, at which point exchange rates between the member states' national currencies would be fixed and the écu become the single European currency.[29] With this evasion the Delors Report was accepted by the Council in June 1989. Even so, there were several indications that the Community still was far from agreement on movement towards monetary integration. In September the United Kingdom proposed making the écu a parallel currency to national currencies and letting financial markets decide whether the écu should in these conditions become a widespread European currency. The position of the United Kingdom came as no surprise, but behind its overt opposition the attitude of other member states indicated a growing scepticism about the implications of the Delors Report.

It has been suggested that it was functional spillover effects from the Single European Act which prompted the Council in December to ignore these disagreements and go ahead with the Delors Plan, as the report was by then called, and summon an inter-governmental conference for an economic and monetary union. In particular it has been argued that it was a response to the fear that the abolition of capital controls would create serious adjustment difficulties among the member states.[30] Only a more thorough analysis of the historical evidence when it becomes available can determine this question. However, we ourselves are not at the present moment convinced by this line of reasoning. External developments, in the form of the dramatic political changes in Germany and eastern Europe, seem to us to have had a more important role in establishing a united front within the Community. The statement of the Strasbourg meeting explicitly referred to those events and stated the determination of the European Council to intensify the efforts towards unification in order to make the European Community the epicentre of a wider Europe embracing both east and west. Behind this cliché can be discerned on the one hand the anxiety of France and the other original member states of the Six to keep a reunified Germany within the Community structure, which made it essential to find some way in which a further German policy could be advanced through the integrationist structure, and on the other hand the desire of the United Kingdom and some of its smaller followers to use the new power constellation in Europe to bring integration to a halt and construct a larger, merely co-operative, framework of interdependence including eastern Europe. Fear of Germany was the cement which forced these opposed interests still to try to find common ground.

At a special meeting in April 1990 Germany secured the full inclusion of the former German Democratic Republic in the Community, in exchange for its agreement to an eventual European Monetary Union with a single currency. The emphasis on speeding up the integration process as a guarantee to France that its security would not be threatened by German reunification was underlined by the decision to call a second inter-governmental conference on political union, a joint Franco-German proposal. At the summit in Dublin in June of the same year this new bargain was consolidated by the Council's decision to set a date for the final stage of monetary union at an inter-governmental conference to be held at the end of 1991. Spillover from the Single European Act was surely insignificant compared to the economic collapse and political retreat of Soviet communism, the withdrawal of

Soviet forces from some eastern European states and the unity of Germany. Only the United Kingdom refused to recognize the centrality of the Franco-German alliance to maintaining peace, exactly as it had done in 1950–2 and 1956–7, and voted against calling the inter-governmental conference on economic and monetary union.

During 1990–1 Council statements increasingly emphasized the need for the European Community to act as one political unit on the international level, not least when the Gulf War proved that such unity of action was still lacking. At the Luxemburg summit in 1991 defence policy was included in the plans for a political union; at the Maastricht summit in December the goal was said to be a European union involving not only economic and monetary union but also a common foreign and defence policy. The Maastricht Treaty text primarily indicates the European Council's will to face the challenges in the Community's external environment. As such, Maastricht reflects new national policy objectives which have emerged within the member states since 1989, not the mere continuation of the commercial policies embodied in the Single European Act. The history of the Community suggests a certain caution with respect to the future viability of the Maastricht agreement. The British and Danish reservations to the agreement on European Mone-tary Union indicated that governments are not equally committed to the inter-governmental bargain on which that union rests, and the state-ments made about a union of foreign and defence policies suggest that in an attempt to strengthen the political and economic model of the Community after the end of the Cold War the member states have overstretched their political commitment to European integration. As this book was completed the Danish population voted down the Maastricht Treaty in a referendum and is only likely to ratify it when it has been amended to give Denmark further exceptions.

Furthermore, the European Union Treaty is a highly asymmetrical treaty which bears very little resemblance to federal ideals. It is an ambitious enterprise: it sets a fixed date for the monetary union and a single currency, aspires to a common immigration, defence and foreign policy, and opens the issue of how to enlarge the Community in the near future. However, the treaty also maintains the choice between inter-dependence and integration as instruments. It makes clear that its intent as far as immigration, defence and foreign policy are concerned is not the federal ideal of a united Europe but only the more pragmatic one of interdependence, with nation-states co-operating closely together in pursuit of common objectives. This is in contrast to its treatment of monetary union, where its intention is specifically integrationist. For monetary union it sets out a timetable, whereas for the other objectives it gives no direction on how they will be fulfilled. Thus of the three pillars of which the treaty consists only one is integrationist, while the other two remain outside the influence of the Court of Justice, the Commission and the Parliament. The concept of the treaty is new in Community history, because it opens the way for a two-tier Europe in which member states with policy objectives held in common can move ahead of the rest of the Community if they wish to use the integrationist framework. This was made clear when the Community chose to ignore the United Kingdom's resistance to the incorporation of any statements about common welfare or social policies in the agreement. Few would at this moment believe that even if the result of the Danish referendum is discounted all the signatories will be ready for monetary union at the date indicated.

The latest developments in European integration do not seem in any way therefore to modify our hypotheses about the process of European integration and the Community. Rather, they seem to bear them out. The European Union Treaty indicates member states' wish to use both integration and interdependence to further national policy advancement for the future and, as in the Treaties of Rome, it leaves that policy-making function to national governments. Despite the increased powers of the European Parliament, the European Council remains the sole policy-maker within the Community and, as before, the question of whether integration will be chosen over interdependence depends on the development of domestic policies. What has changed is not the attitude of the nation-states to integration – it has remained remarkably unaltered since 1950 – but Germany's place in Europe. It may be that this change has altered the scope for independent national economic policy formulation in the other European countries, but this is outweighed by its political consequences. As long as the best way to deal with Germany's disproportionate economic weight in the European balance is still thought to be European integration, there will always be the possibility of an extra gain in European political stability which increases the support for advancing national policies through the integrationist framework. German reunification can only make that extra gain, and the dangers of renouncing it, seem greater.

Both choices therefore still exist. The frontier of national sovereignty, which is approached within varying distances by national policy choices, remains with little alteration where it was fixed in 1952 and 1957. Political parties seeking office continue to present to the electorate the concepts of European 'integration' and 'unification' as grand general ideas, which they either favour or oppose. Would they not be wiser to descend to the detail of the relationship of any particular policy proposal to the available European international frameworks for advancing it?

Not only would that be a step towards acknowledging European political realities, but for ardent champions of the cause of European unity, who unfortunately are normally the first to reject so realistic a political discourse, it might actually advance their cause. For the greatest single piece of evidence that the nation-state continues to dominate all policy choices is surely that political parties continue to advocate major changes of national policy with scarcely any explanation to the electorate of the international requirements needed to make them possible, even in the European Community.

2 Migration as an issue in European interdependence and integration: the case of Italy

Federico Romero

The post-war economic growth of every western European country has been repeatedly affected by vast manpower migrations across national boundaries. This large, protracted migratory phenomenon also influenced the political priorities pursued by the nation-state, domestically and internationally. Crucial choices in the field of migration policy had a profound impact on economic growth as well as on political strategies for internal social cohesion and consensus. Primarily shaped to meet each nation's economic goals, immigration policies – and a deliberate emigration policy in the case of Italy – also had a crucial bearing on the social and electoral processes which determined the broader definitions of the collective interest and the long-term identity of the nation-state. Each government therefore tried to regulate and channel manpower flows according to its own long-term view of national prosperity and political stability. Internationally this translated into an attempt to shape the terms of continental interdependence in accordance with the perceived national interest. As a result, the issue of migration and, more broadly, of the interconnection among the various national labour markets, deeply influenced the entire political and institutional configuration of western Europe.

The various options adopted for the regulation of migrations shed a revealing light on the priorities that each nation pursued, exposing the nature and function of each approach to integration and highlighting the domestic compromises and arrangements which shaped each international action. In this respect, the historical study of migrations and of their regulatory frameworks allows for an analytical and conceptual reassessment of some of the crucial passages in the historical dynamic of interdependence and integration in western Europe.[1]

Throughout the increasingly large migratory cycle which accompanied the post-war European boom up to 1973, the processes of European co-operation and integration revolved around an inherent, recurrent tension between the expanding goals pursued through national economic policies and a deepening degree of interconnection between the various economies. The point is that such growing interconnection was neither spontaneous nor inevitable, but it had been deliberately, albeit cautiously, promoted and cultivated by national governments as a condition for the success of their domestic policies for growth. In the field of manpower migrations, the whole post-war period – through all the different stages in the institutional formalization of interdependence – shows quite clearly a complex and involuted interplay between national requirements for limited migrations of workers and the concomitant national necessity to maintain a complete control of their consequences. This placed the domestic problems and aims of the nation-state at the very centre of every international negotiation on this matter and, more importantly, of every actual framework consequently devised for regulating interdependence.

So overriding was this national necessity to maintain control over the consequences of migration, that even when the concomitance of national policies towards economic growth and the promotion of foreign trade led to the selection of an integrationist strategy to promote them, the liberalization of labour movements within the integrated area was a much less acceptable idea. The liberalization of manpower movements did not travel smoothly down the wide avenue of supra-nationality. Instead, in contrast to the movement of goods, it trudged a narrow path hemmed in by cautious inter-governmental compromises which tried to balance and, whenever possible, conciliate different national interests by retaining elements of interdependence and co-operation to mediate the principles of integration. At least for the EEC's six founding members, manpower requirements appeared largely complementary. But more complex policy goals prevented a simple integration of their labour resources in a common, unified market. As a practical result, most of that vast flow of foreign workers which fed the industrial expansion of western Europe in the 1960s still took place within the framework of bilateral agreements among nation-states. Just a relatively small portion of the overall movement – that represented by Italian emigrants, and only after the mid-1960s – was actually stimulated and governed by the new supranational procedures brought into being by the common market.

In this policy area the crucial domestic importance of a few key political and social issues, which depended – among other factors – on labour-market conditions, shaped the emerging frameworks of European interdependence and integration in such a way as to maintain migration policies under a firmer control of the nation-state than integration would have allowed. Whereas, for example, Italy's strong

'European' inclination directly served its government's strategy for national growth and stabilization, the analogous but inverted necessities of the receiving countries imposed a system of strict regulations upon the liberalization of manpower flows across western Europe. The actual course of European integration in this case does not stem from an allegedly ineluctable historical decline of the nation-state. On the contrary, it seems to embody a negotiated international co-ordination and expansion of parallel domestic strategies, all of which were aiming rather at the economic and political consolidation of the nation-state.

ECONOMIC GOALS AND POLITICAL REQUIREMENTS

At the end of the Second World War dislocations of manpower were such as to feature prominently among the problems that every national reconstruction programme urgently had to take into consideration. Vast numbers of unemployed, displaced persons and refugees were encouraged by governments and international organizations to leave for the Americas or Australia, in a flow of inter-continental emigration which peaked in the 1950s but declined rapidly in the following decade. A few nations, on the other hand, suffered from serious, even though localized, shortages of manpower, which induced intra-European migrations. From the very onset of the Cold War in 1947 these movements took place almost entirely within each bloc of nations: the only major and obvious exception was divided Germany.

West Germany received, up to 1961, a constant flow of East German refugees: their overall net total is estimated by the United Nations at around 2.7 million. Britain continued to attract and employ many Irish workers and in the period 1945–75 also received 300,000 migrants from continental Europe (Poles, Germans, Italians, Greeks). The Scandinavian countries linked up in a Nordic Common Labour Market (1951) in which circulation and employment were liberalized: by 1978 about a million people had taken advantage of its provisions, mostly Finnish workers employed in Sweden.[2] The most geographically widespread and, for our purposes, politically significant migratory flow, however, connected various western European nations after 1946 to one main source of manpower: Italy.

Initially directed to France, Belgium and Switzerland, this last migratory flow would vigorously expand also into the German Federal Republic in the 1960s (see table 1). On the supply side moreover it would gradually extend so far as to include most Mediterranean countries, thereby growing into the major European migratory phenomenon up to the crisis of 1973–4. At the root of this emigration there was, in the immediate post-war period, the apparent complementarity between massive unemployment in Italy and manpower shortages elsewhere in some sectors with a crucial role in early reconstruction (agriculture and construction in France, mining in Belgium, construction and manufacturing in Switzerland).

The inherent instability of this type of demand for labour, together with geographical proximity, made this movement into a highly temporary and fluctuating shift of single workers rather than a permanent emigration of entire families. This was a feature that would become increasingly visible and indeed dominant in the most intense stages of growth of the demand for foreign labour in the 1960s. Migration from southern Europe often followed a seasonal pattern and was always so temporary as to appear almost as a revolving movement between the areas of departure and those of employment. It was primarily made up of young male workers who conceived their employment abroad as temporary and were committed to accumulate some savings in view of an early return back home. It can be more appropriately defined as a phenomenon of intense mobility of workforce between contiguous labour markets rather than as a transfer of population.[3]

Thus from the very beginning to the end of the long post-war boom some of the main labour markets of western Europe grew to be not only interconnected but indeed highly interdependent. But how was this interdependence organized and institutionalized? The solutions varied widely according to each country's specific position and necessities, and a basic contrast between supply nations and demand nations marked the processes of political co-operation and of integration. For Italy the main answer however was relatively clear. It had a fundamental interest in opening up the European labour market for its own unemployed.

From the end of the Second World War, Italy's apparent over-population and scarcity of capital generated a widespread political consensus on the urgency of a vast emigration. Given an official unemployment figure of 2 million units (10 per cent of the labour force) and about just as many workers unproductively underemployed, the Italian labour market presented an apparently intractable economic and political problem. It was thought that the interruption of emigration in the inter-war period had consigned to the new republic a backlog of surplus manpower whose prospects for employment could not be matched, at least in the medium term, by the limited capital resources available to the nation.

Table 1 Migratory movements, 1946–73 (thousands)

Year	Belgium	France		German Fed Rep.*	Italy	Lux.	Neth.	Swit.
	(a)	(b)	(c)	(a)	(a)	(a)	(a)	(d)
1946		30.2			−105.7			
1947		68.2			−188.6			
1948	46.3	57.0			−189.3			
1949	−8.2	58.8			−135.8			
1950	−4.9	10.6	35	378.0	−128.3		19.9	3.7
1951	23.1	21.0	30	137.6	−201.2		−22.4	80.3
1952	18.2	32.7	20	64.9	−180.6		−47.7	85.4
1953	7.2	15.4	19	348.9	−121.6	1.5	−31.6	84.5
1954	3.7	12.3	51	221.2	−143.7	1.4	−18.9	91.4
1955	20.4	19.0	120	310.8	−178.2	1.9	5.2	106.3
1956	20.4	65.4	170	339.4	−189.5	1.5	−11.0	123.6
1957	26.3	111.7	220	416.7	−178.5	3.0	−12.5	149.1
1958	9.2	82.8	140	328.9	−116.4	2.6	12.1	119.0
1959	−0.9	44.2	130	210.7	−112.4	1.7	−16.9	124.8
1960	2.8	48.9	140	394.8	−191.7	2.0	−12.8	162.4
1961	6.1	78.9	180	436.0	−176.9	2.9	6.4	204.9
1962	24.8	113.1	860	252.0	−136.5	3.3	16.9	210.2
1963	40.8	115.5	215	192.8	−56.5	2.0	8.4	199.5
1964	58.1	153.7	185	277.6	−68.3	4.0	13.7	196.1
1965	44.3	152.1	110	343.7	−86.3	4.3	18.7	141.4
1966	33.6	131.7	125	131.6	−90.0	3.3	19.9	140.7
1967	24.0	107.8	92	−176.9	−59.9	−0.4	−11.5	128.0
1968	16.8	93.2	100	278.2	−65.7	0.7	6.0	137.9
1969	19.4	167.8	150	572.3	−28.9	1.7	20.2	140.2
1970	23.0	174.2	180	574.0	−9.3	1.1	33.5	103.7
1971	25.5	136.0	145	430.7	−39.1	5.1	33.0	85.1
1972	19.8	98.1	109	330.8	−3.6	3.2	19.1	89.7
1973	23.8	132.1	120	384.0	−1.4	4.9	21.1	90.1

(a) net migration as balance of total inflow and outflow; negative figures indicate a prevalence of departures
(b) immigration of foreign workers (Algerians and seasonal workers are not included)
(c) overall net immigration (inclusive of Algerians and repatriated French citizens)
(d) foreigners granted first labour permit
*   Up to 1959 immigration in the German Federal Republic is almost entirely composed of refugees from the German Democratic Republic; within two years they are entirely replaced by officially recruited South European workers.

Sources: Various national statistics; United Nations, *Labour Supply and Migration in Europe. Demographic Dimensions 1950–1975 and Prospects* (New York, 1979).

In the framework of the economic policy adopted in conjunction with Marshall Aid, the Italian government considered emigration as a 'vital necessity'. The 'viability' of the national economy had to depend also on a programme of 'rational productive emigration' aimed at bridging the gap between the medium-term reconstruction effort and the long-term goal of national economic security and prosperity in conditions of high employment.[4] The national four-year liberalization and investment plan submitted to the OEEC in 1948 put forward a solution to Italy's international payments problem that relied mostly on American aid but also on the inflow of foreign currency which would result from sustained emigration: about 10 per cent of the cost of Italy's imports was to be covered by the emigrants' remittances. To achieve such a target a net outflow of more than 800,000 people in four years was required. Even if this goal were to be accomplished however, unemployment would still stand around 8 to 9 per cent by 1953, a seriously threatening level for the tenuous and fragile political stability of the newly born republic.[5]

The new conditions of mass electoral competition dictated a rapid decrease of social tensions if the precarious public consent to the centrist government coalition were to be maintained. In the government's own opinion this gave emigration a crucial importance because of its certain contribution towards a high-employment policy, and this appeared even more urgent than its beneficial but largely unpredictable financial effects. The migratory outflow therefore had to be as rapid and 'as vast as possible', and the government's own diplomatic initiatives had to be geared to this goal.[6] Emigration had become an integral component not only of economic policy but also of the government's own survival strategy, and its promotion and implementation a primary goal of the country's foreign policy. The nation-state had to attain abroad – with the negotiation of new outlets in foreign labour markets – the very conditions for its own stability and political viability. The solution of Italy's most urgent domestic problems, and the search for its long-term economic security, had therefore inevitably to be pursued in a new framework of international interdependence. Italy's 'Europeanism' was not only the result of the defeat in the war with a consequent search for respectability, nor just the vague response of a universalist culture to a deeply felt comparative weakness: it was in fact a requirement for the success of the government's policy and a direct function of its effort for the consolidation of the nation-state.[7]

In practical terms this meant, at the best, a full integration, or, at the least, a partial opening, of western European labour markets to Italian emigrants. The process of trade liberalization had to advance hand in hand with the liberalization of labour movements. This became a basic tenet of Italian policy which was determinedly pursued up to the early 1970s in all European negotiations.

The obvious obstacle was that Italy's hope and goal could very well become everybody else's nightmare, and for the very same reasons. The protection of the national labour force and the maximization of its employment was a top priority for the economic prosperity and political stability of every other European nation. The very concept of full employment – no matter how strictly or loosely interpreted – was at the core of every post-war vision of society and reconstructive strategy. In the countries that were supposed to receive the migrants, a policy of uncontrolled liberalization of access to the national labour market could undermine those conditions of high and stable employment whose attainment it was meant to facilitate for Italian manpower. In several cases, foreign workers could provide a much-needed contribution to recovery and growth; unregulated migration, though, could wreck the social and political process of national reconstruction. The same social and political domestic pressures that urged Italy to press for European freedom of circulation and employment prevented the other states from relinquishing their national controls. No government intended, or indeed deemed it politically feasible, to forgo its powers to regulate the access to its territory and to its own labour market, which constitute an essential attribute of sovereignty.[8]

The economic necessities of a group of neighbouring (and allied) nations converged, but their resolution was potentially contradictory and could indeed be disastrous for any participant. The prospect for an organized system of interdependence hinged on the difficult reconciliation of these multiple, delicate and indeed parallel goals pursued by various national governments. Even when a bold step towards sectoral integration was undertaken – as was the case with the creation of the European Coal and Steel Community in 1952 – governments remained deeply reluctant to give up their control of the national labour market. In the post-war boom the only feasible instrument for the organization of workers' migrations turned out to be a system of carefully negotiated, and rather restrictive, bilateral agreements.

A BILATERAL SYSTEM FOR MANPOWER MIGRATIONS

From 1946 onwards Italy signed bilateral agreements with all the countries that experienced some shortage of manpower and needed a specific (and generally temporary) inflow of migrant labour: France, Belgium, Switzerland, the United Kingdom and Luxemburg. These agreements organized the co-operation of each nation's employment services for the recruitment of specific types of workforce. An overall ceiling was generally set to the number of immigrants to be admitted each year, and within this quota the actual level of recruitment was then left to the demand expressed within the receiving economy. Actual recruitment was sometimes managed directly by a government agency (as in the case of France), sometimes left to the employers and their trade associations (as in Belgium and Switzerland). Foreign workers were admitted with temporary contracts and with permits restricted to a specific place and occupation. Renewal of these permits was easy in a country with a prospect of slow demographic growth and persistent labour shortages like France, but strictly regulated in Switzerland, where immigration policy aimed at preventing the permanent settlement of foreigners. There, the migrant was considered as a temporary 'guest worker', whose productive role was to be taken up by some other immigrant one or two years later, so as to constantly maintain the temporary basis of the foreign workforce. The bilateral accords also guaranteed that wage levels would be equal to those of the national workforce and that remittances could be sent back home.[9]

These early agreements allowed for limited but significant migratory flows that prevented labour market bottlenecks and shortages from hindering the reconstructive effort in the receiving countries. Their achievements, at any rate, fell far short of the expectations – and the necessities – of the Italian government. The gross migratory outflow from the country's poorest regions was sustained, and European destinations did indeed attract a relatively large number of workers. But the volatility of western European demand and the temporary nature of employment there resulted in very high rates of return. From 1948 to 1956 the bulk of Italy's net migratory losses (the indicator that really mattered for the government's employment strategy) was made up by emigration to inter-continental destinations. This came as a useful but quite insufficient compensation to the scarcity of permanent European outlets: the overall level of net migration remained simply too low. Italy's minimum target of 200,000 net departures per year was never attained except (and just barely) in 1951 (see table 2). This meant that for the whole period 1948–57 total net emigration amounted to just 73 per cent of what the government had hoped to achieve as a *minimum* goal. Largely determined by cyclical variations in short-term demand, emigration to Europe remained throughout the 1950s simply too limited to satisfy the needs of Italy's economic and political strategy.

Moreover, the bilateral system was particularly unsatisfactory for Italy – indeed for every sending country – from a qualitative point of view. It did not really lead to the permanent opening of foreign markets nor did it entail any international responsibility for the solution of the unemployment problem, which remained a strictly national matter.

Table 2 Gross and net emigration from Italy, 1946–57

Year	Europe		Other continents		Total	
	Gross	Net	Gross	Net	Gross	Net
1946	103,077	99,119	7,209	6,609	110,286	105,728
1947	192,226	136,806	61,918	51,809	254,144	188,615
1948	193,303	91,612	115,212	97,642	308,515	189,254
1949	94,959	+ 2,721	159,510	138,564	254,469	135,843
1950	54,927	16,550	145,379	111,722	200,306	128,272
1951	149,206	95,765	143,851	105,388	293,057	201,153
1952	144,098	71,947	133,437	108,688	277,535	180,635
1953	112,069	40,606	112,602	81,027	224,671	121,633
1954	108,557	32,374	142,368	111,351	250,925	143,725
1955	149,026	62,682	147,800	115,561	296,826	178,243
1956	207,631	87,481	137,171	102,028	344,802	189,509
1957	236,010	108,033	105,723	70,423	341,733	178,456

The + mark signals a prevalence of return movements.

Source: Figures from ISTAT in Ministry of Foreign Affairs, *Aspetti e problemi dell'emigrazione italiana all'estero. Relazione per il 1975* (Rome, 1975) and in G. Lucrezio and L. Favero, 'Un quarto di secolo di emigrazione italiana', *Studi Emigrazione*, 25–6, 1972, pp. 78–9.

Since it depended on foreign demand for labour, it did not decrease the receiving governments' control over their national labour markets. Such a control could be exercised in a more or less protectionist fashion according to cyclical needs and political conditions, but remained none the less unimpaired. When demand was very high the economic priorities of the host countries could occasionally coincide with the needs of the sending countries, but the agreements did not assure any irreversible rights to the latter. Most importantly, the system could not in the least restrain the receiving governments from bowing to internal social and political pressures for the protection of local employment. Their sovereignty was intact, their regulating powers untouched and always available if domestic protectionist considerations called for a containment of immigration. This was well epitomized by the United Kingdom in 1951, when the strong reaction of the National Union of Mineworkers to the arrival of Italian workers in a few Welsh mines convinced the UK government to unilaterally discontinue a specific bilateral agreement that had just been signed for that purpose.[10] Thus, as an organized structure of interdependence, the bilateral system was too limited, unbalanced and inconclusive.

Italy saw its ambitions frustrated not only by scarce and erratic demand but especially by powerful political and institutional resistances which remained beyond the reach of diplomatic pressures and international negotiations. Its government therefore became increasingly persuaded that national barriers to the circulation of manpower had to be brought down or circumvented by other means. The question of Italian unemployment had to be turned into an international issue and dealt with at a multilateral level. Italian leaders argued that the very concept of full employment had to transcend the boundaries of the nation-state and be considered in a larger geographical – and political – context: the growing economic co-operation within western Europe. The various institutions for European co-operation and integration must become instruments for the realization of a 'larger and freer European labour market', which was deemed vital for the accomplishment of the nation's economic strategy.[11]

INTEGRATION AND NATIONAL SOVEREIGNTY

As early as August 1947 Italy had already asked for an OEEC commitment to the liberalization of migration, but to no avail. The United Kingdom and France had no desire to entrust some newly born international agency with the handling of such delicate matters, and no agreement could be reached except to commission an inconclusive study of the issue. In the following years Italian diplomats also insisted that the USA take the lead, and lift the financial burden, in an international effort to promote the massive emigration of refugees out of Europe. Rome hoped that such an international initiative, once under way, could take care also of part of its own unemployed population. After long and frustrating discussions however, the only practical accomplishment was the establishment in 1952 of limited machinery – the Inter-governmental Committee for European Migrations (ICEM) – to finance the journey of trans-oceanic migrants. In a European as well as in a larger context, national prerogatives still blocked the way towards any proposed internationalization of the migratory issue.[12] Attention then turned towards the first crucial European negotiations for an integrative framework, the European Coal and Steel Community (ECSC).

The Italian delegates to the Paris conference argued from the outset that an integrated market ought to embrace the freedom of circulation for workers, and asked for a complete liberalization of access to the coal and steel labour markets of the Six. They found little support. By the end of 1950 there were just over 30,000 Italians working in Belgium's coal-mines (by mid-1951 the figure had risen to 39,430). Exchanges of manpower among the other nations in the industries concerned were insignificant. The Benelux countries opposed an increased mobility.

France and the German Federal Republic made clear that free circulation could be contemplated only for a very few highly skilled workers. Italy however had at that time a very small number of coal-miners and steel-workers with skills and qualifications; its potential emigrants were unskilled workers, in most cases agricultural labourers. The rather restrictive Franco-German formulation was eventually accepted in the Treaty of Paris: article 69 committed the member states to lift every employment restriction based on nationality only for workers of 'proven qualification'.[13]

Upon this basis, the real bargaining started around the criteria for the implementation of article 69. Italy wanted a Community employment service operated directly by the High Authority of ECSC so as to move towards a fully integrated labour market under supranational regulations. But this was precisely what the other countries were not prepared to accept. In 1954 the ECSC finally agreed on a rather restrictive interpretation of the article; steel- and coal-workers with a specific qualification and at least two years' experience could receive a European Labour Card, which enabled them to work in the other member states, but only in their own sector. For the employment service, only a loose co-ordination of the existing national agencies was contemplated, and even that never actually came to life.[14]

In sum, no real power in this area was transferred by the Treaty of Paris from the nation-states to the High Authority and the ECSC rules actually amounted to a substantial restriction rather than an implementation of the freedom of circulation. The European Labour Card was available to only one-third of the Community workers and did not activate any significant migratory movement: in the first eight years of its existence only 1,800 workers took advantage of its provisions![15] From a practical as well as a political perspective this first attempt to solve the issue through integration was a bitter disappointment for the Italians. The Coal and Steel Community did not open new outlets for migrants, it extended only very restrictively the supranational principles and rules to the labour market. It certainly did not represent a noticeable advance towards an international solution of Italy's demographic and occupational difficulties. The only accomplishment was the statement of principle in favour of the freedom of circulation vaguely spelled out in article 69.

But even this abstract concept meant very different things to the different countries involved in the integrative process. The inconclusive but rather revealing debate on the possible outlines of a common market, which took place during the negotiations for the Defence Community Treaty in the Commission for the European Political

Community at the end of 1953, brought their divergences into stark relief. Italian diplomats obviously aiming for a wide interpretation argued that the freedom of circulation formula had to entail the full harmonization of all the factors and procedures regulating access to the labour markets of the Six. France and Luxemburg, on the other hand, conceived of the freedom of circulation only as a long-term prospect for an indeterminate future, when unemployment had been completely drained off from the whole of Europe, possibly through a sustained process of inter-continental emigration. In the meantime, they had no intention of giving up their strong national safeguards. Even the more explicitly integrationist countries however raised substantial objections to the Italian view. Belgium and the Netherlands would not agree to a mutual recognition of qualifications and to the harmonization of social legislation. At least in principle, the German Federal Republic did not disagree on a common European approach to unemployment, but saw its solution only in a future co-ordination of economic policies, while objecting to the destabilizing consequences of any early move towards freedom of circulation.[16]

It was primarily a set of social and political domestic constraints that hampered any movement towards multinational agreements. Up to the late 1950s the fear of an invasion of unemployed foreigners remained quite widespread throughout western Europe, and was obviously very intense among workers. National and international labour unions, even when in agreement with the lofty economic principles of European liberalization and integration, none the less insisted on the retention of effective controls and national restrictions on the movements of foreign workers. It was conceded that new sets of regulations might possibly be agreed upon in international negotiations, but they certainly had to remain effective and responsive to national necessities; no one would take the risk of uncontrolled flows which could endanger income and employment levels for local workers. Even more importantly, this consensus on the defence of national employment was not limited to wage-earners. It included large and differentiated sectors of public opinion, thus placing at the centre of the political process in every receiving nation a consistent, robust, protectionist bias which acted as a powerful impediment to any market liberalization.[17]

These social constraints were compounded by another crucial factor which weighed heavily against the opening of national borders. No government bureaucracy was willing to give up, or transfer to some supranational authority, the vast and entrenched set of national regulations upon which rested its power to control migrations and therefore exercise sovereignty. Since industry was not yet starving for large inflows of foreign manpower, the end-result was that economic growth policies were not at all hampered by protective restrictions, and the search for political stability could comfortably remain anchored to the maintenance of strict controls on access to the labour market. After all, it was precisely these national regulations which allowed the receiving countries to govern the process of national growth (whose tensions Italy was trying to defuse in an international or supranational arena) within a consensual electoral framework.

THE NATIONAL BASE OF INTERDEPENDENCE

The only instance when the Italian strategy seemed to face a promising opportunity was during the Korean War boom. The strong growth associated with the rearmament effort induced NATO planners to look with concern at the imbalance between countries with full employment and localized shortages of skilled workers and other nations with dangerously large groups of idle manpower. In the event of full mobilization, this asymmetry could endanger a productive effort whose resources were already stretched quite thin. NATO however did not have the authority to assume a direct economic role, but its Lisbon summit in 1952 recommended a rationalization of manpower usage throughout Europe. The Mutual Security Agency, the branch of the American government concerned with allocating military aid, then formally asked the OEEC to liberalize the circulation of the European workforce. Such an objective was well beyond the practical reach of the OEEC, which in this respect had even less power than the Coal and Steel Community, but the whole philosophy of the OEEC revolved around liberalization, and the emergence of this new impulse from within the western alliance converged with Italian pressures in bringing the issue to a new negotiating table.[18]

In March 1952 the OEEC ministers set up a Working Party on Manpower Liberalization. It was charged with the task of achieving 'the maximum possible progress' in the removal of all the 'restrictive rules, formalities and other obstacles to the free movement of workers between Member countries'.[19] One of the most intelligent and effective Italian officials, Giovanni Malagodi, was appointed chairman of the working party, composed of British, French, German and Belgian delegates and an American observer. The first meeting significantly began with a bitter row between Italy and the United Kingdom on the failure of the scheme for the migration of Italian miners into the UK. Italy's explicit stigmatization of protectionist attitudes was meant to pave the way for its own proposal, which came immediately thereafter in the form of a full-fledged plan for the liberalization of manpower movements in western Europe. Italian diplomacy produced a complete, systematic and quite astonishing programme for linking its partners into a multilateral framework of interdependence whose essential feature was an automatic progress towards integration. Like the Dutch proposals in 1952 for a customs union, which eventually became the basis of the common market of the EEC, they contained a fixed programme of automatic irreversible stages towards the abandonment of national sovereignty exercised through border controls, in this case on labour.

The plan envisaged the acceptance by every OEEC country of an established annual quota of immigrants, within whose range foreign workers could freely enter if they had a contract with an employer or were called by relatives who could house them for six months while in search of a job. The quotas were to be enlarged every two years under the supervision of an OEEC international board, with similar status to the management board of the European Payments Union, until complete freedom of movement was achieved in ten years' time. The multilateral quotas would not replace the work permit system for organized migrations contemplated under the bilateral treaties, but come on top of it. They were meant not only as a means for a further quantitative increase in manpower movements but, above all, as an entirely new instrument aimed at releasing intra-European migrations from the current institutional, state-organized system of exchange. The fundamental objective was to create an area of liberalization dominated by market criteria – in strict similarity to what OEEC was doing for industrial trade – so as to activate spontaneous flows of workers and family dependants across western Europe. While workers officially recruited through the bilateral schemes had no right to change jobs and take residence, those who entered through the multilateral quota would be totally free to move in the labour market and reside in the country as long as they wished.

Thus, the plan implied a complete break with the very concept of a national labour market: it explicitly aimed at depriving governments of their control on immigration. By superseding the receiving countries' authority to regulate manpower flows with that of an international body, the political goal of full employment was to be uplifted from a strictly national to a Europe-wide objective. The OEEC would gradually assume some direct responsibility for Italy's unemployment.

The Italian negotiators knew all too well that such a programme would impair some of their partners' crucial instruments for full employment policies. Moreover, it would directly endanger trade union power and influence and therefore upset some basic conditions of political equilibrium. But this is precisely what the Italians aimed at. Since they deemed it indispensable to sever the linkage between social protectionism and national governments' resistances to immigration, the plan charged the obstacle head on. In what was probably its most astonishing clause, the plan stated that the host government could not interfere with the provisions of the new immigrants' work contracts even in the case of sub-standard wages and conditions. The receiving government, in short, was challenged not only to give up its powers and controls on access to the country, but also to declare itself not responsible, in the eyes of its own public opinion and electorate, for the economic and social consequences of liberalization. The plan clearly appealed directly – across and beyond any idea of national sovereignty – to foreign firms to hire migrant workers in order to cut their labour costs. This part of the proposal might have been meant as a bargaining chip to be negotiated away later on, but it certainly revealed the distance that Italy was prepared to travel in order to get rid of its own unemployed in an international framework. If put into practice, after all, such a scheme would have exposed the migrants themselves to a condition of utter weakness *vis-à-vis* their employers. It would have created a peculiar group of workers with the right to move across international borders but with no protection under any nation's social legislation.[20]

The Italian proposal was flatly rejected by France, Belgium and the United Kingdom, who argued that they had no intention of endangering the employment of their own workers, scrapping all social guarantees and giving up the administrative instruments which assured their governments' sovereignty on the labour market. Italy was accused of treating workers as 'a merchandise'. The discussion made clear that no country was prepared to forgo the permit system, without which the migrant workforce could not be directed to the sectors whose growth was deemed most urgent and without which, it was argued, no planning would be possible. Moreover, the social and political consequences of such a deregulation of the labour market, both international and domestic, it was argued, would grow unmanageable.

The disagreement looked so irreconcilable as to make the impasse of the working party likely to grow into a major political embarrassment. The British Foreign Office suggested extreme caution in handling such an 'explosive material'. It was apparent that something had to be conceded to Italy, which claimed that manpower liberalization was a 'vital national interest', and threatened to retaliate by obstructing progress in other fields of OEEC action. Eventually France came up with a counter-proposal that envisioned a co-ordinated, light and gradual relaxation of the existing rules on work and residence permits and the establishment of information exchanges between the national employment services. The idea seemed 'innocuous' to the British and thus to be supported in order to overcome the stalemate and soothe Italian susceptibilities while rejecting their radical plan.[21] In the end, Italy found itself completely isolated as the only potential beneficiary of a liberalization which basically entailed only concessions by the other partners. Thus it had to back away from its confrontational posture and settle for the scanty result embodied in the French proposal.

The practical outcome of the working party was then the enactment, in October 1953, of an OEEC Code of Liberalization on the employment of other member countries' citizens. The code in fact amounted to little more than a partial simplification and standardization of the existing national rules on work permits, and it brought little if any liberalization. Its basic features were the following. First, a work permit had to be given to a foreigner if an offer of employment could not be taken up by a national citizen within one month (two for France which obtained a temporary exception). Thus the code sanctioned the legitimate usage of a one-month priority of employment for nationals. Second, work permit renewal would become automatic after five years, but only for the same occupation and only if the sector was not suffering from heavy unemployment. Finally, it was established that the migrants' wage and employment conditions were to be equal to those of the local labour force.[22]

National governments had managed to preserve their full control over the domestic labour market and had merely accepted a limited degree of international harmonization of the administrative rules for the admission of foreign migrants. Indeed in most countries the new rules did not represent a significant departure from the previous ones. Only in the case of Belgium could the OEEC later claim that its Code of Liberalization had made admission procedures slightly more generous. In the first two years of implementation (1954–5) the overall number of permits granted by member states according to the new code grew a little, but an OEEC study found out that this was purely the effect of higher demand, which would have been equally satisfied under the previous rules. In the following years further measures to improve the code and enlarge its scope came under discussion, but they were repeatedly blocked by strong national opposition.[23]

By the mid-1950s western European unemployment had been greatly reduced by sustained economic growth and substantial inter-continental emigration. The German Federal Republic was rapidly approaching high levels of employment and the political urgency for an international solution of the migratory issue appeared limited to the poorer countries of southern Europe. Italy was increasingly isolated in its diplomatic search for new European outlets to ease its own unemployment. After ten years of European economic co-operation, and in spite of a significant experience of sectoral integration, the institutional framework for manpower movements was still almost totally shaped by national regimes. Most national barriers and impediments to the circulation of workers were still there, as effective as ever. The receiving countries' governments activated and regulated moderate migratory flows in accordance with their purely cyclical requirements, which in those years were still relatively modest, and occasionally with their needs for specific skills. All the major attempts to liberalize the circulation of workers throughout western Europe had been effectively frustrated: the OEEC itself had to admit that there was no such thing as a 'European labour market'.[24]

The reasons for this failure were both strong and obvious. The system of bilateral exchanges, after all, served the objectives of the industrialized economies of northern Europe in a satisfactory way. Ever since the end of the Second World War, manpower shortages – however momentarily severe they might be in a sector or a region – had always remained quite circumscribed. The bulk of European industry had not suffered from a generalized shortage of manpower, which, in most cases, was made quite abundant and relatively cheap by massive internal migrations. The bilateral agreements had allowed for rapid and adequate responses to the erratic peaks of demand in construction, mining or – in the case of France – seasonal agricultural work. A vast emigration of the Italian unemployed had been inhibited not just by protectionist restrictions: international demand for labour had simply remained too limited, given the vast internal reserves of unskilled manpower available to almost every European nation.

The era of bilaterally organized interdependence culminated in 1955 when Italy signed a migration agreement with the Federal Republic of Germany, the last among western European nations to begin the recruitment of foreign workers. In spite of a sustained inflow from the east, the Federal Republic was then approaching full employment and facing years of insufficient demographic growth. The Minister of the Economy Ludwig Erhard proposed to recruit Italian workers in order to maintain flexibility in the labour market and prevent the rise of inflationary wage pressure. The trade unions, supported by the Sozialistische Partei Deutschland (SPD) and to a certain extent also by the Ministry of Labour, naturally objected to an indiscriminate liberalization that could lower working standards and curb their own bargaining power. but they were also anxious to maintain a fast pace of economic growth and in the end came to accept some form of carefully regulated immigration. A compromise was reached that was meant to safeguard social consensus while at the same time enabling sustained industrial expansion.

A federal agency was charged with the active task of recruiting foreign workers abroad on a highly selective and strictly temporary basis. The migrant was called only after a precisely motivated request from a firm. The government would issue only temporary permits, making sure that the migrants would leave the country when their contracts expired, possibly to be replaced by other migrants so as to keep the foreign workers' population on a rotating basis and prevent the settlement of permanent communities. At least in theory, national control over the access to the labour market was thus made almost perfect. The guest-workers were meant to come in merely to fill cyclical gaps and to remain only as long as they were needed, in a sort of protectionist planning of the labour supply which (however fallacious it proved to be later in the 1960s) appeared initially capable of conciliating political and economic priorities, foreign labour immigration and domestic social cohesion. The over-ambitious goal was to have the advantages of migration without its social consequences and costs. This policy of temporary recruitment was inaugurated with an agreement with Italy, later to be followed by a string of others with many Mediterranean countries. After three years of very limited recruitment, demand for foreign labour boomed from 1959 onwards, and the German Federal Republic soon became the very centre of the huge migratory flow of the 1960s from southern to northern Europe.[25]

With the German-Italian treaty the industrial regions of western Europe were now thoroughly covered by a network of bilateral schemes for the immigration of Italian, and more generally Mediterranean, workers. But the post-war record of Italian migratory policy remained inadequate. Its quantitative targets had gone widely unfulfilled. In the twelve-year period 1946–57 more than 1.7 million migrants had left for western Europe but, their rate of return being around 52 per cent, net migration was only 840,254 units (see table 3). In the same period, emigration to trans-continental destinations had achieved better results because rates of return were substantially lower: 1.4 million people had left Italy with a net emigration of 1,100,900 units. This fell short of the stated minimum target of 200,000 a year: the actual yearly average for overall net emigration was only 161,750. In spite of a decade of fast economic growth, in 1957 domestic unemployment still hovered around 9 per cent. From a qualitative point of view, Italian policy had been even more drastically frustrated. The bilateral system was a manifestly

Table 3 Italian migration to European countries, 1946–57

Destinations	Exits	Returns	Net
Belgium	216,315	56,904	159,411
France	589,179	208,491	380,688
German Federal Rep.	21,138	13,633	7,505
Luxemburg	25,530	20,667	4,863
Netherlands	5,921	319	5,602
Switzerland	789,820	587,339	202,481
United Kingdom	72,380	4,931	67,449
Other countries	24,806	12,551	12,255
Total, Europe	1,745,089	904,835	840,254

Source: U. Ascoli, *Movimenti migratori in Italia* (Bologna, 1979), p. 47.

inadequate answer to Italy's hope for a liberalized, and possibly integrated, European labour market.

The defeat of all attempts at a multilateral opening of European borders, however, is quite understandable in view of the substantial conflict between two approaches to interdependence which had similar – in fact parallel – origins but steered in opposite directions. An essentially national interest in assuring sustained domestic growth in conditions of political stability fostered Italy's search for liberalization and integration just as much as it prompted the other nations to avoid such a course. It was Italy's national interest, because of the urgent need to drain massive unemployment, that required interdependence to be organized in the shape of an open European market. The aim was not to reduce the nation-state's power and ability to steer the economy, but in fact the opposite: to find in Europe the only space and the only arrangements that could enable the government to accomplish its own economic policy goals.[26]

As far as manpower migrations were concerned, however, the interest of the only major 'exporting' country within OEEC was neither coincident with nor entirely complementary to that of the 'importing' countries. For the latter, all strategic objectives – growth in conditions of high employment, public consent, governments' planning of growth policies – required an effective national control on the labour market. Italy's own employment goals demanded multilateral liberalization, while the very same purpose dictated an opposite solution to France, the Federal Republic or Belgium: protection of domestic employment and controlled immigration. The bilateral agreement scheme – with its national regulation of the inflow – was precisely the type of interdependence which these countries needed in order to pursue their national interest.

In both visions, the approach to Europe stemmed from, and was completely shaped by, the political and economic aims of domestic strategies for the consolidation of the nation-state. The organization of interdependence, and within the ECSC of integration, was in fact the battleground upon which each government tried to shape the most convenient framework for the realization of its own national strategy.

NATIONAL PREROGATIVES WITHIN THE COMMON MARKET

Those conflicting tensions took an explicit and fuller shape with the negotiations for the common market begun in 1955. The resolution adopted at the meeting of the Foreign Ministers of the Six which took place at Messina in May 1955 had directed the inter-governmental committee to work for the 'gradual establishment of the free circulation of manpower'.[27] In the subcommittee on social issues the Italians' argument for a rapid and complete liberalization of labour movements was confronted by numerous insuperable objections, which led to a rather limited and restrictive tentative agreement. Freedom of circulation was interpreted only as a qualified, long-term goal to be approached through a slow, carefully negotiated transition. In three distinct stages, skilled workers first, and later unskilled as well, would be granted access to other member countries, but only in order to respond to actual offers of employment. In spite of Italy's pressure, no right for the unemployed to look for jobs abroad was contemplated. The guiding principle remained the primacy of demand-induced migration: this seemed to be the only type of movement whose liberalization could be accepted within the future common market. The national employment services were asked to co-ordinate their systems for exchanging information, so as to facilitate recruitment abroad, but no mention was made of any supranational authority, since no transfer of sovereignty in this area was actually contemplated.[28]

This approach however appeared immediately too narrow to suit the integrative thrust of the larger political negotiation, and it had to be abandoned when the discussion returned to the ministers' level. The Spaak Report of May 1956 referred to unemployment not as a hindrance but rather as 'a resource' for European growth, to be managed in a communal way with interventionist supranational institutions, like the European funds for investment and for social readaptation, to be operated directly by the High Authority. Consequently, it aimed at opening up and integrating the national labour markets. The report suggested that the Community be entrusted with the task of supervising a system of gradually expanding quotas of migration, whose steady enlargement would lead to a full liberalization of manpower movements by the end of the transition period.[29]

These bold but still vague terms of reference caused an intense discussion in the ensuing inter-governmental conference. The Dutch surprisingly advanced an extensive interpretation of the freedom of circulation as the right to move without restrictions, even for the purpose of seeking employment, in a totally open and truly unified market. But fears of an excessive mobility were still too strong among the other participants, and an agreement was found only on a more limited right to circulate within the Community in order 'to accept offers of employment actually made' (Treaty of Rome, article 48/3). Thus, the common market was simply going to be an area of free circulation for demand-induced migrations only. Other discords emerged on the timing and pattern of transition and on the suitability of a common employ- ment policy. The latter was considered by Belgians and Dutch as an indispensable tool in order to supervise the system of expanding quotas and then regulate the common market afterwards. This supranational approach however was flatly rejected by France and Luxemburg and quietly discarded by the German Federal Republic. National control on labour market and migration policies was still too high a priority for these countries, and this eventually led them to question even the proposal of a system of quotas for the transition.

The final compromise solution was advanced by the Federal Republic, which needed a flexible environment for migrations but was also convinced that their flows had to remain determined only by actual demand. The Federal Republic then proposed to abandon the idea of progressive quotas, which inevitably entailed a substantial form of supranational integration. Instead, the transition would be based on the gradual decrease (and eventually the abolition) of the 'procedures . . . and qualifying periods' that regulated the eligibility of foreigners for available jobs under the national permit systems (Treaty of Rome, article 49). Therefore, no Community planning was necessary or contemplated. The practical and crucial decisions on the actual pace and scope of the transition stages were deferred to the Council of Ministers, where each government could use its veto power. And even the clearing of job offers and applications was to remain in the hands of the national agencies; the Community was simply assumed to exist to facilitate their exchange of information, without taking any direct role.[30]

The actual treaty provisions thus rejected the bolder step forwards proposed in the Spaak Report. Rather than taking a supranational connotation, the procedures for liberalization would remain within the confines of an inter-governmental process where member states retained their basic sovereign prerogatives on migration and employment policies. Expecting the twelve-year transition period to be sufficient to soak up unemployment, the Six had agreed to a gradual easing of their mutual restrictions on entry. But they had firmly rejected the notions of a common European employment policy and of a supranational legal framework for employment policy. As far as manpower was concerned, the six national markets were to be connected in an incrementally liberalized system of interdependence rather than integrated in a common market.

This ambiguous solution diverged quite markedly from theoretical models. Under the Treaty of Rome some elements of liberalization, of (potential) integration and of persistent national sovereignty coexisted within a contractual community of nations where no substantial interest was sacrificed to the pursuit of supranationalism.[31]

In the specific field of manpower movements this ambiguity was particularly biased in favour of national autonomy. Unlike agriculture, there was no element of a centralized common policy. Unlike trade in manufactured goods, internal liberalization was not coupled with measures of external protection and with a common policy. Each government retained full independence in formulating its immigration policy and particularly in dealing with third countries. Migrants from one member state were gradually to come to enjoy the right of free access to the labour markets of the other five countries, but they would not have any specific protection *vis-à-vis* non-Community foreign workers. This issue did not appear particularly important in 1956–7, when migratory flows were still rather limited and overwhelmingly made up of Italians. But in the 1960s boom of migration, when recruitment abroad expanded dramatically, the Italian government discovered with dismay that under the treaty it had no legal instruments to force other member states to call and hire Italian rather than Turkish or Portuguese workers. In spite of the integrative vision outlined by the Spaak Report, the common market did not entail any obligation to give priority to the recruitment of other EEC nations' unemployed, and this would later emerge as the major deficiency of the integrative process in this field.[32]

Throughout the 1960s, the continued vigorous expansion of construction and manufacturing in the whole EEC area and the diminution of internal migrations within nations activated foreign labour immigrations of unprecedented magnitude (see table 4). This sustained boom in the demand for foreign manpower prevented the emergence of protectionist pressures from within the member states and considerably eased the transition process. In fact for a certain period no national government had any motive for obstructing or delaying the internal liberalization of labour movements. With three successive community regulations – in 1961, 1964 and 1968 – the national priorities for employment and the restrictions of the work permit systems were reduced and eventually abolished for all EEC workers and family dependants. Given the protracted favourable economic conditions, complete freedom of movement was actually achieved two years earlier than prescribed in the treaty. As far as labour issues were concerned, the limited degree of integration to which the Six had subscribed with the Treaty of Rome was accomplished precisely because it was no longer socially and politically dangerous.

At every stage of the transition process however, the Council of Ministers consistently rejected the reiterated pressures from the Italian government and the European Commission itself for more deeply integrative measures. All proposals to establish rules and machinery for a rudimentary common employment policy were frustrated, and nation-states particularly rebuffed any attempt to interfere with their full sovereignty on recruitment policies. Even though for a few years Italian workers did often enjoy some informal preference of employment (primarily because they were easier and faster to recruit), no specific formula for an EEC priority of employment could ever be included in the directives and regulations on liberalization.[33]

Towards the end of the 1960s, the cumulative effects of EEC internal liberalization in conditions of sustained growth with high demand for labour and of Italy's own fast economic development eventually changed the nature of Italian emigration. Overall figures for departures decreased dramatically, inter-continental emigration petered out and flows towards western Europe diminished while rates of return grew higher than ever. As a result net emigration almost disappeared, as shown in table 1. Indeed in the early 1970s Italy's secular tradition of long-term, massive emigration was finally terminated, and its relatively prosperous economy began to turn into a pole of attraction for new immigrants from African countries. Many workers from Italy's southern regions kept going to the German Federal Republic for brief periods of remunerative employment which coincided with the peaks of demand, but they increasingly returned and settled back home. In a common market where they could freely enter, leave and re-enter each nation's labour market at any time, their movements in fact correlated ever more closely to the fluctuations of demand. With rates of return now hovering each year around and above 90 per cent, by 1970 Italian migration in Europe had actually turned into an almost rotatory

Table 4 Inflow of foreign workers (thousands)

Year	German Fed. Rep.	France (a)	Switzerland	Benelux	Total
1946		30.2			30.2
1947		68.2			68.2
1948		57.0			57.0
1949		58.8	28.0		86.8
1950		10.5			10.5
1951		21.0	63.0		84.0
1952		32.8			32.8
1953		15.4	67.0		82.4
1954		12.3			12.3
1955		19.0	87.0		106.0
1956	31.6	65.4			97.0
1957	45.3	111.7	119.0		276.0
1958	54.6	82.8		19.3	156.7
1959	85.3	44.2	102.0	13.4	244.9
1960	259.5	48.9	137.8	15.8	462.0
1961	360.5	78.9	176.0	23.9	639.3
1962	396.6	113.1	179.5	31.6	720.8
1963	377.5	115.5	165.0	45.6	703.6
1964	442.3	153.7	159.4	62.1	817.5
1965	524.9	152.1	104.7	61.1	842.8
1966	424.8	131.7	97.6	53.2	707.3
1967	151.9	107.8	90.6	25.2	375.5
1968	390.9	93.2	101.3	23.3	608.7
1969	646.1	167.8	101.8	30.7	946.4

Frontier and seasonal workers are not included. For data on global net migratory flows see table 1 (p. 37).
(a) Algerian workers are not included.

Source: I. Hume, *Migrant Workers in Western Europe*. World Bank Economic Staff Working Paper, no. 102 (Washington DC, 1970).

movement between the German and the Italian labour markets (and their respective welfare systems). This profound qualitative and quantitative change in the nature of Italian emigration to the rest of Europe was primarily due to long-term economic factors, but it was also favoured and accelerated by the new EEC legal framework. From the viewpoint of Italian policy however, integration finally came about only when its impact was of decreasing relevance for the economic security and social well-being of the nation, now well beyond the employment difficulties that had previously determined Italy's integrative policies on migration.

With the full implementation of the common market the organized flows of Italian manpower previously activated and regulated by the bilateral agreements had been superseded by independent, individual movements inside the liberalized framework of the European Community. Among the Six, the liberalization of manpower flows had further increased the influence and impact of market forces and lessened the regulatory authority of national governments. The latter were no longer organizing the recruitment of Italian manpower and directing it to specific sectors. In most cases, Italian migrants directly answered employers' demands. The interaction of supply and demand was no longer channelled and filtered by national public agencies; for intra-EEC migrations their regulatory role had been effectively bypassed. However, no new powers over employment and migration policies had been concentrated at the supranational level. Alongside this dismantling of internal protectionism (made possible only by a decade of persistent growth that soaked up unemployment and eliminated any concern for its social effects) immigration from third countries, now at an all-time high level, remained thoroughly regulated by national rules on admission and bilateral agreements.

The integrative solution therefore appeared as a very peculiar one. It had gone further than the mere inter-governmental co-operation of the bilateral agreements, since the regulatory powers of national governments had been largely devolved to market forces. The integration at market level however remained imperfect, in so far as it stopped far short of an actual unification of employment and immigration policies. On these matters, any substantial move towards supranational regulation had been deliberately rejected. The national labour markets of the Six were irreversibly interconnected into an area within which EEC migrants could follow the fluctuations of demand without being any longer submitted to the administrative controls and national regulations for access which applied to non-EEC citizens. But this was certainly far short of a common market, particularly since it lacked any common policy and external protection. For labour, the EEC merely amounted to a preference zone rather than a full-fledged customs union.

What stands out as the most contradictory and significant feature of this process of liberalization is the persistence of complete national sovereignty over the directions and aims of external immigration policies. Nation-states could freely recruit outside the EC or ban further inflows, and they used this authority on a massive scale. First they used it to recruit vast numbers of non-EC migrants (primarily from Turkey, Yugoslavia and several Arab countries) in the boom years of the late 1960s, and then abruptly to stop their inflow when, with the 1973–4 recession, policy goals decidedly shifted towards labour protectionism. Even within the common market, then, national autonomy in the formulation of labour market policies had remained paramount, and governments had retained most of the necessary instruments for an independent pursuit of their immigration targets and manpower policy goals. The complete absorption of EC unemployment was a stated goal of general policies for economic growth, but it was never elevated to an actual priority to be attained through the EEC regulations on migration. Liberalized access to their own labour markets for EEC workers was all that the receiving countries would concede towards this purpose, but they rejected any binding commitment to assume Italy's unemployment as their own responsibility under a common policy framework. Thus Italy had once more to accept a very partial solution of its own difficulties. The common market certainly helped Italian emigration, but it remained quite distant from Rome's favoured option of a highly integrated and protectionist Europe where its own diminishing stock of idle manpower would be given a clear priority of employment.[34]

Interdependence, therefore, had been reorganized – thanks to a long cycle of fast growth – on the basis of a co-ordination and actual convergence of national necessities but with no break-up or relevant transfer of national authority on the key issues of labour policy. In the field of migration the actual history of the Community-building process did not at all proceed along the allegedly ineluctable route of a functionalist expansion of the supranational dimension, nor did it witness any significant spillover from technical solutions into larger political powers for the Community.[35] Even though it laid out the theoretical premises for further potentially integrative progress, the common market did not substantially alter the pattern of inter-dependence which had prevailed throughout the whole post-war period, and which revolved around the centrality of the nation-state and its basic autonomy in the determination of labour policies.

3 Restoring France: the road to integration

Frances M. B. Lynch

The decision of the French government to sign the Treaty of Rome in March 1957 setting up the European Economic Community marked a sharp break with the policies of protection pursued since the end of the nineteenth century. So momentous was the decision to integrate the French economy with the five western European economies that the British were confident that the French government would not be able to take it. That the French government agreed to such an important surrender of sovereignty is generally portrayed in the literature as a sign of the weakness of the French state – a weakness which was confirmed when the entire regime of the Fourth Republic collapsed one year later.

Its political and military weakness is said to have been highlighted in the Suez fiasco – an episode which Pierre Guillen has argued was critical in tilting the internal debate in France in favour of signing the Treaties of Rome.[1] Its economic weakness is said to be demonstrated by the surge in growth which took place as a result of de Gaulle's decision after the collapse of the Fourth Republic to devalue the franc and to cut real wages, so enabling the French economy to respond successfully to the stimulus of the larger European market.[2] Yet although the French economy seemed to benefit from participation in the European Economic Community, with rates of growth of GNP rising from 4.4 per cent per annum in the period 1950–60 to 5.7 per cent per annum in the period 1960–70 making France the fastest-growing economy in the EEC in the 1960s, this has not been seen as the primary motivating factor. As William James Adams argues:

> despite its own predilection for self-sufficiency, France decided to surrender some of its economic sovereignty on political and military grounds. It did not choose economic integration to raise living standards through specialization in production. Nor did it choose economic integration to expose domestic producers to competition.

Its primary goal was to achieve the greatest possible interdependence between Germany and its neighbours.[3]

In this argument precisely why interdependence should take the form of economic integration is not explained, because by implication it was inevitable. The Treaty of Rome was simply institutionalizing a set of economic relations which already existed, or which would have existed had the state not blocked them. It is at this point that classical economic theory and political bias substitute for an explanation based on historical research.

As this chapter demonstrates, the reason why the French state agreed to sign the Treaties of Rome was due neither to the historical accident of Suez, nor to the force of federalist political ideas, nor to the inevitable process of economic development. It was rather the outcome of a prolonged debate about how best to secure the French national interest – a debate which was driven by the shock of defeat in 1940.

The experience of defeat and occupation had not only discredited the Third Republic and the Vichy state but created a set of new expectations which the Fourth Republic had to meet in order to establish its legitimacy. As elsewhere in western Europe, the state was expected to look after people's material well-being as well as their physical security. These new demands necessitated both a new machinery of government to articulate them and a new international framework to support and sustain them.

The French played no part in negotiating the new international monetary arrangements which culminated in the Bretton Woods Charter, despite the attempt by two of de Gaulle's supporters in London, Hervé Alphand and André Istel, to set out the French position in a draft plan in 1943.[4] The emphasis was on domestic reconstruction. It was to ensure control over domestic policy and policy-making that de Gaulle set up the Commissariat au Plan under Jean Monnet in 1946. One of the many weaknesses of the inter-war machinery of government had been the vertical structure of policy-making. Each ministry represented a particular sectional interest, but in the absence of a horizontal body designed to co-ordinate or choose among conflicting interests, policy tended to be dictated by financial criteria. The result had been disastrous for the real economy; in 1938 the level of industrial output was 25 per cent below that of 1929.

As in other countries, the French planners saw economic development based on industrial expansion as the key to restoring the legitimacy of the new state. Only by expanding the industrial base would the new regime be able to solve the structural problem of the balance of payments deficit and enable incomes, including agricultural incomes, to rise. Industrial expansion would draw labour off the land, which would provide an extra incentive for mechanizing French agriculture and making it self-sufficient.

The planners inherited a number of ideas and instruments of control from both Vichy and the resistance which were to enable the plan to be implemented. These included controls over prices and external trade, the nationalization of key sectors, and the creation of a national credit council which would supervise the allocation of credit according to the priorities set by the plan. The ultimate objective as stated by the plan was to enable the French economy to be reintegrated into the international economic and monetary system – the first elements of which had been set out in the Bretton Woods Charter, signed by France in December 1945. However this did not inhibit the French government from adopting in the transitional period policies which were quite antithetical to the principles of Bretton Woods. The most notorious example was the decision to adopt a multiple system of foreign exchange rates for the French franc in January 1948 in an attempt to redirect imports away from the dollar area. Although the United States condemned this, it did not alter its support for the broad objectives of French economic policy as articulated in the Monnet Plan. This support took the form of a dollar loan in 1946 followed by dollar aid and its counterpart in French francs under the Marshall Plan.

The first real division over economic policy both within France and between France and the United States came in 1949–50 when the United States in the interests of promoting a multilateral trade and payments system in Europe diluted its support for national investment plans. The European Payments Union set up in 1950 was designed to increase the interdependence of European economies in order to reduce their dependence on the United States. Where the scheme divided the French was in its integral association with the earlier British and American scheme for liberalizing intra-European trade by the progressive removal of non-tariff barriers supervised by OEEC. When in February 1952 in the face of a payments crisis, the French had to reimpose trade controls, critics of this scheme seemed to be vindicated. The EPU provided the first real debate in France, as late as autumn 1949, over the nature and terms by which the French economy would be reintegrated into the international economy.

In 1949 the Ministry of Foreign Affairs had identified two ways of increasing trade. One was the market solution. This would entail exposing both competitive and uncompetitive sectors to foreign competition in the hope that the uncompetitive sectors would be stimulated into taking the steps necessary to survive. The alternative was to draw up a list of those sectors which felt that they could withstand exposure to foreign competition but there was little doubt that such a list would be so short that it would not stimulate trade and competition.

For France the situation was complicated by the trading relations within the French Union. To adopt the second, progressive solution the government would have to consider first the effect on exports from the departments and territories overseas (DOM-TOMs) to metropolitan France, and second, metropolitan exports to these countries. These took place in a closed protectionist system. North African producers already felt menaced by metropolitan French imports of Mediterranean food-stuffs within the context of bilateral deals and were conscious of their own higher price levels. The reason that North African prices were uncompetitive was partly because these countries imported higher-priced French goods, particularly investment goods and textiles. Because French textile producers enjoyed a virtual monopoly in the North African market, it was certain that textiles would not feature on any list of goods to be exposed.

Unlike the textile industry, producers of investment goods and agricultural machinery were actually being encouraged under the Monnet Plan to expand output to satisfy the needs of North Africa and the overseas territories. If these countries were allowed by any change in international arrangements to turn to the sterling area, French industry would be saddled with overcapacity. The Ministry of Foreign Affairs felt that it would be possible in the short term to reconcile the two apparently conflicting objectives: namely an increase in intra-European trade with the maintenance of a closed trading system in the French Union, but not in the longer term.[5]

The debate over the EPU revealed the main cleavages of opinion within France which were to remain until 1957. On one level the dispute was simply over the timing of trade liberalization. It was argued that France should retain control over its external trade and payments until the Monnet Plan had been fully completed; in other words, that modernization had to precede liberalization.[6] On another level it was argued by the Ministry of Foreign Affairs that France would have a deficit with the sterling area and the German Federal Republic which it would be unable to cover with a surplus from the rest of OEEC. Therefore the EPU would not lead to the rebuilding of French reserves, the restoration of convertibility of the franc, and the reintegration of the French economy into the international economic system. This analysis was based on the inter-war experience when France had depended on the receipts from invisible transactions – and in the 1930s on its gold reserves – to balance its external payments. French gold reserves had been further depleted between 1945 and 1947 to help finance the needs of reconstruction before Marshall Aid arrived, so that by 1949 they amounted to a mere 464.6 tonnes compared with a maximum of 4900.4 tonnes in 1932.[7] It was assumed that receipts from invisible transactions had also largely disappeared. This reasoning led to the recommendation that France would be better off expanding trading links with complementary economies in eastern Europe and the French Overseas Territories in the short term at least.

A third argument centred on the nature of the trade liberalization programme and on the inclusion of the German Federal Republic in it. Within OEEC, the United Kingdom and France had very different views about the best method of reducing quantitative restrictions on trade.[8] Whereas the British advocated a simple percentage reduction in each of the three main categories of 1948 private trade, the French Ministry of Finance wanted it to be done on the basis of common lists of products to be liberalized. Only in that way it was argued would liberalization lead to an increase in intra-European trade and competition between producers. However it was the British proposal which was adopted by OEEC. In view of the arguments which the announcement of the French proposals for a common list provoked within France, this was probably the wisest course of action. Within the Ministry of Industry, which had not been consulted, the Directorate of Mechanical and Electrical Industries objected to the fact that steel was not on the list whereas industries using steel were to be liberalized.[9] Given the lower price of West German steel, all users of French steel would be at a comparative disadvantage and yet they were to be exposed to European competition before the steel industry itself.

This of course was not the only factor identified by the Ministry of Industry as responsible for West German economic superiority. The inadequacy of Allied military action during the war and their reparations policy after the war meant that the German Federal Republic had a production potential in 1950 equal to that of 1938. The stock of machine tools in France – 500,000 – was one-third that of the Federal Republic and they were twice as old, averaging twenty years. Whereas French industry was saddled with debts, the West German monetary reform had amortized those of the Federal Republic. West German industry also benefited from cheaper basic products – the price of coal was 15–20 per cent less and electricity 25–30 per cent less than in France. West German social charges were lower. Vertical concentrations in West German industry led to savings in fiscal charges. Overcapacity and surplus labour in West German industry would reduce marginal costs of production, allow increases in productivity, and enable West German industry to dump abroad in the future. The conclusion though was not that French industry should be protected permanently against West German exports, but that trade liberalization should be gradual and be accompanied by a harmonization of the two economies and an end to all West German discriminatory practices: in other words that something closer than interdependence as it had been earlier defined was to precede liberalization.

A fourth argument put forward by the Confédération Générale de Travail (CGT), the main communist-dominated trade union, was that exports from the French overseas territories would be exposed to competition on the French market with exports from the overseas territories of other OEEC countries, and that this would undermine the cohesion of the French Union. Rather than be forced to liberalize trade and payments with western Europe as a condition for further American aid, the CGT preferred to cut back on imports from the dollar area, accept a decline in living standards and forgo American aid.[10]

The main supporter of the EPU was the Ministry of Finance, on the grounds that it was only by restoring competition among European producers that the price and productivity gap with the United States would be closed and with it Europe's need for dollar aid. Without making it a precondition for accepting the EPU it continued to argue that competition would only be restored if countries agreed to liberalize trade in the same products.[11] It also considered that the attempts to re-create a trading structure based on the supposed complementarity of industrialized countries and developing ones were completely misguided. Few developing countries wanted it. France had no option but to trade and become competitive with other industrialized economies.

Two events of major importance were responsible for overcoming some of the criticisms of the EPU within the French administration. One was the announcement of the Schuman Plan which was directed towards removing the most significant advantages which the West German steel industry benefited from at the expense of its French counterparts. An initiative of Jean Monnet, head of the Planning Commission, it succeeded in removing some of the grounds for objection to the EPU of both the Ministry of Foreign Affairs and the Ministry of Industry. The second was that, quite contrary to expectations, as the West German economy got going again, its demand for imports from France increased and far outstripped French imports from the Federal Republic. Thus instead of running a deficit with the Federal Republic, France had a very healthy surplus.

As a result between July 1950 and April 1951 France registered a net surplus each month with the EPU. This enabled the government to comply with the OEEC trade liberalization code so that by February 1951 it had removed quotas on 75 per cent of its 1948 private trade. After that the situation deteriorated and it was not until autumn 1954 that French payments with the EPU were back in surplus.

The obvious conclusion to be drawn is that the critics were correct and that France could not survive when exposed to a degree of competition within Europe. But in fact it could be argued that the deterioration in the payments position was due entirely to the effects of the Korean War. After the war broke out both the French government and French producers took the decision not to join in the international race to stockpile raw materials. Their argument was that it was an exaggerated response to the international situation and would be inflationary.[12] As a result French exports increased quite dramatically – particularly to the German Federal Republic, the United Kingdom and the United States, between the second and fourth quarters of 1950. But in 1951 the restrictions first on German imports and then later on British imports – both countries temporarily restoring the import restrictions earlier removed under the trade liberalization scheme – together with the inflated price of raw material imports from the sterling area caused the serious reversal of the French payments position in EPU.

The balance of payments deficit which reached a crisis in February 1952 was tackled in the same way as in the 1930s. Trade liberalization was suspended, planning was abandoned and an orthodox deflationary policy was implemented by the Pinay and Mayer governments in 1952 and 1953. Between 1952 and 1955 the French economy remained one of the most protected economies in OEEC.

This was tolerated initially by France's partners on the grounds that the state of the French balance of payments in EPU did not permit any relaxation of import controls. The evidence presented by the French was that in the period between October and December 1953 when imports had been liberalized slightly the volume of imports had increased by about 30 per cent in both industry and agriculture.[13] Nevertheless the government was under increasing pressure from the rest of OEEC to participate in the trade liberalization programme again. The Ministry of Foreign Affairs, under the guidance of Georges Bidault, wanted to resist this pressure on the grounds that the best way to overcome what was still seen to be a structural deficit in the balance of payments was to restrict imports and exploit the resources of the entire French Union to the full. The option of devaluation, which had been tried several times since the war to solve the balance of payments deficit, would not work since, it was argued, it did not solve the underlying causes of inflation in France. These were held to be lower levels of productivity and higher wages relative to France's competitors in OEEC. However to cut wages, devalue and liberalize trade would lead to the sort of stop-go policies which were to become so familiar in the United Kindom and which would, in the Ministry of Foreign Affairs' view, soon undermine investment and growth and further damage French competitiveness.

But this was a policy which the rest of OEEC and the French Ministry of Finance were opposed to on the grounds that prolonged protection of the French economy destroyed European trade flows and would actually make it harder for French industry to compete. For this reason Edgar Faure, when he became Minister of Finance in June 1953, advocated devaluing the franc and resuming the OEEC trade liberalization programme. But because of the opposition of the Ministry of Foreign Affairs he agreed to set up a commission chaired by Roger Nathan to investigate the reasons for higher prices in France which caused the balance of payments deficit.

The conclusions of the Nathan Commission were that it was essentially the policy of protection which was responsible for the proliferation of small firms and for the higher prices in France. Lower productivity was not the real reason since levels of productivity varied from one firm to another and depended very much on the size and degree of concentration of the firms. Nor were higher wages the reason, since wages in France were higher than in the German Federal Republic, Italy or the Netherlands but lower than in the United Kingdom, Belgium or Switzerland. French interest rates were higher than in the United Kingdom, Belgium or Switzerland but lower than in the Federal Republic or Italy.[14] This more or less reinforced the view of the Ministry of Finance, so that Faure continued to advocate a devaluation of 15 per cent and a resumption of trade liberalization.

Bidault as Foreign Minister was not prepared to accept this. He insisted that France was unable to liberalize trade and should return to earlier ideas and implement the Second Plan, left in abeyance since 1952, to improve the levels of productivity and competitiveness of the economy. This would prepare for the day when the economy could eventually be liberalized.

A problem with putting the Second French Modernization Plan into practice was that it would be hard for France to insist that the EPU be retained if it was at the same time refusing to co-operate in its trade liberalization programme and there had been plans afoot since 1952 in the United Kingdom to get rid of it. With the improvement in British reserves in early 1954 the French government fully expected the United Kingdom to announce in the summer the convertibility of sterling, which not only would probably have meant the end of the EPU but as a consequence might have entailed also the convertibility of the Deutschmark, leaving France with the choice of retaining a non-convertible currency or being forced into a more competitive multi-lateral system at a time not of its own choosing.

Whereas the American government had previously been opposed to British plans to make sterling convertible on the grounds that it would break up the EPU and undermine the process of European integration, the situation was rather different in 1954. In view of its declining commitment to the European Defence Community treaty and its associated Political Community and in view of its reluctance to participate in the OEEC trade liberalization programme, France could no longer claim, as it had been able to in 1950–2, to be taking the lead in the integration of Europe. If the franc did not become convertible this would obstruct the workings of the ECSC through which the French steel industry was exporting increasing amounts of steel to the German Federal Republic. It would also undermine the modernization of French industry which was being stimulated with imports of German machines, machine tools and parts – the demand for which far exceeded the capacity of France itself to supply. But if the franc did become convertible then French industry would lose most of the protection which it enjoyed in the French overseas territories. Since many of these countries did not have tariffs it was largely through exchange control that France was able to ensure privileged access for French exports. Not only would convertibility open up these markets to foreign competitors but it would reveal the full extent of French privilege at a particularly sensitive time politically.[15]

The compromise worked out was that France would agree to participate in the OEEC trade liberalization programme but on condition that it could apply import taxes on a selected range of products. This would enable France to maintain its credibility as a European leader particularly in view of the threatened convertibility of sterling and the break-up of the EPU, while exposing French industry to a greater degree of European competition, without endangering the balance of payments. The imposition of import taxes had the advantage over a devaluation of the franc in that it was not applied to raw material imports or imports into the overseas territories. A further condition was that France would implement the Second Plan which had been drawn up in 1952 but not adopted for financial reasons and in view of the likely move to make sterling convertible it was agreed to set up a commission to explore the consequences of forming a customs union with the overseas territories.

FRENCH POLICY TOWARDS THE FRANC AREA[16]

An integral part of the strategy for restoring France after 1945 had been to strengthen the French empire, renamed the French Union for political reasons. As in France itself, it was recognized that this could best be achieved by improving living standards largely through a programme to stimulate economic development. Originally the plan for the social and economic development of the overseas territories was to be spread over ten years but in 1948 this was reduced to four years to bring it into line with the European Recovery Programme (ERP). Each of the three North African countries drew up its own plan and in 1948 these plans were also dovetailed with the time-scale of the ERP. One of the main issues at the end of the war had been whether these development plans should be carried out by giving the colonies full tariff autonomy, and thus not oblige them to import from metropolitan France if they could buy the imports more cheaply elsewhere, or whether France should control trade with these countries even more tightly in order to make them run a balance of payments surplus with the rest of the world and thereby help solve France's external deficit.

In 1934 the French government had considered the conclusion of a French-style Ottawa agreement with its colonies. It was rejected however because in certain important products the French colonies were considered to be competitors either amongst themselves or with respect to France. The government chose instead to restrict the trade in, and in some cases the production and transport facilities for, colonial products.[17]

In 1941 and 1942 the Vichy government, largely for practical reasons, had given the colonies full tariff autonomy for the duration of the war, so that after the war a decision on their future had to be taken. The reason that tariffs were the central issue was largely because in its white paper on trade and employment published in December 1945 the United States had talked of eliminating imperial preferences and of rejecting any preference or customs agreements which were not a full customs union. The French government itself was divided over the issue. The Ministry of Overseas France was in favour of giving complete customs autonomy to the colonies to enable them to buy at cheap world prices and to protect their own economies from competition from metropolitan France. Other ministries called for a return to a system of preferences to provide metropolitan France with both supplies and markets. The steel industry wanted colonial markets, especially if the colonies were going to be industrialized, whereas agriculture wanted greater complementarity between metropolitan and colonial agricultural production.

What the French government realized was that whereas the United States treated the countries of the French Union as a set of quite distinct customs territories, the entire franc zone, despite having different currencies, was treated as one unit in the IMF. Alphand, head of the economic section of the Ministry of Foreign Affairs, who was himself in favour of granting a large degree of autonomy to the colonies, felt that it was a matter for the French government and not the American government to decide. But sometime in the course of 1946 American policy softened somewhat and the US administration began to accept the continuation of a preferential regime if it was needed to safeguard the vital interests of a country. The Ministry of Overseas France in turn modified its opposition to preferential tariffs and in October 1946 argued that a preferential regime would be acceptable provided that it did not result in higher prices for the French Overseas Territories.[18]

However the whole debate was to prove largely irrelevant, since in the years after the war France controlled the trade of the DOM-TOMs through the use of exchange controls and quotas rather than tariffs. Largely on account of the shortage of foreign exchange and their development needs the countries of the French Union ran a trade deficit with both metropolitan France and the rest of the world between 1948 and 1952. The size of the trade deficit with metropolitan France was 537,600 million francs in this period. Over the same period French investment in the DOM-TOMs totalled 1,340,000 million francs of which 662,700 million francs were loans from the French Treasury and 533,800 million came from the counterpart of Marshall Aid.[19]

While metropolitan assistance to the Overseas Territories under the first plan was 55 per cent subsidy and 45 per cent loans from the Fonds de modernisation et d'équipement (FME) through the intermediary of the Caisse Centrale de la France d'Outre-mer, 100 per cent of the metropolitan contribution to the development plans of North Africa took the form of loans from the FME. Largely for political reasons the first plan put more emphasis on social rather than economic investment in North Africa which meant that those economies were not growing fast enough to finance the increased demands on the general budget arising from the better provision of social amenities. Given that most of the resources of the FME came from the counterpart of Marshall Aid, as this ended the metropolitan budget had to assume all the costs. For these two reasons the financing of the second plan for North Africa threatened to be contentious. Either investment had to be cut or the contribution from metropolitan France had to be increased.

Furthermore because the metropolitan contribution took the form of loans rather than grants, albeit at interest rates lower than those prevailing in the market, France did not gain the benefit of any political capital.[20] When the FME was replaced by the Fonds d'expansion economique (FEE) the French government lost all control over the uses of it made by the North African governments. The loans simply became part of the local budget.[21]

As we have seen, the Ministry of Foreign Affairs saw the trade and payments arrangements within the French Union as offering a more stable and secure basis for restoring French independence than the closer association with western Europe advocated by the United States and supported by the Ministry of Finance. However in 1954 this concept of stability was called into question. Quite apart from domestic political unrest in North Africa, it was events in western Europe which threatened the French system of economic control. Currency convertibility would remove the main form of protection which France enjoyed in many of the markets of the French Union. Second, the agreement reached by OEEC in April 1954 to extend trade liberalization to members' overseas territories threatened France's trade monopoly even more directly and immediately.

Trade liberalization in OEEC between 1949 and 1952 had not been applied automatically to all the countries of the French Union. The French government decided to extend it to Algeria, New Caledonia and the overseas departments as well as Saint-Pierre and Miquelon but not to Morocco, French Equatorial Africa, Togo and Cameroon. Each of the latter group had an international statute which prevented it from discriminating in favour of OEEC member states.[22]

Even if the franc were not made convertible immediately after a declaration of sterling convertibility, France would still have to begin to revise tariffs if it were to get preferential access to these markets or even renegotiate their international statutes in view of the cost to the French exchequer of financing development in them. Since any upward tariff revision was contrary to GATT, one alternative was to turn the entire French Union into a customs union. It was to assess the implications of such a policy as well as to draw up a balance sheet of the existing arrangements that a major study was initiated on 10 May 1954 under the direction of General Corniglion-Molinier, a minister of state. He set out to identify a coherent long-term direction to the economic relations between metropolitan France and the departments and territories overseas. Quite apart from the external pressure to change the system it was coming under internal attack both in the colonies and in France itself. The DOM-TOMs blamed their relative underdevelopment on having to import investment goods and other manufactures from metropolitan France which, apart from steel, were at prices higher than world prices, whereas the French complained at having to cover both the external and the domestic budget deficits of the colonies while domestic agriculture faced increasing competition from colonial exports.

There was plenty of evidence to support each case. A study quoted by the Ministry of Overseas France calculated that in 1953 the overseas territories had paid 1,320 million francs above world prices for flour, 1,870 million francs for cars and lorries and 16,090 million francs for investment goods. In the case of Algeria, which was by far the largest single market in the franc area for goods from metropolitan France, the price difference was considerable. In 1954 Algeria imported 21 per cent of all French car exports. Belgium–Luxemburg, the second largest market, was far behind, taking 12 per cent. Furthermore the unit value to Belgium–Luxemburg was much lower, 42 million francs compared to 53 million francs to Algeria. Similarly Algeria was the single largest market for metallurgical goods taking 16 per cent of all exports. The average unit price was 19 million francs compared with an average unit price of 7 million for exports in the same category to Brazil. Whereas metropolitan goods sold in the DOM-TOMs at a level of prices on average 19.7 per cent above world prices of similar goods, goods from the DOM-TOMs sold in France itself at a price level only 9.5 per cent above that of world prices. Thus French industry benefited to the extent that it was able to export to the departments and territories overseas at much higher prices than to the rest of the world, and that when it exported to Europe at a loss it was able to make this up on exports to the DOM-TOMs.

Not surprisingly given such a level of protection and given the emphasis of the Monnet Plan on increasing production to supply the markets of the franc area France ran a large trade surplus with the rest of the franc area. Between 1949 and 1955 it amounted to 1,075,800 million francs. In this period however the French invested 1,340,000 million francs of public funds in those territories and less than 100,000 million francs in private funds. Any reduction in the level of protection enjoyed by metropolitan producers in these markets threatened to undermine confidence in the investment plan. Yet as the study directed by Corniglion-Molinier concluded, given the very high level of trade between the DOM-TOMs and metropolitan France – 72.5 per cent of all their imports and 76 per cent of their exports – it would be difficult if not dangerous to increase the links by forming a customs union. The Ministry of Foreign Affairs still believed that in the short term a policy of liberalization in the context of OEEC could be combined with a protection of the French Union as long as the time was used to modernize production in both France and the DOM-TOMs.[23]

In February 1955 the Commissariat au Plan carried out its own investigation into the implications of integrating the French Union into Europe of the Six. The broad conclusions were that it would benefit Europe because the French overseas territories would provide markets, sources of supply and investment opportunities. It was expected that it would also probably benefit the overseas territories because they would pay less for imports, which would lead to an improvement in their living standards, to an increase in their exports, and possibly to an increase in productive investment provided that such investment was not solely for the purpose of extracting raw materials. But the planners concluded that it would probably not benefit France. In economic terms France would lose valuable export markets or would no longer be able to charge higher prices to pay for subsidizing exports in world markets. And if France had to carry the costs of financing unproductive investment while sharing productive investment with others then it would bear a disproportionate burden.

On the other hand it was clear that the French government could no longer cope with the burden of financing investment in the overseas territories on its own and it was failing to mobilize private investment. At the same time it was under increasing pressure to develop these economies if only because of the example from elsewhere in Africa. It was for that reason that the planners saw an advantage in some form of closer association between the French Union and western Europe if in return for opening up the markets of the French Union they could secure a contribution to investment in their economies.[24] Thus even before the Benelux relaunched proposals for a common market in spring 1955 the French planners were already coming to the conclusion that the future of the French Union lay in some form of integration with Europe of the Six.

THE ROLE OF AGRICULTURE IN FRENCH ECONOMIC DEVELOPMENT

After the war official policy, enshrined in the Monnet Plan, had been based on expanding the basic sectors of the economy. Agricultural machinery was selected as one of the six priority sectors on the grounds that the mechanization of agriculture would release labour for the expanding industrial sectors while improving the productivity of those remaining on the land. It was accompanied by a pricing policy designed to restructure cultivation to match more closely changes in domestic consumption. This meant that output of wheat was to decline relative to that of meat, dairy products, fruit and vegetables, with the ultimate objective of making France as nearly self-sufficient as possible in foodstuffs. This was to correct the pre-war situation in which France, despite having a third of the labour force employed in agriculture, was a net food importer. However, one bad harvest in 1947 revealed how precarious this policy was. As a result of the relatively low price for wheat, the area sown was cut back and France had to import extra wheat from the United States, causing the severe balance of payments crisis of 1947.

This led to a shift in policy in 1948. Under the revised version of the Monnet Plan the whole of agriculture was made a priority sector in terms of access to investment and supplies. The understanding was that if surpluses were generated as a result, the government would not allow prices to fall but would negotiate export contracts instead. And to confirm its commitment the French government registered as a net exporter in the International Wheat Agreement. However since voting strength there was based on trade rather than production France had only seven votes out of 2,000 and thus had no effective influence over prices. Partly for that reason and partly because in the conditions of global food shortages which prevailed until 1952 better deals were available, the French preferred to dispose of their surpluses by negotiating bilateral contracts in which agricultural products were exchanged for industrial raw materials.[25]

However by 1953 the situation had changed. The global food deficit had turned into a surplus. The price of wheat exported under the International Wheat Agreement fell from 87 dollars per tonne to 73 dollars compared with French producer prices of 102 dollars.[26] It was in this context that the French planners announced their second plan to increase agricultural output by 20 per cent above the 1952 level. While it was clear that considerable gains in productivity could be achieved from investing in French agriculture there was no incentive to do so if as a result output increased and prices fell. And indeed the budget submitted by the Ministry of Agriculture for 1954 reflected this fear on the part of French farmers. The President of the Committee for Agricultural Production and Rural Equipment wrote to the Planning Commissariat in October 1953 expressing its concern that the planned increase in output would lead to overproduction and a crisis similar to that of 1930–6. The commission also complained about subsidized production in the overseas territories competing with French agriculture. Yet the expansion was justified by the planners on the grounds that of the three possible policy options for agriculture, expansion was the only one which would stimulate the development of the whole economy.

One option was to increase productivity without increasing production simply by ending protection and by running down the agricultural labour force. This was ruled out on the grounds that the industrial sector was not large enough to absorb the labour transfers. The other option was for the state to continue protecting agriculture but not take any part in restructuring or modernizing it. This would result in a widening gap between living standards in industry and agriculture and an acceleration of the rural exodus with the youngest and most able leaving first. Since the planners felt that both of these options would provoke considerable political discontent and instability and exacerbate the balance of payments deficit neither was entertained for serious consideration.[27]

Of course to try to increase agricultural production and exports required the co-operation of farmers and this was seen to depend on state guarantees that an increase in production would not lead to a collapse in prices. This meant guaranteed export markets. But as the French governments' experience between 1947 and 1952 had demonstrated, it was exceedingly difficult to negotiate export contracts with foreign governments until export surpluses actually existed. Yet without such contracts French farmers would not increase production. To break the vicious circle the planners argued that if need be France would have to be prepared to import food in the first instance in order to provide exports. It would also have to subsidize these exports if it was necessary to find purchasers.

So whereas under the revised version of the first plan the objective behind increased agricultural production was dollar saving with exports being a welcome but uncertain bonus, by 1953 the experience of an expansion in agricultural production together with falling prices and peasant riots led to a change in policy. While the underlying objective of the second plan was still to modernize the sector it was now argued that the most painless, indeed perhaps the only, way to do this was by negotiating export contracts. This new awareness necessitated a much clearer understanding of the food import needs of other European countries and of how French agriculture could be restructured to meet those needs best.

What was essentially a policy choice based on domestic factors was then given a wider but quite spurious justification by the planners. French agricultural surpluses which were intended as a result of diverting increasing amounts of public funds into agriculture would, the planners argued, meet Europe's need for increasing amounts of basic foodstuffs. They seemed to think that rising incomes together with a greater equality of income distribution in Europe would result in a higher per capita consumption of foodstuffs whereas most of the historical evidence pointed to the contrary. The second assumption,

Table 5 Relative shares in Europe's food trade, 1952 (per cent)

	Imports	Exports
United Kingdom	38	
German Federal Republic	20	
Switzerland	7	
France	7	8
Belgium–Luxemburg	7	8
Netherlands		19
Denmark		18
Italy		8
Sweden		8

Source: French national archives Commissariat au Plan CGP, 'Projet de rapport général des Commissions de la production agricole et de l'équipement rural', 22 September 1953.

equally mistaken, was that rising prices in developing economies, from which Europe had traditionally imported cheap food, would lead to a closure of the price gap and a reduction in trade between Europe and the developing economies and particularly of exports of manufactured goods in exchange for imported food.

If France was going to benefit from these assumed trends and increase its food exports its main competitors in meat and dairy products would be Denmark and the Netherlands, and in wheat the United States and Canada. In sugar the main exporters were the United States and Central America which together accounted for 50 per cent of Europe's imports, with the rest supplied by Denmark, France and Benelux. Since French agriculture was relatively undermechanized and productivity per worker was lower than that of its major competitors the planners were quite confident that France had considerably more potential for growth and price reductions than had its main competitors. But France would only be able to exploit this potential market in Europe if it undertook the modernization which had been called for since the war. However it was not until 1954 as table 6 shows that public investment in agriculture mirrored the public rhetoric. Although there were substantial wheat surpluses for export in 1950 and 1951, in general it was not until after 1953 that the problem of finding a market for food surpluses became a serious one.

When the French National Assembly failed to ratify the European Defence Community (EDC) treaty in August 1954, Prime Minister Mendès-France tried to recapture the initiative by proposing the creation of a Franco-German economic committee to bind the two economies more closely together. However in view of the West German

Table 6 Public expenditure in agriculture and industry (as percentage of OEEC total)

Year	Agriculture	Trade and industry
1947	1.6	10.0
1948	1.1	23.0
1949	1.8	21.5
1950	1.3	16.6
1951	1.8	8.2
1953	1.5	6.6
1954	4.6	9.6
1955	5.5	10.6
1956	5.3	9.8
1957	3.7	8.9
1958	4.2	7.8

Source: C. André and R. Delorme, *L'état et l'économie. Un essai d'explication de l'évolution des dépenses publiques en France 1870–1980* (Paris, 1983).

government's hostility to any structure which brought together industrialists and civil servants along the lines envisaged by the French, all that actually emerged from the initiative was a commercial agreement governing non-liberalized trade. Since the German Federal Republic had liberalized most of its imports of raw materials and manufactured goods the main French interest in the agreement was to get guaranteed markets for some key agricultural products, particularly wheat and sugar. On the other hand since France was still edging tentatively towards liberalizing 20 per cent of its 1948 private trade by December 1954, the German Federal Republic was anxious to get greater access to French markets. For that reason the Germans wanted to negotiate a three-year agreement allowing for some exceptions to be negotiated on an annual basis, whereas the French wanted the reverse. In the end the Germans agreed to the French proposal and offered long-term contracts for French agricultural products to a value of 9,000 million francs above the level of the current year. This was to include 500,000 tonnes of wheat in the first year and 400,000 tonnes in the two subsequent years, as well as 250,000 tonnes of other cereals each year, but the Federal Republic refused to give any commitment for sugar, meat or milk products.

At the same time the German side insisted on being able to export to France goods of the same value which were still under quota restrictions. This meant that as the French reduced their import restrictions they would have to find additional items which the Federal Republic could export freely. The total value of imports into France from the Federal Republic which were subject to quantitative restrictions was 18,000

Table 7 French wheat exports to the United Kingdom and the German Federal Republic, 1951–4

Year	United Kingdom		German Fed. Rep.	
	Quantity (1,000 tonnes)	Price (per 1,000 tonnes in million francs)	Quantity (1,000 tonnes)	Price (per 1,000 tonnes in million francs)
1951	32.3	34.9	227.5	30.0
1952	21.9	36.6	55.8	24.8
1953	17.1	22.7	175.5	30.5
1954	332.5	20.8	371.0	23.3

Source: *Statistique mensuelle du commerce extérieur de la France.*

million francs. Since the Germans were proposing to import an extra 9,000 million francs of goods and demanding full equality of treatment, this would effectively mean widening French quotas by 50 per cent in respect of imports from the Federal Republic.

In the final negotiations at the end of April 1955 France tried to avoid complete reciprocity, bargaining for exports of 500,000 tonnes of wheat to the Federal Republic each year for three years as well as 85,000 tonnes of sugar, without having to widen quotas on the same value of imports. The real worry was that if the French accepted reciprocity with the Federal Republic they would find it difficult not to extend it to the United Kingdom and Switzerland which until then had not made any such demands in return for French agricultural exports.[28] And as table 7 indicates, in 1954 the United Kingdom had imported nearly as much wheat as the German Federal Republic although at a lower price. What is clear is that when Benelux proposed to reopen negotiations to set up a common market among the six member countries of the European Coal and Steel Community the implications for French industry, in terms of exposure to competition, were not very different from what the West Germans were demanding in return for accepting French agricultural exports.

NEGOTIATING THE TREATY OF ROME

It was the French Ministry of Foreign Affairs which still remained opposed to joining a European common market when Benelux re-launched the idea. Given that the option they had favoured earlier of a closer association within the French Union was being dismissed at the official level, the Quai d'Orsay was in the embarrassing position of not having an external economic policy at all both before and for some time after the Messina conference. The internal debate revolved once again around the ability of French industry to compete in a common market.

The situation at the beginning of 1955 was that, given the way it was calculated within OEEC, trade liberalization in France had reached 79 per cent – albeit with special taxes on imports. The breakdown for the three main categories of imports was 96 per cent for raw materials, 65 per cent for manufactured goods and 64 per cent for agricultural products. Import taxes were applied only to 3 per cent of raw materials – mainly lead, some fertilizers, cement, tar and some skins. The increase in imports of raw materials which had taken place was not considered to be due to liberalization but to the increase in demand from industry itself. It was thus not felt that the formation of a common market for raw materials would make any difference – except that national tariffs, which were 5–10 per cent, would be removed to be replaced by an external tariff. French production should not decline. The problems lay elsewhere.

As far as manufacturing industry was concerned a special committee was set up in 1955 to calculate the effects of trade liberalization on machine tools, agricultural machinery and automobiles. The main European producers of machine tools were the German Federal Republic and the United Kingdom where production was over three times higher than in France. Other suppliers were Switzerland and Italy where production was less than in France. They had all removed their quantitative restrictions on imports. Tariff protection on machine tools ranged between 7 and 25 per cent in Italy, but only between 6 and 8 per cent in the Federal Republic, and was fixed at 20 per cent in the United Kingdom, which was similar to France. It was concluded that the main reason why the French machine tool industry was not competitive was that social and fiscal charges were higher in France and that France did not have the same need as the Federal Republic to export given that the German machine tool industry was so over-equipped. But the committee did not fear the effects of a common market on the French machine tool industry, judging the market to be much less open to new suppliers than the trade in consumer goods. It recommended a gradual liberalization accompanied by an import tax. Since preserving the special taxes on imports would not have been possible either in OEEC or the separate negotiations with the Federal Republic, the committee's recommendations were not acceptable either to the industrialists themselves or at ministerial level.

Price disparities were also a problem for agricultural machinery. But in this case the reasons were not considered to be the higher wages and

Table 8 Structure of costs in the European car industry

	Price of steel products	Weight of steel price in car retail price before tax	Per cent difference in car price due to steel price	Level of wages including social charges	Weighting of labour costs in car retail price before tax	Per cent differences in car price due to labour costs	Total per cent difference
France	100	20	–	100	40	–	–
German Fed. Rep.	100	20	0	75	40	10	10
United King- dom	80	20	4	93	40	2.8	6.8
Italy	100	20	0	74	46*	6	6

* Including the obligatory cost of retaining surplus labour

Source: Quai Branly, Interministerial Committee for Questions of European Integration, SGGI 121.9.

social charges in France but rather the lack of concentration and specialization in this sector in France and the high cost of investment. If the French were to specialize in the production of petrol-driven engines for tractors leaving diesel ones for the German Federal Republic then trade liberalization could, it was argued, be very beneficial.

The car industry was heavily protected by tariffs in all the main producing countries. Tariffs were highest in Italy at 35–45 per cent, 30–35 per cent in the Federal Republic, 33.3 per cent in the United Kingdom and 30 per cent in France. The Federal Republic had, though, removed its quotas. French car imports represented 1 per cent of production and were fifteen times less than car exports. But the committee identified a number of obstacles to trade liberalization. French prices were higher than those of France's main competitors mainly due to higher wages and social charges as table 8 indicates. Other explanations for differences in car prices were that French prices incorporated a margin for financing exports which amounted to about 1.5 per cent of the construction price. Prices in both the German Federal Republic and the United Kingdom were said to benefit from greater economies of scale. If French car production could reach the same level, it was argued, savings of 2–4 per cent could be achieved through replicating the same scale economies. At the same time it was suggested, somewhat oddly, that the West German car industry was under much greater pressure to export since car ownership was very much lower in the Federal Republic than in France –

Table 9 Output and exports of motor vehicles, 1955

	Passenger cars	Commer-cial vehicles, etc	Total	Exports	Exports as percentage of production
United Kingdom	897,500	339,500	1,237,000	536,300	43
German Fed. Rep.	692,000	216,400	908,800	409,000	45
France	553,300	171,700	725,000	164,000	22.5
Italy	230,800	38,000	268,300	74,650	28

Source: Quai Branly, Interministerial Committee for Questions of European Integration, SGGI 121.9.

one car for every thirty-four inhabitants there compared with one car for every fourteen inhabitants in France. This justified rather than explained the situation since the lower level of car owner-ship in the Federal Republic could have resulted in fewer exports and a greater concentration on exploiting the potential of the domestic market.

The only condition under which the French car industry could be liberalized was in the committee's opinion if a compensation tax of 15 per cent were added to tariffs of 30 per cent and if the car industry was liberalized at the same time in both the United Kingdom and Italy. Even then the risks to the French car industry were, it was estimated, serious.

The committee also investigated the effect of trade liberalization on intermediate products and consumer goods. Nearly half of total French imports of these goods came from the German Federal Republic, Italy, Belgium and the Netherlands. Even with an import tax imports tended to be very sensitive to trade liberalization. This was with tariff protection of 25 per cent and import taxes of more than 10 per cent. The committee selected three sectors for detailed study: the cotton industry, artificial textiles, and paper and card.

Its conclusions for the cotton industry were extremely pessimistic. Most OEEC countries had removed quotas and their tariffs were lower than those in France, while the French industry was further protected by an import tax of 15–20 per cent. This was necessary because apart from the usual explanations for higher French prices – namely, higher wages and social charges – the cotton industry faced declining demand and was saddled with overcapacity. Thus even though the industry was relatively concentrated, the institution of a common market would still, it appeared, threaten a large number of French firms.

The situation for artificial fibres was little better. France was the only country in OEEC not to have removed quotas on rayon and one of the few not to have liberalized staple fibres. French tariffs were also higher – 20 per cent and 18 per cent compared with 13 per cent in the Federal Republic and 10 per cent and 6 per cent in Benelux. The committee considered that liberalization, if accompanied by an import tax of 15 per cent, would compensate for differences in price due to differences in labour costs. But if tariffs also were eliminated, as in a common market, then the fact that French prices were 15 and 30 per cent higher than those of the other member states would have serious consequences.

Only the paper industry presented few problems. Quotas had been removed, tariffs on paper and card were 18 and 25 per cent and they also had special import taxes of 7 and 15 per cent. Most imports came from Scandinavia although the German Federal Republic supplied some. Provided that the industry was given time to reorganize itself into larger production units the committee saw few obstacles in a common market of six.

The committee's overall conclusions were that the problems raised by liberalizing trade within 'Little Europe' were really no less than within OEEC. Since imports from the Federal Republic, Benelux and Italy represented 70 per cent of imports from OEEC, unless the formation of a customs union were accompanied by a devaluation of the franc, safeguard clauses would be crucial for most branches of industry. But the alternative of retaining quotas temporarily would not ensure that industries made the necessary conversions to ease their entry into a common market. This was true even for modernized industries for which demand was growing such as the car industry, the machine tool industry or the electrical construction industry.

It is somewhat surprising, given the pessimistic nature of this committee's conclusions, that the French government did sign the Treaty of Rome and that French exports did so well as a result. Since subsequent studies showed that the devaluation of 1958 was not the only factor responsible for this successful performance it indicates that French industry was stronger than it liked the French government to believe.

The Ministry of Foreign Affairs was equally dissatisfied and sceptical about the findings of the committee and consulted Milton Gilbert, the director of Statistics and National Accounts at OEEC.[29] It found him sceptical about the worth of studies which tried to compare prices and competitiveness. Gilbert dismissed the view which had been held consistently by the Ministry of Finance that the French external deficit was an indication of the lack of competitiveness of the French economy and could be solved by devaluing the franc. It was, said Gilbert, not a global problem which could be tackled with global remedies. On the other hand it was practically impossible for a government to carry out detailed studies comparing production costs to find out which industries were not competitive and why, since industries would never reveal the real situation. The only purpose of such studies was the political one of justifying or recommending particular levels or forms of protection.[30]

What Gilbert recommended was that specific factors should be identified which distorted costs and prices so that these could then be harmonized. These included disparities between male and female wages, the length of the working week and the age of retirement.

This was not a new argument of course. It had already given rise to studies carried out by the High Authority of the European Coal and Steel Community as well as the Institut National de Statistique et des Etudes Economiques (INSEE) and the French Ministry of Industry, and with very conflicting results. The High Authority argued that rather than a comparison of wages and social charges only, all costs to the employer needed to be taken into account. These included family allowances, perks, costs of recruitment and professional training. While social security costs in France were higher than in the other member states, all costs were not. In the car industry social charges were 45 per cent of hourly wages in France, 35 per cent in the German Federal Republic and 25 per cent in Belgium, but the overall costs of labour were 0.55 dollars per hour in France, 0.53 dollars in the Federal Republic and 0.76 dollars in Belgium. The average hourly wage in the steel industry was 284 francs for the Federal Republic and 262 francs for France. Indeed the differences in the overall wage cost between regions in the same country was often greater than between countries. Once again in the case of coal, the differences in the overall wage cost between France and the German Federal Republic was 36 francs per hour, while that between Lorraine and the mines in the centre of France was 59 francs and between Lorraine and the Nord/Pas-de-Calais mines 47 francs.[31] The French contention that taxes were higher in France was also rejected. While it was true that indirect taxes were high in France, these were completely reimbursed when production was exported, whereas imports were subjected to the same tax as national production.

However the French government refused to accept these findings also. One major omission of such a study based on the coal and steel industries was, it argued, that since virtually no women were employed in these industries the great disparity between male and female wages which affected such industries as the textile industry, was ignored. Since,

Table 10 Production costs in the woollen industry

	France	UK		Belg.	Neth.	Italy
Wages: male	100		122	107	84	65
female	100		104	88	56	55
Obligatory charges on wages (as % of wage)	52			30.9	30.7	68.2
Cost per man-hour	100	male	88	92	72	72
		female	75	76	48	61
Energy: electricity	100		72	110	115	75
coal	100		64	104	93	117
petrol	100		73	68	56	108
Maintenance	100		70	96	74	70
Amortization:						
spinning equipment	100		89	87	86	80
weaving equipment	100		85	90	90	91
Wool credits	100		99.53	99.43	99.2	100

Source: Quai Branly, Interministerial Committee for Questions of European Integration, SGGI 121.9, Direction Générale des Prix et des Enquêtes Economiques, 23 May 1956.

it argued, France was the only country to apply the Geneva Convention relating to equal pay for women, this was critical to explaining differences in production costs.

A comparison of costs in the woollen industry goes some way to bearing out this contention (table 10), although it does not show the relative proportion of male and female labour in the different countries. INSEE had carried out its own study published in May 1955 which concluded that of all the factors entering into the calculation of wage costs, the length of the working week and therefore of overtime and differences between male and female wages, were the most important. This made the calculation of average costs fairly irrelevant. In France overtime pay started at 40 hours, in the United Kingdom at 45 and in the German Federal Republic, Benelux, Italy and Switzerland it was at 48 hours.

The debate remained inconclusive leaving France still with no clear line of policy on how to fit its great effort at national reconstruction into the evolving multilateral international economic system. What forced the issue was the United Kingdom's first proposal in July 1956 to OEEC for a free trade area covering OEEC members including the Six, but excluding agriculture. Although the Spaak Committee, to which the proposals for a customs union of the six ECSC states had been referred without any positive commitment on the French side, had made no recommendations regarding agriculture which pointed the way to solving France's problems, it accepted that it would be included in the common market but would require special treatment. As we have seen, French plans for developing the economy were seen to depend on the success of the policy of agricultural modernization which in turn depended on securing access to the West German market for food exports. The fear was that the British proposal of a free trade area might be more attractive to the West Germans and undermine at a stroke French economic policy as well of course as French foreign policy in Europe which aimed at closer links with the Federal Republic. When the government met to decide its policy towards the common market in September 1956 it was ironically the Minister of Finance, the Socialist Paul Ramadier, who now opposed it. His position was based on the deteriorating situation in Algeria which, he argued, would require France to operate a closed economy if not a war economy for some time. But his was a minority voice.

Both Prime Minister Guy Mollet and Foreign Minister Christian Pineau argued that a policy of European integration was the only way to solve France's economic and colonial problems. What was agreed was that provided a number of conditions were met including the harmonization of social legislation and arrangements for the French overseas territories then France should sign the treaty.[32] Despite the opposition of the German negotiators to any harmonization of social legislation on the grounds that the French problem was a monetary one which should be solved by altering the exchange rate, Adenauer for political reasons overruled them during his highly secret talks with Mollet in November 1956.[33]

Similarly, although everyone apart from Belgium rejected the connection made by France between trade liberalization and investment in the member states' overseas territories, a compromise was reached. Von Brentano, the German Minister of Foreign Affairs, proposed that in return for an annual investment allocation of 100 million dollars shared among the Six over a period of twelve to fifteen years, the same programme of trade liberalization would apply on trade with these countries as on trade within the Six. The Italian government, which was already committed to a ten-year investment programme in the South of Italy, objected to such a long-term commitment in the overseas territories of France, Belgium and the Netherlands. As a compromise Spaak suggested that the German proposal apply in the first instance for five years. In that case, the Germans argued, it should take the form of a Marshall Plan – in other words investment with no commercial strings or obligations. But Pineau found this politically unacceptable on the grounds that it would mean that French territories were being subsidized by the German Federal Republic.

The compromise arrangement which was eventually settled upon was that the six states would contribute 581 million dollars in investment over five years with France and the German Federal Republic contributing 200 million dollars each. But there were to be different arrangements for agriculture for France and its overseas territories. France was offered long-term purchasing contracts for agricultural exports until such time as the special arrangements for a common agricultural policy, announced in the treaty, were completed. The overseas territories were excluded from this, but they were to have preferential tariffs. In return the tariff concessions which they granted to exports from the five other common market countries at the end of the five-year period were not to be the same as for France but rather to be equal to the difference between French tariffs and those previously applied to the other five.[34]

CONCLUSIONS

Despite frequent changes of government under the Fourth Republic there was a basic continuity in the debate over the best framework in which to promote French economic development. The Ministry of Finance, which until the Socialist Paul Ramadier took over in 1956 was held by centre-right politicians, advocated a policy of increased interdependence in OEEC as a prelude to participation in the one-world system announced by Bretton Woods. The assumption was that greater exposure to competition would lead to an improvement in productivity and help correct the external deficit. But the Ministry of Finance no longer had the monopoly which it had enjoyed in the inter-war period over economic policy-making in France, and particularly where foreign economic policy was concerned it had to take account of the views of the Ministry of Foreign Affairs. Although the political leadership of this ministry changed quite frequently between 1954 and 1956 there was considerable continuity in its recommendations throughout the entire period from 1945. Basically it opposed trade liberalization on the grounds that it would weaken the French economy, escalate the disintegration of the French Union and exacerbate the external deficit. But its preferred policy, which was based on economic expansion within the protected confines of the French Union, was not viable in the long term. France could not continue to resist the pressure from OEEC to participate in the trade liberalization programme, because it wanted to retain the EPU with its easy credit arrangements and wanted also to resist moves by the United Kingdom to take over the leadership of Europe by dismantling European institutions and re-establishing the one-world system of Bretton Woods according to its own timetable. Furthermore the trade and payments arrangements within the French Union were coming under pressure from both France and the countries of the Union.

Where the planners played a key role was in offering a long-term perspective for economic policy. In many respects the first plan had avoided the critical problems raised by French economic interdependence by arguing that as a result of an investment programme implemented within the protected confines of the French Union the French economy would be able to participate freely in a one-world multilateral trade and payments system. By 1952 this had been proved to be wrong. A basic problem was that although the investment programme increased the external deficit, without it French industry could not meet domestic demand. As the level of protection was reduced this demand was met from imports which in the absence of external aid could not be financed. Moreover although the internal financing of investment in metropolitan France was increasingly met from private sources, as American aid declined, this was not true for investment in the French Union. The longer-term solution advocated by the planners was based on an expansion of agricultural exports and the participation of other countries in the investment programmes of the French Union. Mendès-France hoped to achieve these economic objectives through bilateral inter-governmental arrangements particularly with the German Federal Republic. However given the conditions demanded by the Federal German government in return for accepting French agricultural exports, the result was not particularly advantageous for France and risked setting a precedent for other governments to follow. While the integration of the French economy with the other five European economies was not a French initiative in 1955, the form which it took owed much to French conditions drawn up to ensure what was perceived to be the French national interest.

As the debate outlined in this chapter has shown, integration was a policy choice which was not forced on the French government through the pressure of technological developments, or trading patterns, or external political events such as the Suez fiasco. While the need to contain the German Federal Republic played a part in the decision this does not in itself explain the form which the European Community was to take. Where the decision was to a certain extent inevitable was that by 1956 it was clear that the French government could no longer achieve its objectives within the existing framework of interdependence in OEEC or in the alternative one offered by the one-world system of Bretton Woods and GATT.

4 Between interdependence and integration: Denmark's shifting strategies

Vibeke Sørensen

Denmark is often referred to by economists and historians as an almost perfect example of how a small country can pursue high rates of economic growth through adjustment to international market forces. Behind this judgement lies the theoretical assumption that small states like Denmark cannot impose their own strategy with respect to their national destiny and will reap maximum economic benefit from fitting into a world economy which is largely shaped by strategies of larger nations.

In reality however Denmark has demonstrated a remarkable will to shape its own national destiny in the post-war period and was largely successful in doing so until the early 1970s. Despite particular difficulties arising from dependence on agricultural exports and from internal political division, Denmark has advanced its national policy objectives within the changing international environment of the post-war period in much the same way as other western European states. This chapter considers the way that a small open economy, in contrast to France which was both large and protectionist in the early 1950s, could attempt to shape the international framework to suit the choices which emerged from the interplay of domestic politics. It demonstrates also however that there was never any durable consensus on the basis of which a firm commitment to either interdependence or integration could be made. The choice wavered between the two, with ideas of a nordic community substituting at different times for both.

Where Denmark perhaps can be said to have varied from the rest of western Europe is in its largely agrarian economy and the particular organization of the national polity to which that gave rise. Historically, specialization in a few agricultural export staples for the British and the German markets achieved a high national standard of living based on imports both of capital and consumer goods. Given this economic structure, industry remained small and, apart from a few sectors, dependent on domestic demand and on the economic fate of the agricultural export base. Since the 1930s however, agricultural value-added and employment have been declining, a policy problem which focused political attention in the cities on the question of employment and, consequently, on the need for industrial development.

In the 1950s Denmark had particular problems of managing such an industrial development, because its economic structure was based on a complementary pattern of foreign trade as distinct from the rapidly growing interchange of manufactured products which was typical of the foreign trade of most other western European countries. Denmark had a catching-up problem with respect to the division of labour in Europe after 1945 which led government and manufacturing industry to believe that a certain insulation from the German economy was required. Where other governments increasingly saw foreign trade in manu-factures with the German Federal Republic as beneficial to industrial and economic development, Danish governments were more concerned to protect the industrial sectors which they wished to promote, as well as industries supplying the domestic market which still provided the major share of employment. Danish foreign economic policy therefore was preoccupied less with the construction of an international framework which would ensure the continuation of industrial trade with the German Federal Republic and more with finding ways to restrict and control that exchange and accommodate it to the speed of Danish industrial development. One of the major factors behind the choice of integration, the desire to commit the Federal Republic to the pattern of trade which developed in western Europe after 1949, was therefore missing, or much less strong, in Denmark. As drafted, the Treaty of Rome was perceived in Copenhagen by the groups in power as more of a threat than a support to Danish industry and commerce. This was however not solely the consequence of the dominant role which agriculture had played in Danish exports since the mid-nineteenth century; it was also due to differences in historical development between Denmark and its neighbours in the inter-war period.

The political basis for the development of the modern nation-state in Denmark was laid down in the 1930s. In contrast to the widespread political and ideological upheaval elsewhere in Europe, Denmark experienced a remarkable political stability in that decade which served to strengthen the existing power structures of government. Less than 10 per cent of the vote was lost to anti-parliamentarian movements and a coalition government between the Social Democratic Party and the Radical Party remained in power from 1929 until 1940 and the German invasion, when it was widened. This political stability is partly explained in turn by the fact that the economic crisis of 1929–32 was less severe in Denmark than elsewhere and partly by the fact that a political consensus on managing the crisis was relatively quickly established between the Social Democrats, the Radicals and the Liberal Party, temporarily turned protectionist by the closure of the German and British markets. Democracy and a broad popular allegiance to the national polity were maintained, despite the rapid growth of a right-wing agrarian protest movement. Most farmers and smallholders remained wedded to democracy and political co-operation.[1]

Between 1931 and 1940 the crisis measures gradually developed into a Social Democratic strategy for national development based on the protection of employment and expansion of industrial production. These policy priorities clearly required a greater insulation from the international economy than was provided by the free trade which had earlier prevailed, in the agricultural sector too, until 1929. Limitation of foreign competition in the domestic market from 1931 and a policy of low interest rates led to a rapid recovery of industry and in 1933 subsidies and a series of social measures together with devaluation were introduced to maintain the incomes of those hardest hit by the crisis, the farmers and the unemployed. After an initial decline in 1932, GNP grew by between 2 and 2.5 per cent annually for a decade, a growth rate exceeded only by Germany and the other Scandinavian countries in that period.[2]

This political consensus survived the German occupation and the Social Democratic Party's post-war policy was strongly influenced by the experience and problems of the inter-war period. In particular this was so with reference to the persistent unemployment, which after a sharp decline in 1933–4 remained fixed around 20 per cent. The fact that a 50 per cent increase in industrial employment had been insufficient to absorb labour made redundant in agriculture was seen as strengthening the need for expansion and modernization of industry if the party's policy objectives, full employment and social reform, were to be realized in the post-war period. This perception, of course, had important consequences for the party's approach to the internationalization of the economy in the post-war period. While it was recognized, at least theoretically, that insulation of the economy as practised in the 1930s was not a viable long-term strategy for a small economy like Denmark, the party was equally convinced that increased participation in international trade in the post-war period should not be allowed to jeopardize the progress made by industry during the 1930s. Consideration for employment and the development of a modern competitive industrial export sector were together seen as requiring a continued measure of protection of the industrial sector.[3]

These policy objectives however faced the Social Democratic Party with the problem of how to maintain its co-operation with the farmers and the Liberal Party. The distinction between farmers and smallholders in the landholding structure of Danish agriculture, crucial to the original success of the agricultural sector in the nineteenth century, was crucial, too, to the shifting attitudes of Danish parties to international economic arrangements.[4] Whereas the larger landholders, farmers, had had a relatively wide range of international opportunities available, the smallholders had concentrated heavily since the late nineteenth century on producing butter and bacon for the British market. The farmers had entered into the 1930s consensus only when forced by the closure of international markets and had, despite large state subsidies, suffered a heavy loss of production and exports. Through the Liberal Party, they had prevented the Social Democrats from instituting the tariff reform for which industry and trade unions had been campaigning since the turn of the century. Other forms of import restriction were seen as a more efficient means of conducting trade policy in a world thought to be only temporarily protectionist. After 1945 the farmers were determined to free themselves from the state regulation and import restrictions of the 1930s. Import restrictions, they believed, hampered agricultural exports within the system of bilateral trade agreements which dominated European trade in the early post-war years, whereas a rapid expansion of agricultural exports, before production elsewhere in Europe caught up again, would be crucial to securing future market shares. Likewise, state trading was seen as subjugating agricultural exports to more overall national interests, i.e. the need to secure raw materials and capital goods for industrial production, and thus as a limitation on the historical freedom of the farmers independently to market their products via the co-operative system. After strong political pressure, the export boards under the Ministry of Agriculture were in fact privatized in 1950.

Seen in retrospect, Danish farmers appear not only to have under-estimated the strength of protectionist feelings in Europe, but also to have overestimated their ability to compete against state cartels and high tariff barriers. The farmers themselves had already in 1944 pointed out that Danish agriculture in the post-war period would meet growing protection; a situation in which it would have seemed logical to give up the ideology of free trade and instead try to achieve an agreement based on state regulation and subsidies to maintain agricultural income. This was what actually happened after 1958, but not before Danish farmers, by sheer force of will, had made a last attempt to force their cost-efficient products on to European markets. However, even the most efficient producers cannot for long compete against subsidies and domestic price arrangements and all the farmers achieved was to postpone an outcome which seems inevitable. Why Danish farmers did not switch to state protection earlier is perhaps best explained by domestic political reasons. Only a return to the free trade of the 1920s would turn the internal terms of trade with industry back in favour of agricultural production and thus restore the political influence which the farmers had begun to lose during the 1930s.

The broad political consensus of the 1930s consequently broke down in late 1945 when a Liberal-led government came to power. The farmers and the Liberal Party made it clear that they aimed at a return to free market forces by proceeding to dismantle all restrictions on trade with the United Kingdom. Fear of state intervention brought agriculture and industry together and the Liberals and the Conservatives joined forces to oppose Social Democratic dominance. The breakdown of the pre-war consensus had a profound impact on post-war development in Denmark; separately neither the Social Democrats nor the Liberals were strong enough to form stable majority coalition governments until 1957.

Social Democratic governments were therefore dependent on their old coalition partner from the 1930s, the Radical Party, which was strongly committed to the support of the smallholders and also to nordic co-operation rather than to agreements with other western European countries. This political division served to constrain Social Democratic policy and prevented an alliance with private industry and the Conservatives around a policy of industrial protection and development. Even so, these political problems could not change the fact that the national choice made in the 1930s, in favour of employment, social reform and industrialization, which had been the Social Democratic Party's road to power, remained fixed as the dominant policy objective of the national polity after 1945.

After 1945 high economic activity and excess demand had a favourable effect on industrial production, which by 1947 had reached the 1938 level while agricultural production still lagged behind. The main objective of the Liberal government was to facilitate the import of inputs for agricultural production. Even by early 1946 however, Denmark had accumulated a large deficit on its sterling balance and was forced to reintroduce controls on trade with the United Kingdom. Before the war Denmark had used its surplus with the United Kingdom to pay for imports from Germany and the continent, and post-war reconstruction therefore depended heavily on sterling convertibility. When a Social Democratic-led government returned to power in 1947 the balance of payments had not improved and suspension of sterling convertibility in August 1947 made it highly unlikely that it would do so in the near future. Despite the use of import restrictions since early 1946, the Danish balance of payments had turned from a surplus of 271 million kroner to a deficit of 660 million kroner in little less than two years.[5]

This indicated that the balance of payments would require very careful management if the policy of industrialization were not to be jeopardized by balance of payments constraints. However there was no political agreement on economic policy. The Social Democratic government was concerned with reconstruction and the new possibilities of demand management, so the use of an expansionary economic policy to preserve employment and encourage industrial development had priority over measures to control the balance of payments. Marshall Aid, which came as a timely relief, for a while allowed the government to ignore the balance of payments and continue its expansionary economic policy to support reconstruction.

Government policy met with opposition from the Conservatives and industry, though for other reasons than the trade policy. The Conservative Party represented an old-fashioned alliance of often conflicting interests of industry, trade and large farmers. It was incapable of providing coherent political leadership for industrial interests. The industrial sector was small and, apart from the shipyards and certain sectors of the engineering and machine industry, orientated towards the domestic market. The administrative use of import restrictions since the 1930s had allowed uncompetitive sectors to expand. It is suggested that, as late as 1957, 60 per cent of Danish industrial production was still protected against foreign competition.[6] One unfortunate consequence of the non-selective protection of the 1930s was the development of an old-fashioned and conservative industrial sector, unlikely to provide visionary ideas for industrial change in the post-war period.

The main political problem became how to adjust industry to international markets without jeopardizing employment. Both government and trade unions thought that this problem could be overcome by leaving the system of restrictions intact and using instead selective investment support to encourage new industrial development. In industry however, such ideas were met with solid opposition. Since the collapse of several large banks in the 1920s, industry had relied heavily on self-financing; selective state intervention in what industry considered private business decisions was strongly resented. If the government wanted to encourage industrial investments, the Industrial Council argued, it should do so by fiscal policy. Tax exemptions for depreciations and private investment funds were however still perceived by government and trade unions as an unacceptable way of increasing private wealth.[7]

Industry was also highly sceptical about government initiatives to expand industrial production. It was obvious that such an expansion had to be aimed at exports, since the domestic market was small, but private industry, providing little over 10 per cent of total exports, found the prospects for such exports highly uncertain. It was generally believed that in order to compete in European markets industry would have to undergo drastic restructuring and mergers to achieve larger economies of scale. The export success of the 1960s achieved by small firms producing for world market niches was not foreseen by industry in the 1950s. On the contrary, it was thought that the small size of industrial firms would prevent Danish industry from breaking into western European markets dominated by large mass-producing companies. Instead, industrial leaders looked towards Scandinavia and less developed overseas markets where competition was thought to be less fierce.

Given the hostility of the farmers and the lack of co-operation from industry, the new government was unable to assert its policy objectives in the long-term programme of 1948 which had to be submitted to OEEC under the terms of Marshall Aid. The planning of the programme ran into difficulties, especially because of the attitude within industry. The administration's original draft had been skewed towards industrial development, but the almost total absence of investment plans in industry and the industrial opposition eventually changed the programme. Although the final version reflected the rapid expansion of industrial production since 1945, the programme finally maintained that agricultural exports should remain the basis for the Danish economy in the post-war period.

Already in 1948 the government recognized that it would be unable to assert its more ambitious policy objectives against this political opposition. In this situation, all the government could hope for was that the new post-war European framework, which had been initiated with the Marshall Plan, could be used to advance Social Democratic policy objectives, in particular a more permanent relief from the balance of payments deficits which, it was gradually realized, would be the inevitable consequence of industrial development.

However the government itself was also to a certain degree influenced by the belief in agricultural efficiency as the foundation of Denmark's prosperity. It initially expected agricultural earnings to pay for capital goods and raw material imports until the industrial sector could take over as the main currency earner. But without sterling convertibility this was going to be harder than first thought. Although Denmark for a while had been able to export to continental markets, this option disappeared during 1948–9 as agricultural production caught up on the continent and left Danish agricultural exports highly dependent on the British market. Concerned about long-term market security, the farmers insisted on tying agricultural exports to the British market during 1948–9 in a series of long-term contracts based on fixed prices. These contracts tied more than 30 per cent of total Danish exports to the United Kingdom over a period of from five to seven years and were the first real indication that the government would not be able to rely on agriculture's foreign exchange earnings other than in sterling to finance industrialization.[8] Protectionism in Europe also raised the daunting prospect of a rapid decline in Danish agricultural income.

Although the government had not fully grasped this prospect in 1948–9, it attempted to find a more permanent solution to its payments problem through the inherited European structure of interdependence. Denmark, the government hoped, would be accepted as a structural debtor within the European Payments Union. This was a hope quickly dashed by the Americans; the Economic Co-operation Agency (ECA) firmly believed that once the trade liberalization programme, which was based on widening the existing quota restrictions, went ahead in OEEC, efficient production of agricultural exports would enable Denmark to recover very quickly from its balance of payments problem.[9]

The OEEC however was hardly an adequate forum for solving the Danish problem. High tariffs and state trade, which was exempt from the liberalization programme, prevented a general liberalization of agricultural trade in western Europe until a solution was found for some countries through European integration. If anything, interdependence as encapsulated in the OEEC liberalization programme served to compound Danish difficulties: Denmark had the lowest tariffs in Europe and most of its industry was protected by quantitative restrictions. It was consequently highly vulnerable to the OEEC programme of quota removal.[10] Maintenance of tariffs in the rest of Europe meant that loss of domestic market shares would not be compensated by easier access to foreign markets. The inherited framework of interdependence, as it developed in the immediate post-war period, was thus singularly unsuited for the advancement of Danish policy objectives.

This was confirmed by a serious balance of payments crisis in August 1950 which necessitated a drastic reduction of imports as well as of economic activity. The crisis meant the end of the low interest-rates policy which, as in the rest of Scandinavia, was seen as a crucial element in Social Democratic policy. The trade unions rejected austerity measures and the government chose to leave the implementation of a deflationary policy to a new Liberal–Conservative coalition government (1950–3). The balance of payments crisis meant the end of the reconstruction policy and the start of a stop-go policy from which Denmark escaped only after large-scale international borrowing was initiated from 1958.[11] The payments crisis in 1950 was seen by both industry and trade unions as a direct consequence of the OEEC trade liberalization programme and therefore as a bad omen for the problems that participation in European co-operation would bring in the future.

In 1950 two important national policy objectives were clearly outlined: first, the necessity of securing agricultural markets to protect the balance of payments and agricultural incomes and, second, the necessity of industrial development to provide employment and social welfare for the whole population. For a small country this was a formidable challenge which would require close co-operation between government and economic interests. As it was, the country was deeply divided and, in the absence of an adequate international framework which simultaneously could facilitate these objectives, both the Social Democrats and the farmers began to consider possible alternatives to the inherited system of interdependence.

The most important change in Denmark's international economic relations in the 1950s was in fact the growing trade with the German Federal Republic about which the first post-war governments had been so cautious: imports from the Federal Republic increased steadily after 1949 while industrial exports to it began to grow after 1953, although more slowly. Nevertheless, while against all expectations the dollar deficit was balanced as early as 1954, Denmark still remained locked in a permanent payments deficit with continental Europe and in particular with the Federal Republic and Benelux. Even when depleting its EPU drawing rights Denmark only managed its recurrent balance of payments crisis with these countries through heavy cut-backs in economic activity.

Predictably, the reactions within Denmark to this new economic trend reflected the existing policy divisions. The farmers began in 1951 to show more interest in the German Federal Republic and other European markets, which they expected would show a more dynamic growth for such exports as meat, live animals, eggs and cheese, while the smallholders, with little possibility of diversifying production away from the heavy concentration on butter and bacon, continued to look towards the British market. But neither trade unions nor industry itself believed in industry's ability to compete in the German market and continued to maintain that expansion of manufactured exports should be directed towards Scandinavia and less developed markets overseas.

It was in this situation of confusion and crisis that the farmers' organization in late 1951 began to investigate the possibilities of a European integrationist arrangement for agricultural trade. In 1950 the farmers had ignored an initial Dutch invitation to participate in the development of such an arrangement. But when the six signatories of the European Coal and Steel Community (ECSC) during 1952 reached agreement on the European Defence Community, Danish farmers gradually began to fear that the idea of a high authority for the agriculture of the Six, put forward by the Dutch Minister of Agriculture, Sicco Mansholt, might soon become reality and the prospect of being excluded from those markets now spurred them into action. A common market of the Six in agriculture, without Danish participation, would give Dutch agriculture a permanent advantage in the German market, deprive the farmers of important bargaining power, and leave them totally dependent on the shrinking British market.

The Liberal–Conservative government, which had taken over in 1950, was more inclined than the Social Democrats to follow the farmers' new line towards European integration and already in 1951 had informed the United Kingdom that it would support all European initiatives that could help break the OEEC impasse on agricultural trade. More attention to industrial needs which was necessary to support the coalition with the Conservatives, now led, furthermore, to a closer investigation of the possible benefits of membership of the ECSC. Since 1945 Denmark had experienced difficulties in obtaining coal and steel at what industry called 'equitable' prices. To the irritation of the United Kingdom, the Liberal–Conservative government began to explore the possibilities of improving the conditions of farmers as well as of industry within the integrationist framework. It was quickly realized that the economic advantage that could be obtained from the ECSC was too small to justify membership in what appeared to be at the time in the process of becoming a European Union involving both foreign policy and defence. In January 1953 the government decided to abandon the negotiations. The separate agricultural proposals, which collapsed as an arrangement between the Six, lingered on among all OEEC countries as 'the Green Pool'. Farmers opposed a transfer of the Green Pool negotiations back to the OEEC. When the Green Pool negotiations during 1953 threatened to become part of the larger European scheme of political integration envisioned in the Defence Community, the government became highly apprehensive about leaving the initiative to the farmers and eventually overruled the farmers' organization, the

Agricultural Council. When the disagreements among the Six ended with the defeat of the Defence Community in the French national assembly in 1954, a new Social Democratic government was more than willing to support the British and Dutch demand to transfer the Green Pool negotiations back to the OEEC and the framework of interdependence.[12]

The Social Democrats, trade unions, industry and the smallholders were more sceptical with respect to the growing economic interdependence with the German Federal Republic. While for the smallholders it was a question of preserving access to the British market, the party and the unions were apprehensive for both political and economic reasons. The Industrial Council remained fearful of German trade competition. Although European market developments in the 1950s in general helped to reinforce the necessity of structural change among private business, this was a realization enforced by economic hardships, a development in striking contrast to the belief in the dynamics of economic growth which grew in train with the high rates of industrial growth elsewhere on the continent. During the 1950s Danish industry went through a difficult period of restructuring and rationalization, which did help to promote exports, but also resulted in the liquidation of many firms and a loss of employment. There is a distinct difference between adjustment in order to capture the rewards of market opportunities and adjustment necessary to offset market penalties; Denmark was to some extent penalized by European market developments and the OEEC liberalization programme during the 1950s. The sluggish growth which was the result of the stop-go policy did little to bolster industry's failing confidence with respect to western European markets and played a large role in strengthening the fear of closer economic ties with the Federal Republic.

The passivity of Danish industry in the face of these developments was striking. The Industrial Council was dominated by the interests of industries selling to the domestic market and was therefore not a forum from which new visions and large-scale plans for industrial change would be likely to emerge. Denmark also lacked a powerful state bureaucracy which could have overcome this passivity by a plan for industrial development. Instead, industrial policy was developed gradually and often rather haphazardly by government and administration in close consultation with industry; a story which still needs detailed historical investigation.

One overriding concern of industrial policy is clearly discernible in the post-war period, that of expanding the small Danish steel industry as a basis of industrial development. An investigation of Danish consumption of steel compared to that of Norway, Sweden and the United Kingdom by the Directorate of Supplies found that the lower per capita consumption in Denmark was closely related to the higher prices paid by Denmark to British and continental suppliers.[13] This difference was an effect of Denmark's status as a consumer country and was perceived as a particularly salient problem for long-term industrial development. The shipyards, which were export earners, were highly dependent on the supply of steel plates and had already in the 1930s in alliance with the machinery industry begun to campaign for domestic steel production. As a joint enterprise between private industry and the state a steel rolling mill had been set up during the war. This enterprise was expanded in 1947 with another rolling mill, bought in the USA, producing plates for the shipyards on the basis of domestic scrap, a purchase which allowed Denmark to increase its production 400 per cent between 1947 and 1955. Throughout the 1950s 20–25 per cent of Danish steel consumption and 75 per cent of the shipyards' consumption of plates was provided domestically.[14] However compared to other European countries steel production remained low (237,000 tonnes in 1955) and it was recognized that Denmark on its own did not have the economic resources or the domestic market to sustain a larger or a more differentiated steel production.

The perception of the need for larger-scale industrial development together with the importance of providing a measure of protection for industry had already persuaded Social Democrats and trade unions early in the post-war period to consider nordic co-operation. The many plans to create a Nordic Customs Union between 1948 and 1957 were to a large degree a Social Democratic project constructed for the international advancement of their industrialization objective, although wrapped in ideological clichés about Scandinavian unity. From the start of the Marshall Plan in 1948 the project was couched in integrationist terms to please the Americans, but the institutional arrangements planned for the projected Scandinavian customs union were in fact wholly inter-governmental.

The first negotiations for a Nordic Customs Union under the propulsion of the Marshall Plan had been buried by 1950, but an inter-governmental committee had continued working with new instructions to investigate the possibilities for a nordic free trade arrangement. This committee delivered its report in 1954. The Scandinavian trade unions proposed in 1951 the creation of a nordic common market and a nordic investment bank to support industrial development.[15] The idea of a customs union was initially also supported by parts of Danish industry as a means of compensating for the negative effects of the OEEC liberalization programme; a customs union would provide the higher tariff protection which agricultural interests were blocking domestically and help to strengthen the Scandinavian countries' bargaining power with respect to the rest of Europe.[16]

A Nordic Customs Union however would not give agriculture any market advantages, as both Sweden and Norway were determined to preserve agricultural protection. In the early 1950s, the Agricultural Council had only very reluctantly agreed to the plans for a customs union. The farmers' strong interest in the Green Pool negotiations then made it clear that market solutions excluding Danish agriculture were only politically viable as long as they did not jeopardize agricultural exports to non-nordic markets. The Radical Party and the smallholders were less negative towards a Nordic Customs Union because the United Kingdom was expected to take an encouraging commercial attitude towards it, thinking that it would buy a large part of its imports in the British market.[17] In the beginning of the 1950s there was thus political support within the two parties which had formed the central structure of the 1930s policy consensus for a Nordic Customs Union and there was considerable interest in industry and the Conservative Party as well; only the farmers were openly hostile to the nordic project. Despite this hostility, the government gave its full support to a Nordic Customs Union when the inter-governmental committee presented its white paper on nordic co-operation in the spring of 1954. At a conference the following October, the Danish, Norwegian and Swedish governments appointed an *ad hoc* committee, the Nordic Economic Co-operation Committee (NECC), to investigate the conditions for the creation of a customs union.

Most existing research into nordic co-operation has concluded that the customs union negotiations were primarily a means to achieve a better position for the Scandinavian countries in European trade negotiations during the 1950s.[18] According to this literature, none of which is based on government archives, the nordic negotiations were motivated by external policy considerations rather than by the economic advantages of co-operation. European developments obviously were an important incentive after 1956, when nordic co-operation within the negotiations for a European free trade area were politically conditioned by the wish to create a better bargaining position for the Scandinavian countries. But research in government archives now suggests, at least in the case of Denmark, that it was economic motivations which were the driving force behind the country's support for the nordic plans in the early 1950s. The source most revealing of these economic motivations is the nordic white papers published by the NECC during the 1950s, economic studies of the benefits of larger markets, larger units and technological know-how.[19] In the case of Denmark, a customs union was seen as providing both a larger market for industrial expansion and a preferential trading arrangement that could compensate for the insulation from the German economy which was thought necessary. Earlier research into nordic co-operation has also ignored one powerful political motive; a co-operation of this kind between Social Democratic parties might build an international framework for the establishment of a new political alliance between labour and industry as a basis for the preservation of the Social Democratic consensus model.

The existing literature for example is unable to explain what motivated the decision to continue the investigations into the creation of a customs union in October 1954, when the French rejection of the European Defence Community appeared to have brought commercial negotiations between the Six to a standstill as well as having ended the attempt to create a European Union. Scholars have emphasized the strong opposition towards any customs union in Norway and have questioned the sincerity of the Danish and Swedish commitment to the project.[20] However seen in relation to overall economic developments in Europe, in particular the unexpected upswing in intra-European trade from winter 1953/4, which in Denmark immediately elicited a balance of payments deficit, the Danish and Swedish agreement to move ahead with the nordic plans is more understandable. This upswing confirmed the rapid development of the German Federal Republic as the dynamic centre of European commerce and consequently the necessity of accelerating industrial restructuring and development to prevent Scandinavian industry from falling further behind in the European division of labour. The existence of a catching-up problem in relation to the rest of Europe was, of course, less strongly felt in Sweden than in Denmark, but even in Sweden traditional export staples like timber, paper products, and iron and steel accounted for over 70 per cent of exports by value in the late 1940s, indicating the need for the expansion of new manufactured exports.[21] Seen from this point of view there were, in fact, very good reasons to maintain the nordic alternative in 1954 and to attempt gradually to overcome opposition in Norway. The Danish Foreign Ministry's archives covering Danish European policy in the period 1954-7 support this assumption. The Danish decision in October 1954 was seen both by government and administration as a commitment to be taken seriously when defining Danish European policy in general.[22]

The main reason however why research into nordic co-operation until now has underestimated these economic motives, is the general evaluation that the economic foundations for a nordic common market did not exist. The raw material-based Scandinavian exports, such as pulp and paper, had their markets outside Scandinavia and the intra-nordic level of trade in them was therefore relatively low. This has been interpreted as an indication that the potential for the expansion of intra-nordic trade was equally limited. Seen from the liberal assumption that countries trade with each other to exploit differences in comparative advantages this is a logical conclusion, which seems to be confirmed by the relative stagnation of intra-nordic trade in the 1950s compared to the increase in the Scandinavian countries' trade with the continent. Danish exports to Norway and Sweden, for example, accounted for a fixed share of 10–12 per cent of total exports throughout the decade, while exports to the German Federal Republic alone increased from 11 per cent in 1953 to 21 per cent in 1959.[23]

But such a conclusion tends to overlook the fact that already in the 1950s intra-nordic trade was dominated by the exchange of manufactures. In 1957 raw materials and semifinished goods accounted for 30 per cent of intra-nordic trade, but manufactures for 44 per cent. In 1960 exports of machinery from each of the three countries to their proposed partners were larger than their exports of machinery to the Six and the United Kingdom.[24] The Scandinavian countries thus had a potential for intra-trade exactly in those sectors that their governments wished to promote. This trade potential was realized in the 1960s when membership of EFTA led to a dramatic increase in intra-nordic trade.[25] Its relative stagnation during the 1950s might actually help us to understand why the early Nordic Customs Union was not realized before the later proposals for a free trade area and why, later, EFTA completely changed the Scandinavian agenda. In contrast, between the Six there was a rapid increase in intra-trade supporting the creation of the customs union by demonstrating concretely its possible benefits. The nordic project rested on a belief in an as yet unexploited intra-trade potential in manufactured products, while the interest in the free trade area was stimulated by a desire to secure the traditional Scandinavian export staples against discrimination in their European markets. The latter responded immediately to considerations of the balance of payments and full employment, the former to less pressing, longer-run strategic considerations of Scandinavia's place in the European division of labour.

The economic motivations for the nordic common market in the mid-1950s were thus the same as those behind the Treaty of Rome in 1957 and the Single European Act, the search for economies of scale, improved competitiveness, and technological development. Only the means and methods by which these goals were to be achieved were different. In the nordic plans co-operation between producers played an important role. In order to overcome the restraints of small national markets and limited economic resources, such co-operation under a degree of state supervision was thought necessary in order to match the modern large-scale plants being developed in the USA and Europe in industries like steel, chemicals and cars.

Investigations of the conditions for the expansion and co-ordination of the Scandinavian steel industry formed an important part of the NECC's brief in 1954. The three countries had planned an expansion of their domestic steel production on an individual basis of from 10 to 20 per cent over the decade after 1955, which would bring the total Scandinavian production up to 4.5 million tonnes by 1965. There was very little intra-Scandinavian trade in steel; net imports into Denmark and Norway accounted for 60–80 per cent of consumption, into Sweden for 40 per cent. This relatively high level of dependence on the rest of Europe was felt to be more problematic after the creation of the ECSC which, in economic terms, was perceived as a re-creation of the European steel cartel of the 1930s. An increase of intra-Scandinavian trade to cover 85 per cent of total consumption was seen as offering benefits in the form both of security of supplies and of stabilization of prices.[26]

Both issues were especially important in Denmark. In 1951, 74 per cent of Danish steel imports by value came from the ECSC which by early 1953 was already constituted as an export cartel.[27] A committee was set up under the Ministry of Trade and Industry in that year to conduct consultations with private industry on commercial problems in relation to the ECSC. The discussion in this committee gives a relatively clear picture of how Danish officials and industry perceived their supply problems. Some industries, particularly those importing steel, hoped to continue to profit from price competition among producers, while the shipyards were more concerned with the long-term security of supplies. The Directorate of Supplies and the Ministry of Trade and Industry were rather sceptical about the future possibilities of exploiting price competition. They saw the ECSC investment policy as a sign that the steel market would be more co-ordinated, a development that would work against price cycles and so make it more difficult for Denmark to pursue its traditional import policy. The implementation of quotas by the ECSC on exports to third countries in 1954 was seen as confirmation of this.[28]

Danish officials complained strongly about these quotas both in GATT and to the ECSC. During 1955, the complaints were discussed several times with the High Authority of the ECSC, Denmark claiming that the prices paid by Danish industry were 15–20 per cent higher than those paid by Community consumers. The Danish position however was seriously weakened by the fact that higher prices had not reduced consumption. On the contrary, Danish imports of steel had increased since October 1954 when prices started to go up. Discussions in GATT gave the clear impression that Denmark was acquiring a reputation for complaining without reason and the High Authority pointed out that Denmark could not expect to enjoy the same advantages as member countries without accepting the commitments of membership.

The nordic plans for co-operation within their own iron and steel market elicited a response from the ECSC in 1955. This is hardly surprising considering that such a market would have been the ECSC's largest customer for coal, coke and steel and its largest supplier of iron ore (in 1954, 54 per cent of ECSC imports). In October the Dutch member of the High Authority, Dirk Spierenburg, suggested that Denmark should consider a closer relationship to the ECSC. The proposal was that Denmark, without becoming a member, would achieve 'equal' treatment with respect to prices and supplies if it agreed to keep coal and steel imports tariff free and in times of surplus production to implement certain restrictions on imports from third countries. The proposal was clearly aimed at obstructing the nordic plans and was therefore after careful investigation rejected by the government in August 1956. Discussions with private industry showed that both the shipyards and the steel traders were now in favour of the nordic solution to the Danish supply problems.[29]

However this solution too was not without problems. Although all three participants were small economies, they were also very different. Both Norway and Sweden produced more steel than Denmark and an important issue of disagreement was that of fixing the level of a common external tariff. Sweden wanted a tariff on raw materials high enough (5–6 per cent) to prevent dumping, while Denmark insisted on maintaining tariff freedom on such imports, although the shipyards were less adamant. The greater problem was the different production structure in the three countries. In Denmark and Norway, steel production was concentrated in two or three enterprises with a measure of state guidance. Production in Sweden was highly decentralized in forty-three mills, of which only five had a production capacity over 100,000 tonnes.[30] When Norway insisted on the restructuring and planning of Scandinavian steel production as a prerequisite for membership, this inevitably encountered strong opposition from private industry in Sweden. Norway and Denmark favoured a concentration of steel production in a production cycle beginning with the blast furnace and continuing through to a few large rolling mills, with special steel and other products delegated to smaller plants. This would have meant a restructuring of the larger Swedish industry.[31]

The political attitudes behind these disagreements are relevant. Denmark and Norway were concerned to submit Swedish industry to a higher level of state control in order to strengthen an inter-governmental bargain which required a deflection of their trade away from traditional suppliers and, as long as the Swedish government was not ready to step in and overrule private industry, could not see much future in the nordic plans for a steel market. Even so, the negotiations were continued and the proposal for a nordic steel market made up the central part of NECC's final report in 1957. By this time however, ambitions had been lowered; instead of state supervision and planning, co-operation among the Scandinavian steel industries was to be left to the operation of free market forces within the customs union.[32]

The idea that, by pooling their economic resources within a customs union, the three countries could achieve the larger freedom of action in their economic relations with Europe which could promote industrial development was in fact totally dependent on the attitude of Sweden which, as the largest and most industrialized economy, was designated the important role of growth point within the project. Even if we assume that the Swedish Social Democratic government was fully committed to the nordic project, it was clearly reluctant to alienate powerful domestic interests in order to bring it to life. It can be safely assumed that once the United Kingdom's free trade proposal in 1956 changed the agenda for the country's relations with Europe, Sweden would have been even less inclined to make economic sacrifices for the sake of nordic co-operation. Even so, despite this uncertainty about Swedish intentions, the Danish government clearly found that the project provided a much more adequate framework for the advancement of its industrial policy than closer association with the ECSC.

If we look at the development of the economy in this period, it is not difficult to see why. After a period of stagnation, Danish agricultural exports began declining in 1953 while industrial exports showed a promising increase. In the Social Democratic Party this strengthened the conviction that it was industrial interests which should have priority in commercial policy. As far as agriculture was concerned, the party's main loyalty was to the smallholders who were dependent on the British market, and the government was relatively unaffected by the problems of the larger farmers. Nevertheless between 1954 and 1956 it did try to improve their situation by an active participation in the campaign within GATT and the OEEC against high tariff levels. This did not diminish the wish to maintain industrial import quotas. The defeat of the campaign for lower tariffs strengthened the government's conviction that a domestic tariff reform was necessary to substitute for the protection provided by quantitative import restrictions which were under increasing threat from the OEEC trade liberalization programme. But this would require a majority in parliament, which the government did not have. The nordic project seemed easier, for it might eventually provide such a majority, as well as a strong motivation for an administrative reform of a tariff law which in its main elements dated back to 1797.

The Messina conference in May 1955, marking the beginning of the negotiations among the Six for a customs union, did little to reduce the commitment to the nordic project. It was, rather, the British proposal in July 1956 to create a large free trade area, including the Six, which completely changed the situation. The free trade area at first seemed to be the perfect framework for the realization of the nordic project. Technically, the relationship of a Nordic Customs Union to the free trade area, it was thought, might be the same as that of the customs union of the Six to the larger area. The free trade area would embrace two customs unions, and the United Kingdom would not practise the discrimination against the traditional Scandinavian export staples which it might have done had the nordic project been realized in isolation.

For Denmark however, the main problem was that the British proposal excluded agricultural products. The government therefore immediately concentrated all its efforts on changing this. A Nordic Customs Union without agriculture had only been accepted very reluctantly by the Danish farmers; participation in a large free trade area which excluded Danish agricultural exports was not politically viable. This was soon confirmed by the farmers' organization which, after having nervously followed the negotiations between the Six, now demanded that Denmark should participate in these negotiations. After the Liberal Party in January 1957 supported the farmers' demands, the question of European integration became an important issue in the spring election. Unable to ignore the demands of the farmers, the Minister of Foreign Affairs travelled to Brussels and achieved a vague promise that membership of the Six would remain open for Denmark if the government should decide to apply.[33] The Six's attitude helped the government to withstand the political pressure from the opposition until the formation of a coalition government with the Radicals gave the Social Democratic Party a parliamentary majority behind its European policy for the first time since 1945.[34]

The pressure on the government was also to some extent reduced by the fact that the United Kingdom, after political pressure from the Six and Denmark, finally conceded in October that under certain conditions agricultural products might be part of the negotiations for the free trade area. For the first time in the post-war period it then seemed possible to reconcile the policy objectives of the farmers with those of the Social Democratic Party within the same international framework. Such a reconciliation was badly needed for Denmark to free itself from balance of payments constraints. European developments since 1953 had increasingly emphasized the necessity of entering some form of officially regulated agricultural market; competitive advantage was not enough. Between 1953 and 1957 the value of agricultural exports to the United Kingdom fell by 17 per cent while that of exports to the German Federal Republic grew by 12 per cent.[35] The gains in the Federal Republic however were on a market where output sheltered by protection and government subsidy was growing consistently, so the prospect there was not too favourable. Nor did they compensate the losses elsewhere, so that the total value of agricultural exports stagnated. By the late 1950s the issue of subsidies for agricultural production was coming to the fore.

The increase in economic activity in 1957 only generated a larger balance of payments deficit, finally convincing the government that Denmark had a structural payments problem and would not in the near future be able to earn enough foreign exchange to finance the manufactured imports which industrial expansion required. The realization that the stop-go policy now had become a vicious circle and a serious risk to the policy of industrialization led to a series of changes in government policy during 1957–8. With a majority behind it the government could introduce a series of new industrial policy initiatives, among which were the tax-based investment supports for which private industry had been arguing since 1945.[36]

More difficult was the issue of tariff reform over which the government coalition disagreed. A tentative alliance on this issue between the Social Democrats and the Conservatives had emerged already in 1956 with the introduction of a selective tariff increase to protect employment in the textile industry, which had suffered growing competition from overseas producers.[37] On the same basis, a series of smaller tariff changes were introduced in 1957 and 1958. The Social Democratic Party still aimed at a comprehensive tariff reform, which would transfer protection from quantitative restrictions on to tariffs and thus secure a continued protection of development sectors like pharmaceuticals, electronics and electrical machinery. In the circumstances after the Treaty of Rome this looked more feasible by the choice of nordic co-operation, as long as the free trade negotiations could reconcile the nordic project with the opening of markets in the United Kingdom and the other free trade area members to agricultural exports. One thing was certain however, unilateral membership of the European Community was not at any time considered. It remained confined as a policy to the Liberal Party and the farmers.

Effective national policy, including a reversal of the structural weakness in the balance of payments, appeared to require the success of the free trade negotiations, and so depended on the willingness of the United Kingdom to move more in the direction of the integrationist stance of the Six, or France's willingness to modify the Treaty of Rome to accommodate the United Kingdom. A government inquiry into the effects of the different international possibilities on the domestic market was published in 1958 and had a profound impact on the debate on European integration. It concluded that about 40 per cent of industry would on a short- or medium-term basis be exposed to foreign competition.[38] Significantly, the report also stated its firm belief that the opening of OEEC markets by a free trade agreement with the Six would provide large export opportunities for Danish industry which would compensate for, if not exceed, the loss of domestic market shares.[39] This latter conclusion however was totally ignored in the ensuing public debate.

The reactions to the report within industry and trade unions indicated the continued preoccupation with the effect of foreign competition on the domestic economy rather than with the prospects of exports. The report concluded that in terms of foreign competition on the domestic market it would not make any difference whether Denmark became a member of the Six or only of the free trade area, while membership of a Nordic Customs Union within the free trade area would provide a certain protection. The plans for the Nordic Customs Union were based on a more rapid mutual dismantling of tariffs and trade restrictions than in the Six and the free trade area. The establishment of a nordic common tariff would therefore give Danish industry at least a temporary protection within the Scandinavian area. Predictably, the report concluded that a Nordic Customs Union within the free trade area would make the transition period to the larger European market less risky for Danish industry. For agriculture, it recommended that the problems of agriculture would be best solved in a common agricultural agreement, based on the rules of the Treaty of Rome, including the whole free trade area.[40] The treaty had as yet set no rules for the promised common agricultural policy of the Six, but the idea that when this happened they would be acceptable to the United Kingdom was without doubt unjustified optimism.

At the meeting of the Nordic Council in February 1957, all three Scandinavian Social Democratic parties spoke very strongly in favour of the creation of a Nordic Customs Union within the free trade area and in October the NECC presented its five-volume report on the creation of that customs union.[41] Despite its agreement to postpone the final decision until the free trade agreement had been signed, the Danish government believed this to be the most positive solution for Denmark, because of its benefits for employment and industrial development. It was against this background that the three Scandinavian ministers for economic co-operation as late as July 1958 decided to expand the customs union plans to cover a number of typical home market sectors which until now had been considered too sensitive to be included in the nordic project.[42]

It was only in autumn 1958 that it began to become clear that French opposition might lead to the breakdown of the free trade area negotiations. The prospect of failure and of an economic division of western Europe, rather than a more widespread commercial co-operation, quickly altered priorities, not only in Denmark, but also in Sweden and Norway. The gradual erection of the European Community tariff walls from 1 January 1959 was a threat not only to Danish agricultural exports, especially to the German Federal Republic, but also to other Scandinavian export staples. The gloomy prospects for products like paper, aluminium and iron which made up a large part of Norwegian and Swedish exports to the Community played an important role in provoking the collapse of the free trade negotiations. With respect to these products, France claimed that Scandinavian producers had an unfair natural advantage which necessitated tariff compensation for less fortunate producers.[43] The French insistence on this issue, as well as on the demand for a transition period for the establishment of the free trade area, placed Sweden and Norway in a situation very similar to Denmark's. Even if the negotiations could be brought to a successful conclusion, the outcome might very well be a free trade area discriminating for some time and perhaps even permanently against the traditional Scandinavian export sectors which still were the most important earners of foreign exchange.

This new threat explains several changes in the nordic priorities during 1958. Co-operation now became more concentrated on the two issues which divided opinion within the free trade negotiations, agriculture and the question of the rules of origin of imports. It was the agricultural issue particularly which altered opinions in Norway and

Sweden. In principle, both countries preferred a free trade agreement without agriculture, but Norway had strong fishery interests demanding access to European markets and both countries now realized that some sacrifice of protection was necessary to strengthen the bargaining power of the Scandinavian bloc. At a meeting in Saltsjöbaden in September 1958 all agreed to postpone the nordic negotiations until an agreement on the free trade area had been reached. The statement from the meeting underlined the necessity of establishing a common nordic policy with respect to the free trade area negotiations, in order to prevent arrangements between the larger countries which could increase discrimination against the Scandinavian export staples, fish, agriculture, timber, paper, aluminium and ferroalloys. The fear was that a trade-off between the United Kingdom and the Six could result in an arrangement excluding important Scandinavian exports. In the first instance a common stance had to be found on the agricultural question which could satisfy Danish requirements.[44]

In reality the breakdown of the free trade area negotiations in November 1958 also meant the defeat of the nordic project. Afterwards, Sweden and Norway focused on the possibilities of creating an alternative commercial framework including the United Kingdom. Officially the opinion that the nordic customs could be included in an 'outer' free trade area was maintained, but it was clear that this option now had much lower priority. Also a certain hostility towards the customs union was now detectable within private industry. After the collapse of the free trade negotiations, under the leadership of Swedish industry the Scandinavian Industrial Councils decided against the Nordic Customs Union and together with the Federation of British Industries pledged its political support to the EFTA project.[45]

But for Denmark the necessity of securing access for agricultural exports to the Six remained. EFTA could not so easily be envisaged as a reasonable substitute for the whole of the OEEC market. When the possibility of creating an 'outer' free trade area had been first discussed between the Scandinavian countries, the United Kingdom and Switzerland, before the breakdown of the negotiations with the Six, both the United Kingdom and Denmark had warned against actions which could provoke a split in the negotiations.[46] After November 1958 the United Kingdom moved towards a confrontation with the Six. Between the breakdown of the talks on the wider free trade area in November 1958 and the final agreement on EFTA in July 1959, the Danish government had to work on two fronts. An attempt to bring the parties back to the negotiating table had the highest priority, but was clearly unrealistic considering the growing interest in EFTA in the United Kingdom,

Sweden and Norway. More realistic was the attempt to obtain tariff concessions for Danish agricultural exports within EFTA and the Community, which eventually resulted in a series of agreements on agricultural exports with the United Kingdom, the German Federal Republic and Sweden.[47] These agreements secured the continuation of Danish agricultural exports and made it politically possible for the government to override the farmers and the Liberal Party's demand for membership of the Community.

Although the potential benefits from the officially regulated agricultural market being planned by the Six were still highly uncertain, the tariff reductions achieved within the EFTA framework were clearly an inferior solution to the Community for the maintenance of Danish agricultural income. However after the breakdown of the free trade negotiations such benefits for agricultural exports could be achieved only at the expense of industrial production and agricultural exports to the United Kingdom. Although frustrated by the development of European markets, the Social Democratic coalition government maintained its national choice for industrial development and employment in 1958. By exploiting an inter-governmental rather than an integrationist framework, it was able to override a powerful domestic interest group.

Membership of EFTA prepared the way for the tariff reform that the Social Democrats and the Conservatives had been campaigning for since the early 1950s. EFTA created the basis for a political alliance between the two parties on the issue of a tariff reform before trade would be liberated between the EFTA Seven. Maintenance of protection was secured by reducing tariffs on raw materials used in domestic production and increasing those on finished products which were produced in Denmark. The government also acquired the right to implement anti-dumping tariffs in accordance with GATT rules.[48] The tariff reform of 1960 was an important supplement to the industrial policy initiatives undertaken by the government in 1957 in order to promote industrialization; it reflected the rapid increase in industrial exports after 1957 and was a sign that the Danish economic structure was becoming more similar to that of the rest of western Europe.

The government's success in overruling the farmers had been politically possible only because of the Radical Party's and the smallholders' insistence on maintaining economic ties to the United Kingdom, an insistence which indicated that if the United Kingdom decided to apply for membership, the Social Democratic Party and the trade unions would be unable to maintain their preference for inter-governmental co-operation in the face of a united front of farmers and smallholders. Within the party there was also a growing recognition that the rapidly falling agricultural income could, in the long term, be financed only through participation in the Community's agricultural policy. The political implications of this recognition were obvious; it meant giving up the preference for nordic co-operation. It was the beginning of a gradual change in the party's Scandinavian policy. Instead of a separate customs union, nordic co-operation should now, so the Social Democrats thought, be realized within an enlarged Community including the United Kingdom and preferably also Norway and Sweden.[49]

This change of policy did not have support in the trade unions where nordic co-operation was still perceived as the best international framework for the advancement of Social Democratic policy objectives. The trade unions had little sympathy for the farmers and saw the choice between integration and interdependence as a clash between the interests of the farmers and the workers. Predictably, the trade unions found that the interest of workers and industry should have priority in Denmark's commercial policy. When the government decided to follow the United Kingdom in 1961 and apply for membership of the Community, this led to a temporary split between government and trade unions over the question of European integration. The government's claim that membership of an enlarged Community was required to protect the weak balance of payments and provide markets for both agricultural and industrial exports was rejected by several of the large unions, which for ideological as well as economic reasons saw pursuit of growth through participation in an integrationist framework encapsulating the German Federal Republic as irreconcilable with Social Democratic policy.[50]

Consideration for trade union opinion resulted in the inclusion of a series of conditions for Danish membership of the Community which the government presented in Brussels in 1961. These concerned Danish reservations with respect to the articles of the Treaty of Rome pertaining to the free movement of capital and persons and social legislation. The fact that no agreement existed among the Six on these issues made these conditions a mere formality and allowed the government to pursue the more important objective of gaining the quickest possible access to Community markets for its agricultural products. These conditions were accepted by the Six and the negotiations for Danish membership of the Community were very close to their conclusion when President de Gaulle in 1963 announced his opposition to the membership of the United Kingdom. For Denmark membership of the Community without the United Kingdom was clearly unsustainable for domestic political reasons. For a while the government refused to recognize the consequences of the French veto, but was eventually forced to realize that developments elsewhere in Europe, once again, had destroyed the frail consensus which had been reached on an international strategy, albeit this time integrationist, to reconcile agriculture to the requirements of industrial expansion.

The prospect for a change in French attitudes looked bleak and the government had to face the fact that agricultural income support would have to be borne entirely by the state budget for the foreseeable future. This was a daunting prospect indeed; yet, apart from the difficulties of financing agricultural policy, Denmark remained remarkably unaffected by its exclusion from the Community during the 1960s. Rapid economic expansion and full employment in the early 1960s proved that industrial policy was working. Despite two applications for membership of the Community, the 1960s were characterized by a withdrawal from European arrangements after the five hectic years between 1956 and 1961. For many Social Democrats and trade unionists this was a welcome development. A customs union among the three Scandinavian members of EFTA was blocked by the non-Scandinavian members, but EFTA none the less was a closer approximation to the ideas of the Nordic Union than the Community. The rapid economic growth also served to direct political attention away from the structural balance of payments problem and towards social reform and welfare.

During the 1960s public expenditures increased dramatically, leading to the development of a public sector which in terms of organization and finance was distinct from parallel developments elsewhere on the continent.[51] All social groups expanded their share of the economic growth in the 1960s except for the farmers and the smallholders. While the latter were more or less extinguished as a distinct social group, the farmers experienced a slower, although persistent, decline. State subsidies in 1965 accounted for 20 per cent of their group income. The Social Democratic government accepted the demand of the Liberal Party that the structure of agricultural production be maintained by subsidies until membership of the Community could provide better conditions for the farmers. In fact when membership came it led only to a short-lived increase in agricultural prosperity and all the Liberal Party achieved was to postpone the restructuring of Danish landholding into the larger units which already in the 1960s seemed inevitable.

But seen from the point of view of industrial development the EFTA experience was much more positive. In 1968 the Community's external tariffs were in place while EFTA in 1967 had already dismantled all internal tariffs and quantitative restrictions. In 1959–60 the Scandinavian countries had agreed to a common labour market, free movement of persons and equal access to the three countries' social security systems; nordic economic co-operation continuing within the framework of EFTA. Common action on commercial policy between the three countries was initiated in 1966, with considerable success in the 'Kennedy round'. The British decision in 1964 to introduce a 15 per cent import tax without consulting its EFTA partners had raised doubts in the Scandinavian countries about the viability of EFTA as an effective international framework and emphasized the need to strengthen these nordic arrangements.[52]

During the 1960s all three countries underwent rapid industrial and technological development and increased their exchange of manufactures with other OECD members. This new trend was supported however by the rapid development of intra-trade in manufactures among the Scandinavian countries themselves. Sweden and Norway in the 1960s became the most important market for Danish industrial exports. Nordic intra-trade in manufactures increased by about 200 per cent in value compared to the roughly 100 per cent increase in the three countries' trade with the rest of western Europe.[53] The highest growth in nordic intra-trade took place in those sectors like chemicals, machinery, transport equipment and electronics which the governments had promoted since the early 1950s.

In February 1968 a new Danish governing coalition formed from Radicals, Liberals and Conservatives, tried to bring the complete nordic project of the 1950s to life again in the form of the Nordek proposal. This was obviously a Radical Party initiative, but as long as de Gaulle's presidency blocked membership of the Community the Liberal Party was less hostile towards nordic schemes than in the 1950s. Nordek was a much more ambitious enterprise than the Nordic Customs Union and stronger inter-governmental institutions enabling Nordek to negotiate on behalf of its members were now included in the proposal. A co-ordination of the member states' economic policies was proposed so as to ensure that in the longer term Nordek could develop into a community with some integrationist aspects. As before, Sweden was to be the generator of growth in order to allow Norway to realize its wish for investment capital and to provide Denmark with better conditions for agricultural exports. Unlike the 1950s, Sweden now seemed willing to accept that role.[54] Danish farmers however obviously found the prospect of an extra income of 200 million kroner from better access to Swedish markets unsatisfactory compared with the 2.4 billion kroner they expected to gain through membership of the Community. Although the Nordek proposal brought the Radicals and the Social Democrats together, this did not mean that the latter gave up their European Community policy; their idea was that a nordic economic community should be established with a view to a broader European arrangement.

In December 1969 European events again interfered with the nordic plans, when the European Community summit in The Hague, after the unexpected resignation of de Gaulle, decided to reopen the question of Community enlargement, a development which immediately weakened support for Nordek in Denmark. Within the Social Democratic Party this event opened a split over the commitment to Community membership. Finland's rejection of Nordek in March 1970, at a time when the agreement had already been concluded, was caused by the insistence of Denmark and Norway on maintaining their freedom to apply for Community membership, should they want to do so. Finnish membership of an international arrangement comprising two Community members was seen as irreconcilable with the policy of neutrality. In Denmark, the Liberals and the Conservatives took the Finnish rejection as putting a definite end to nordic co-operation; political attention, they argued, should now be directed to achieving the best possible entry conditions into the Community. Because trade unions continued to support Nordek the issue of membership became a highly sensitive one for the Social Democrats. The party attempted to maintain its old policy that membership of the Community need not exclude participation in nordic co-operation. This conclusion however was quickly challenged by an official Community statement that membership did not allow participation of that nature in another regional organization.[55]

Seen against the background of the rapid economic and social developments in the 1960s, it is understandable that the issue of membership became so controversial. That decade seemed to confirm that the national choice already made in the 1930s in favour of employment, social reform and industrialization, could be more than adequately pursued within a nordic framework in relative isolation from the German economy. To a large part of the Danish population, membership of the Community increasingly appeared to be a question only of securing Community subsidies for the farmers. Membership, it was feared, would reverse the industrial expansion and social welfare gains of ten years and return Denmark to that automatic adjustment to international market forces which the farmers since their late nineteenth-century successes had always advocated.

Denmark became a member of the Community in 1973, at a time when the oil crisis and collapse of international monetary stability provided new and difficult challenges for Community states. The economic crisis provoked a political revolt against high social expenditure and taxes which achieved greater political salience in Denmark at the time than elsewhere. As elsewhere however, Denmark first attempted to face these new challenges with the traditional post-war policies and instruments. It was the failure of these policies to reduce unemployment and inflation which led to a gradual shift of emphasis in economic policy away from the use of public expenditure to support economic activity to a more market-orientated approach to economic policy. This finally put an end to the patterns of political consensus and national strategy which had emerged in the 1930s and brought a realignment of politics around more liberal ideals. The Social Democratic Party had to change fundamental beliefs and policies and in the course of this change it recognized that such new economic policies appeared to require an integrationist framework for their advancement. Since 1982 a Conservative–Liberal coalition government has in fact been more willing than the Social Democrats to consider such policies and to advance them actively through the European Community. The Single European Act, which the Social Democratic Party rejected, is an indication that increasing the economic exchanges with Germany to include services and state procurement is seen as the best way to pursue economic growth and international competitiveness. Whereas the national strategy of the 1930s – employment, social reform and industrialization – was thought to be more adequately pursued within a framework of interdependence which nevertheless still guaranteed a certain insulation from the German economy, the new national strategy as it has developed since the early 1980s is clearly more efficiently advanced within the integrationist framework of the European Community. For a narrow majority of the population however, the extension of that strategy into monetary union and foreign policy and defence co-operation as embodied in the European Union Treaty proved too much to swallow.

5   Inside or outside the magic circle?

The Italian and British steel industries face to face with the Schuman Plan and the European Coal Iron and Steel Community[1]

Ruggero Ranieri

It is well known that the relationship between western Europe's steel industries for the best part of the nineteenth and twentieth centuries lends itself to be analysed under the category of interdependence. Raw material distribution as well as regional and national specialization have shaped patterns of trade according to the different demands of steel users, mainly in the mechanical industry, a fact which spreads the sensitivity to steel price differentials well beyond the borders of the industry itself. Moreover competitive pressures are sharpened by the low degree of price elasticity in the demand for steel goods, while the capital intensive nature of steel-making enhances the risk inherent in that competition. The result has been that steel producers have been seen repeatedly to yearn for price stability, particularly in times of recession, a concern which has led them to engage in a range of collusive practices on the regional, national and transnational levels. Such exercises however have often had the effect of creating greater instability for other steel makers or steel users, who happened to be outside that particular set of market-sharing arrangements and were, therefore, exposed to aggressive market penetration on the part of the cartel.

Underlying it all was the fact that the political frontiers of nation-states in continental north-western Europe bestrode what were to all intents homogeneous metallurgical regions, a situation in no way altered by the drawing and redrawing of the political map in the large border area between France, Belgium, Germany and Luxemburg in the years between 1870 and 1945. Clearly in this area interdependence between steel producers was particularly intimate, encompassing the whole of the northern European coal basin, stretching from northern France to the Rhineland, to the more southern Lorraine–Luxemburg–Saar iron-ore mining region. As the scale of output increased in the latter part of the nineteenth century, so did the advantages of vertical integration throughout this area, as well as the degree of geographical concentration and specialization. Reciprocal raw material flows, of which that of Ruhr coking coal was crucial, intensified. Transport networks were integrated, technological links were forged, mergers and amalgamations became more frequent.[2]

To this was added an increasingly elaborate network of cartels, culminating in the international ones of the inter-war period, of which the first one was the International Steel Cartel (ISC), established in 1926 between the German, French, Belgian and Luxemburg steel associations. It was based on national production ceilings and integrated by bilateral trading quotas. After its collapse it was replaced in 1933 by the International Steel Export Cartel (ISEC), which was based on an equally binding allocation of export shares.

There is some agreement to the extent that these cartels functioned under German leadership and represented an extension of the German model of business regulation. They appeared to be 'ponderously staffed, bristling with regulations and clauses' and they 'brandished noisily an array of phenomenal weapons with which they attacked the market'.[3] The ISEC in particular was 'a formidable structure, encompassing eight national groups with eighteen separate export cartels. . . . Each product had its own agreement administered by different national groups. This allowed the national groups to set specific policies for each product in each market.'[4] On the other hand, it may be possible to exaggerate the cohesiveness of these organizations. It should be remembered that their rules were often flouted by individual firms and that they were based on short-term contracts and therefore subject to periodical renegotiation between the national groupings. A fundamental difference within them was that Belgian and Luxemburg producers were mainly interested in maximizing exports, whereas the French and the Germans usually aimed at protecting their domestic markets. This however changed during the 1930s when the French, due to a deficiency of domestic demand, increasingly teamed up with the Belgians in focusing on the export of semifinished products.[5]

Subject to greater dispute is the cartels' relationship with governments. In recent scholarship there has been a tendency to consider them as an example of peaceful business diplomacy, thus overturning the notion that they were pliable instruments in the hands of nationalistic and militaristic groups.[6] Whatever view is taken about the inter-war period however, it is beyond doubt that the balance between the public and the private sphere in the industry changed significantly after the war, steel becoming a founding element of the mixed economy and the main object of national reconstruction plans. The negotiations on the status of German heavy industry between the Allies also indicated that international steel matters had ceased to be the preserve of secretive deals between private businessmen. In fact the basis of the peaceful post-war settlement was ultimately provided by the Schuman Plan for a common market in coal, iron and steel, which served the essential purpose of reconciling France and the German Federal Republic over the problem of the Ruhr.[7] The plan was designed by Jean Monnet, who was also the architect of French post-war domestic steel policies, to re-establish the unity of continental heavy industry under a new supra-national pattern of management with a strong technocratic bent. During the negotiations leading to the European Coal and Steel Community (ECSC) however, the Schuman Plan was fundamentally reshaped by a number of compromises between the states and the industries involved.[8]

As soon as industrialists in the United Kingdom and Italy learned about the Schuman Plan they thought it was a new continental cartel. Sir Andrew Duncan, chairman of the British Iron and Steel Federation (BISF), at a meeting of the Federation's Executive Committee on 16 May 1950 expressed doubts as to whether the newly proposed High Authority was going 'to be the controller or if the real intention was merely an agreement among governments along Cartel lines'. He then suggested that 'the British steel industry should have no wish or interest to speak against the French and Germans getting together, or even their being joined by the Benelux countries', although he was quick to add that 'it would be unwise to give such a welcome as to imply that we ourselves were interested in joining'.[9] Very similar concerns were voiced during gatherings of industrialists at the Ministry of Industry in Rome, with perhaps the difference that the Italians hoped that by talking directly to the French the worst threats could be somehow averted.[10] Such reactions betrayed the fact that both the Italian and the British steel industries had experienced a difficult relationship with their continental neighbours. The comparative strength of the British industry lay in open hearth production, as opposed to Thomas converter steel which was best produced in Lorraine, in Belgium and in the Ruhr, and it was precisely massive imports of Thomas steel shapes which had succeeded in making dramatic inroads into the British market during the inter-war period. The British steel industry also shared with continental producers the position of being a leading world steel exporter. The Italian steel industry, in contrast, was a much smaller operation, based mainly on open hearth and electric steel, making but little blast furnace steel, and unable as a result to supply the domestic market with bulk commercial steel products, especially those best manufactured in Thomas converters. These were therefore imported, in great measure from France, Belgium and the German Federal Republic.

According to their different strengths the two industries had secured different terms from the continental inter-war groupings. Italy negotiated something which may be defined as a membership at the margins, by way essentially of bilateral quotas, mainly with France, of supplies of pig iron, scrap and semifinished steel products for Italian domestic re-rollers. Also continental producers were granted a share of the Italian market for finished products, in exchange for which the rest of Italian domestic production was allowed to enjoy very high protection.[11] In the British case continental encroachments were resisted by deploying high tariffs, thereby forcing the international cartel to sit down and negotiate reciprocal quotas. The dispute had bequeathed lasting organizational consequences for the British steel industry, which, having for a long period operated shorn of protection and with only a limited degree of cartelization, had been forced to tighten its structures – the BISF was created in 1935 – and accept to be managed under close government supervision. The Import Duties Advisory Committee (IDAC), first of the many public bodies which were to supervise the industry in the years to come, was set up in 1932.[12]

PROJECTING EXPANSION: THE SINIGAGLIA PLAN AND THE SCHUMAN PLAN

The Italian steel industry also underwent an important transformation during the 1930s, when a large part of it, roughly equal to one-half of its overall capacity, was brought under state ownership as a result of the creation first of the Istituto per la Ricostruzione Industriale (IRI), a state holding company, in 1933, and then of its subholding company Finsider in 1937. A powerful and independent technocracy of state industrialists was thus created, holding their own views on the direction in which they wanted to see the industry move. Most influential were the views first mooted by Oscar Sinigaglia and later taken up by Agostino Rocca, general manager of Finsider from 1937 to 1940. The essential focus of these was that a larger share of steel production should be made in integrated plants – the so-called '*ciclo integrale*' – comprising the entire cycle of steel-making operations from the smelting of coke and iron ore in blast furnaces down to the refining of pig iron in converters or open hearth furnaces and to the finishing operations by rolling mills. Restructuring plans to this effect were put on stream in the late 1930s and although their implementation was seriously delayed by the war their influence was to be felt in the post-war years when Oscar Sinigaglia, who had fallen out of favour in the final years of the Fascist regime, was appointed at the head of Finsider, a post he held from 1945 to his death in 1953.[13]

What came to be called the Sinigaglia Plan was a programme designed to concentrate and standardize production and achieve economies of scale, particularly by adopting the latest American technology in the field of sheet and tin plate production. Central to the belief of Finsider's managers was the fact that Italy's steel production had suffered from an insufficient degree of specialization and market integration. Higher productivity levels and lower costs, they believed, could be achieved only by closing down obsolete mills and by concentrating production in a few big steel plants located by the sea, which would enjoy a number of crucial advantages. First, their raw materials could be carried comparatively cheaply by sea: second, each of them would be modernized and equipped to turn out more cheaply only a limited number of finished products, thus virtually gaining a monopoly of sales on the domestic market. Clearly the emphasis of the Sinigaglia Plan was on growth and productivity and it was especially concerned that the steel industry should be able to supply engineering producers with cheap semifinished products, thus enabling them fully to take advantage of the capacity increase which they had achieved during the late 1930s and the war. Expressed in Sinigaglia's words a 'strong and healthy steel industry' would enable production of 'ships, wagons, boilers, machine tools, metal shapes' to be stepped up and more generally would spearhead the drive to widen the country's industrial base. The three chief industrial plants selected for modernization were Bagnoli, near Naples, which would produce bar and other shapes needed for the mechanical and construction industries, Piombino, specializing in rail and other heavy section, and finally Cornigliano, the showpiece of the whole programme. Cornigliano, having endured wartime destruction and German dismantling, required to be rebuilt from scratch and was meant to develop a large new capacity for thin sheet, by installing a wide hot strip mill of American design, possibly to be financed by a US loan in the context of the Marshall Aid programme.[14]

Clearly such a far-reaching programme, leading to a massive overhaul of the country's steel industry, would not go unchallenged. Strong objections to it were raised by private steel firms, operating mostly in northern Italy, whose spokesmen were the Falcks, an influential dynasty of Milanese steel industrialists, owning a number of steel mills in Lombardy. Together with other private steel makers they had lately enjoyed a degree of success, for, having suffered very little wartime destruction, they had been able to expand their operations and increase their profits in the sellers' market which prevailed after 1945. Moreover their overhead costs were much smaller than those of Finsider's plant and they were flexible both in the use of raw material and in the quality of output. This was essentially because they were comparatively small-scale, relied heavily on scrap-fed electric furnaces and catered for regional markets in which they enjoyed good connections. Not surprisingly therefore, they felt threatened by the plans of the state-owned sector, which were designed to deprive them of some of their most cherished markets, and to undermine the nationwide cartel structure, which served them so well. Moreover most private steel makers did not like mass production. According to Giovanni Falck for example, steelworks in Italy should concentrate on diversity, high-quality products and small instalments and should not engage in producing bulk cheaper steel.[15]

Other objections to the Sinigaglia Plan came from both the right and the left of the political spectrum.[16] The '*liberisti*', free traders who had a long record of criticizing the unfair and damaging protection with which they believed the steel industry had been fostered, obviously disliked the state bias of the Sinigaglia Plan, whereas left-wing parties and trade unions were not impressed by its rationalizing intent, which was bound to lead to widespread redundancies. Some sectors of liberal opinion however were beginning to look more seriously at Sinigaglia's attempt to reduce costs and increase productivity. Ernesto Rossi for example, writing in the columns of *Il Mondo*, accused private steel producers of using free market arguments in an attempt to perpetuate the old mould of high protective tariffs and low productivity. Inside the left there were also those who looked favourably at Sinigaglia's effort to widen the country's industrial base. In this respect a more powerful ally for Finsider proved to be the Turin-based automobile company Fiat, whose dynamic managing director Vittorio Valletta was determined to resume plans first considered during the inter-war period to turn out cheap automobile models. In 1948 Valletta had agreed to buy for Fiat a large share of the hot strip which was to be produced at Cornigliano.[17]

Even so the array of forces stacked against the Sinigaglia Plan seemed formidable. Yet by 1948 the plan had succeeded in becoming the government's official steel policy. How was this feat accomplished? To understand this one needs a better appreciation of the role played by public industry during the reconstruction and beyond. It is often claimed that a group of free marketeers, of which Epicarmo Corbino and Luigi Einaudi are perhaps the best known, having been put in charge of the economy, set out to dismantle the economic controls imposed during the Fascist period, and then, in order to check inflation, engineered a credit squeeze. Its fiscal and monetary equilibrium thus conveniently restored by a sound spell of deflation, the country, so the conventional account continues, was then ready to reap the benefits of the favourable international cycle leading into the great boom of the 1950s.[18] Critics rarely challenged this picture; they sought, instead, to concentrate on its negative social effects and on the opportunities which were missed for higher employment, better public spending and a more balanced growth.[19] Lately however an alternative picture has begun to emerge, according to which the credit squeeze was not savage enough to stop a strong investment drive, which was being channelled largely through the state sector. Although there was no effective planning at the national level, resources were allocated on a sector by sector basis to a number of key industrial projects such as the Sinigaglia Plan. In other words a compromise was achieved at the highest level between deflation and expansion, between orthodox monetary policy and state investment.[20]

It is true that the IRI enjoyed a rather uncertain status throughout the post-war period and there were calls for its assets to be privatized. Nevertheless it was granted enough funds and enough support to reorganize itself and eventually resume its role as the financial nerve of the state sector.[21] Nor was its previous management, among whom were some of the state's most skilled cadres, allowed to disperse. In fact Donato Menichella, who had been IRI's director general between 1934 and 1943, was appointed to succeed Einaudi as governor of the Banca d'Italia in 1948 and is known from that influential position to have played an important role in facilitating the approval of the Sinigaglia Plan. Moreover, if there was a measure of uncertainty surrounding the role of the IRI, it seems to have been turned to the advantage of IRI's subholdings such as Finsider, providing them with an unprecedented freedom of manoeuvre. Finsider's managers were able to bargain for the success of their plan both with the emerging political leadership, especially elements of the Christian Democratic Party who were seeking new allies outside the traditional economic elite to establish their own credentials, and with the powerful ministerial bureaucracy which represented a strong element of continuity with the 1930s. Finally there was the fact that the Sinigaglia Plan was particularly appealing in a period of economic and political reconstruction, playing as it did on a judicious mixture of national strength and industrial expansion on one side, and modernization and competition on the other.

The international scene also proved extremely favourable to the Italian steel plans. This was essentially because the former leadership of the European steel cartel was in tatters: Germany's heavy industry was in a state of temporary collapse and the French were putting all their efforts into increasing their steel capacity. Robert Lacoste, the French Minister for Industrial Production, was very outspoken in his comments to the Italians in the summer of 1947, telling them that, together with the

Germans, they should forget about steel production and concentrate on the finishing skills.[22] About French ambitions Sinigaglia however remained sceptical: there was no reason to believe that the French would be more successful this time than they had been after 1919 and it was very likely that soon German industry would reassert its leadership. The French were, in his view, fighting an uphill struggle and the Italians, by playing alongside them, stood a chance of renegotiating market shares and raw material flows.[23]

Equally enticing for Sinigaglia was the prospect of being able to secure US backing. Sinigaglia believed that Finsider should unreservedly adopt the latest American technology, especially in so far as the production of sheet and tin plate was concerned. In those fields American firms had greatly progressed, achieving gains in productivity and economies of scale hitherto unknown in Europe. Clearly the new wide hot strip mills were expensive and less flexible than the older hand sheet mills, which were better suited if orders of small instalments had to be met. If however the scale of demand should increase, they provided enormous cost advantages. Driven by this realization and betting on the expansion of the market, Finsider proceeded to forge a close link with Armco International, a leading sheet producer based in Middletown, Ohio, and at the same time to bid for a substantial Marshall Plan loan to cover a large part of the costs of purchasing and installing the new equipment.[24]

In order to ensure the application's success the US administration had to be reassured on the trade liberalization issue, since they did not wish to be seen to finance a state monopoly bent on building uncompetitive steel plant shielded by high protection. Moreover many American officials lent some attention to the arguments of Italian private producers, such as the Falcks, according to which Finsider's plans were overambitious and would simply lead to overcapacity. Finsider's management however proved adept at countering such claims.

As far as the call for a free market was concerned, were not the Italians, they argued, trying to establish a level playing field among European producers? Should they not be allowed free access to raw materials so that they could lower their costs and compete? Nor indeed, it was claimed, was there any desire to increase steel output; rather it was a question of rationalizing production in order to achieve lower costs. This was not altogether true, since Finsider was really aiming at increasing its steel output well beyond the targets reported to OEEC and the Economic Cooperation Administration (ECA), which disbursed Marshall Plan funds. Could Italy be blamed however for endorsing the concept of mass production, which seemed to warm so many hearts in Washington? In the end therefore Finsider had its way, securing a loan of around $34 million, to which an Export-Import Bank dollar loan as well as Marshall Aid 'Counterpart Funds' were added. The total amounted to about two-thirds of the sum granted to the entire Italian steel industry, more than enough to provide the much-needed hard currency to speed up the rebuilding and modernizing of Cornigliano.

Relations with Europe were viewed both from the supply and the demand side. The former was essentially a question of raw materials, such as coking coal and iron ore. The obvious source for coking coal was the Ruhr, all the more so since Italy's coking plants had been built during the late 1930s on German specification. Suitable iron ore was believed to be the one mined in French North Africa, both because of its high quality – especially the non-phosphoric ores of the Ouenza in eastern Algeria which could be used in Cornigliano's open hearth furnaces – and because of its comparatively cheap c.i.f. costs at Italian coastal locations. Finally there was the question of securing a number of finished products on the European market, for however intense the drive for self-sufficiency, there was still bound to be a number of shapes both of common steel and special steel which domestic producers would simply not be able to deliver. This, in turn, raised the issue of the nature and the degree of protection. Although the reorganization envisaged by the Sinigaglia Plan was meant to achieve lower costs, this could not at a single stroke eliminate the gap with the more efficient producers in northern Europe, which had been in the past offset by high tariffs and convenient quota arrangements. Moreover such a difference in prices was not without an effect in increasing the friction between steel users, who favoured more imports, and steel producers, who wanted to regulate the market more tightly – a tension which increased when the post-war sellers' market gave way at the end of 1949 to tighter and more competitive pricing.[25]

When the Schuman Plan was announced, the first issue to concentrate the mind of industrialists both in the private and in the state-holding sector was that of securing adequate protection. Private industrialists, such as the Falcks, believed there was a good chance of repeating the arrangements of the inter-war period: one should put up a very high tariff and then bargain for quotas of what was most needed, in their view coal, scrap, pig iron, and common shapes of Thomas steel. Finsider, on the other hand, produced a more ambitious set of ideas which reflected their own priorities and also showed them to possess perhaps a better grasp of the situation.[26]

At this point it is useful briefly to consider developments on the diplomatic front. The option not to join the Schuman Plan was never seriously considered, since the French had officially asked for Italy's participation only a few days after the plan was announced and Italy's foreign policy for diplomatic reasons had been firmly directed towards integration as preached, however vaguely, by the Americans and defined by the Italian government.[27] The foreign policy establishment was quite impressed by some of the more liberal noises which surrounded the inception of the Schuman Plan and many had convinced themselves that it was unfortunate, but extremely likely, that the steel industry would have to be sacrificed in the process. Finsider however, who had the ear of the economic section of the Ministry for Foreign Affairs, considered the Schuman Plan simply as an attempt by the French to impose their own priorities on the reorganization of the European steel market. They also believed that it offered the Italian state industry an opportunity to achieve protection by way of inter-governmental deals and supranational guarantees. When the conference that was to work out the implications of the French initiative convened in Paris at the end of June 1950 the brief and composition of the Italian delegation fully reflected these objectives of Finsider, giving a commanding voice to the state-owned sector.

As far as the Sinigaglia Plan was concerned two dangers had to be faced and both became apparent during the discussion over investment plans in the new Community.[28] On one side there was the traditional cartel position, defended primarily by the Germans and the Belgians, which sought to make profitability the bench mark for new capacity. Clearly this was designed to forestall investment outside the old steel-making centres and would have particularly hampered the programmes of the newcomers, such as Italy and the Netherlands. The authority of such views was not irresistible. Much more weight was carried by the ideas of the French planners, who seemed to envisage something in the nature of a European plan, although, at closer inspection, it appeared to be dangerously slanted on the side of French national interests. According to Monnet and his adjutants strip mill plants together with heavy steel-making capacity should be essentially concentrated in France, whereas Italy would be allowed only a small number of plants for special steel production. Not surprisingly Sinigaglia, much as he might have liked Monnet's planning concept, vehemently disagreed. He did not object to a High Authority supervising steel investment, but wished to see it chaired by somebody not belonging to any of the countries of the pool, rather perhaps by an American, 'on whose fairness we may wholeheartedly rely'.[29]

As a way of thwarting French objectives Italian negotiators concentrated their efforts on what most people might have regarded as a side-show, a request to be granted free access to suitable quantities of

Algerian iron ore. Although those minerals were important, it was fairly clear that they would not remain so for very long, given that vast new iron ore fields in other countries were becoming available. By leaning very heavily on the French on this point however the Italians were signalling that the preservation of their national plan was the main price that the French would have to pay if they wanted to keep them in the pool. This is why exchanges on the issue became so heated, reaching a point where the Italian government threatened to withdraw its delegation. So politically sensitive had the question become, that it had to be solved in the context of a high-level Franco-Italian conference, held at Santa Margherita near Genoa in February 1951, in the course of which, after having obtained their pound of flesh, the Italians promised the French that they would go along both with the Schuman Plan and with the European Defence Community. Not surprisingly the quotas of Algerian iron ore on which the Italians insisted were never taken up, not because they were in themselves exaggerated as the French had always claimed, but because firms chose to supply themselves elsewhere. The issue therefore is best understood as a highly symbolic one. After all, many would agree that European integration has been from the outset a fairly elaborate rite. Such rites usually find their appropriate symbols: Italian participation in the European Communities was dressed up in terms of uninspiring quotas of minerals from a fairly unknown location in eastern Algeria.[30]

The fine print of the rest of the Schuman Plan negotiations reveals that most of the efforts of the Italian delegation were devoted to the issue of protection.[31] Protection inside the Community was secured for domestic steel production by maintaining a tariff against the rest of the pool, which would be progressively scaled down. Price alignment by firms from the rest of the Community on the Italian market was ruled out for the length of the transitional period and coking plants were also allowed to shelter behind tariff barriers, albeit temporarily. According to the Italian delegation, an even better way of smoothing the transition for Italian steel would have been to grant it internationally funded subsidies, as in the case of Belgian coal. The complexity of such an arrangement however proved too daunting. In the event, no overall quota was set and, in this respect at least, private steel producers saw their preference for tariffs vindicated. The fact remained that, in the same way that in the inter-war period tariffs had proved to be no substitute for market-sharing, it now became apparent that they could be appropriately manipulated by the government and made to tie with particular industrial policy objectives. The records we possess of the first stages of the operation of the common market for steel show that the Italian ministerial authorities, prompted by Finsider, were doing precisely that: they were putting pressure on the High Authority and moving the tariff posts in order to stop Italian firms from buying sheet produced abroad.[32]

For all practical purposes the Italian state-owned steel industry achieved most of what it had sought. The plant of Cornigliano came on stream in 1954 and started covering the demand for flat products on the part of the fast-expanding automobile and consumer durable industries. Other steel plants were also allowed to complete their modernization programme without having to suffer undue competition from the rest of the Community. Firms outside the Community wishing to sell in the Italian market were, to some extent, discouraged by high duties, which Italy was allowed to keep for a number of years after the foundation of the ECSC pending their harmonization to a lower level.

The nature of the European arrangement, in other words, seemed to dovetail remarkably well with the aims of the Sinigaglia Plan, inasmuch as it was designed to phase in liberalization in order that appropriate adjustments to it could be made. Although the agreements embodied in the Treaty of Paris were often shaky, perhaps ambiguous, and the powers granted to the new Community institutions uncertain, there were at least two other areas in which the ECSC made a considerable difference for Italian firms. One was represented by the scrap arrangements, negotiated between a cartel of European producers and the High Authority, which favourably affected the costs of electric steel producers by granting them a compensation for the higher prices of scrap imported from outside the Community. The other, perhaps more significant for Finsider, was the subsidies which the High Authority granted to the workers dismissed as a result of the restructuring taking place in many Italian steelworks.[33] There was in fact a dispute as to whether it was proper for the Community to finance the costs of what was, after all, essentially a national investment programme, given that the treaty expressly linked the granting of subsidies to cases which could be connected with the effects of the common market. To argue along such lines however was not only hopelessly ineffective, since it soon became clear that there was no sensible way in which the distinction could be drawn, it was also conceptually wrong, since the common market had been made possible only by the accurate, often painstaking, consideration of each member country's national steel policy.

It could be claimed that what might have impeded the realization of the Sinigaglia Plan would have been a new tight cartel arrangement among producers in continental Europe, which might have undercut Italian prices, thus effectively vetoing the building of any new significant blast furnace or rolling mill capacity. This was not completely out of the question, but it was prevented by a number of international developments, very significant among which was the difficulty experienced by the old continental grouping in reforging its former links, due, among other things, to the parlous state in which the German steel industry was kept for a number of years after the war. The other risk lay in the possibility that the integrationist intentions of Marshall Aid would become reality in a European plan seeking to concentrate investment in locations seemingly offering the best opportunity costs. One such attempt was foreshadowed, albeit not very forcefully, by the ECA when the Marshall Plan was first launched, but was soon abandoned in favour of more feasible policies designed to promote expansion in single European countries. Later it was the French planners who presented similar proposals, but their ideas were barely able to disguise a strong national bias and therefore did not stand much of a chance. On the other hand, history has bestowed its favours to plenty of no less unfair and prejudiced schemes and the launching of the Schuman Plan appeared to be one of those moments when anything could have been possible. Fortunately, on the Italian side negotiators kept their nerve and employed a hard-headed and shrewd tactic to further their objectives.

THE BRITISH STEEL INDUSTRY AND THE DILEMMA OF A COMMON MARKET

Before examining the response of the British steel industry to the Schuman Plan it is useful to address a preliminary question, the answer to which might help put the debate which took place inside the industry in better perspective. What would have been the advantage for the British steel industry in joining the Schuman Plan or in establishing a closer link with the Six? The answer is no simple matter for it involves reconsidering the whole basis upon which the industry operated. Nevertheless there seems now, as indeed there seemed at the time, a good case for asserting that the industry suffered from a degree of artificiality and overprotection and that joining the Community afforded an opportunity to amend those flaws.

The first thing to note is that the industry's prices were fixed. This was done on a statutory basis by the competent ministry. From 1939 to 1955 this was the Ministry of Supply, acting in close collaboration with the BISF and, for most of the time, on the advice of the various public bodies which were set up to oversee and control the industry – namely, the first Iron and Steel Board (ISB) appointed from 1946 to 1949, the Iron and Steel Corporation during the brief phase of nationalization, and the second ISB appointed in 1953. The process involved assessing the average costs of producers and fixing maximum prices for the great majority of steel shapes, which by common agreement inside the industry became the actual prices charged by steel producers in the domestic market. This arrangement had been worked out during the late 1930s and enshrined in legislation during the war and the fact that it remained intact and virtually unchallenged for a long time thereafter conveys a strong sense of continuity in the industry's operations. The implication, clearly, was that the British steel market was not to be a competitive one, or that the better firms would only compete among themselves in quality and timing of deliveries, as well as, of course, in the amount of profits they were able to make.[34]

Another point that should be noted was the nature of the pricing system. The arrangement that had come into force was a rather rigid one, since it consisted of charging uniform delivered prices, meaning that transport costs were incorporated in the final price as well as being equalized over an entire zone; in other words the same price would be charged irrespective of different transport costs within each zone. Furthermore prices for each product in the various zones were roughly the same, which entailed that only customers who happened to be outside them would suffer any disadvantage. Since the zones were so conceived as to include all the main steel-consuming areas of the country, this amounted to little less than having a single price throughout most of the British market. There was therefore very little encouragement for concentrating either the steel-making or the steel-using business at the most favourable locations.[35]

The level at which prices were fixed was equally significant. The idea here was twofold: to avoid fluctuations and to keep prices low. The idea of keeping prices low in its turn depended on the fact that steel was considered an essential input. It was primarily meant to supply with cheap steel the heavy investment programme in the basic industries, including the steel industry itself, and at the same time allow a strong growth in indirect steel exports, among which the products of the mechanical and motor vehicle industries figured very highly. Clearly such a strategy was attuned to the post-war conditions of the British economy, in which the burden of redressing a very grave balance of payments deficit fell primarily on the engineering sector.

By 1950 indirect steel exports had climbed to over two and a half times the volume that they had been before the war. This was also facilitated by keeping restrictions on the amount of direct steel exports, so that more steel would be available to domestic users.[36] The pattern of low steel prices also meant that it was made one of the duties of the newly formed National Coal Board to supply the industry with cheap coke, while the price of another essential raw material, scrap, was fixed at a very low level, far below the prices prevailing on international markets and markedly below those prevailing in other controlled markets such as the continental European ones. This was achieved by putting a ban on scrap exports, lest they provide the stimulus for domestic price rises. On the other hand much scrap was imported, especially from the German Federal Republic after 1948, and these imports, together with the other equally vital ones of iron ore, pig iron, semifinished and finished steel products, were purchased by a central agency managed by the industry, which then proceeded to release them for sale at the lower domestic price. Most of the cost of this operation up to 1949 was funded by the government, whereas after that date it was borne by the so-called Industry Fund, made up of levies collected from each producer according to his output of steel and to a lesser extent to his consumption of scrap.[37]

The first case, a straight government subsidy, simply revealed the extent to which the government would go in keeping prices low. In fact, government financing of finished steel imports was continued up to August 1951. But even after most of the subsidies were discontinued, a fact which inevitably brought along with it some increase in prices, the rationale of the system remained the same: it was designed to keep the British market insulated from the effect of higher foreign prices and to enhance stability by spreading costs across the industry. This generated a number of imbalances among steel firms. For example, producers using domestically mined iron ore, which was cheaper, found themselves subsidizing producers using more expensive, higher-quality imported ores. Equally there was a inbuilt bias in favour of scrap, as opposed to pig iron, and this seems to have been a significant factor in delaying the fulfilment of the targets set by the first post-war plans for extending blast furnace capacity. Nevertheless, there can be few doubts that considerable stability was achieved, since steel prices were nudged up very gently between December 1945, when wartime prices were first increased, and the date of the first significant hike in April 1949, after which they were again kept virtually stable until August 1951 despite mounting inflation.[38]

An important facet of the British steel market was that purchases were conducted from the centre and licensed by the government according to a tight system of quotas covering the vast majority of steel products, a regime which prevailed well into the 1950s. Many, in fact, inside the industry conceived of the planning exercise undertaken in 1945 as a way of achieving virtual domestic self-sufficiency. Such a goal however was somewhat beyond the industry's reach and during the First Plan, whose

Table 11 British imports of iron and steel products (000 tons)

Year	All imports	Imports from Belgium–Luxemburg, France, the German Fed. Rep. and the Netherlands
1948	567.9	312.0
1949	1252.9	827.4
1950	742.3	555.1
1951	849.8	335.2
1952	2200.5	1041.8

Source: BISF, Statistical Year Book, various years.

duration was stretched to 1952, the assumption on which the industry and government worked was that there would be an annual quota of around half a million tons of imports, most of which would be drawn from continental producers.[39] In fact, as table 11 shows, total imports, although subject to large yearly fluctuations, were on average much larger than this. The share coming from the five major continental exporting countries (Belgium, Luxemburg, France, the German Federal Republic and the Netherlands) was always around 50 per cent of the total, sometimes more. Among the continental countries the main sources of imports were Belgium, France and, at some distance, the Netherlands.

For a few years after 1945 most raw materials and steel goods were traded directly by the state, but in 1949 they were moved again to private trade under government licence. By that time however the UK was committed to the gradual elimination of import quotas inside the OEEC and this process, however grudgingly embarked upon and haltingly conducted (the events of the Korean War reversed the progress that had been so far achieved and entailed a new battery of restrictions), did pose a challenge to the arrangements prevailing inside the steel market. The BISF in fact resisted liberalization, whereas on the government side some pressure seems to have developed to move away from the quota system.[40] This, in its turn, focused attention on the nature and extent of tariff protection.

Throughout the time that imports had been managed by the state, mainly under bilateral agreements, tariffs had, clearly, been virtually meaningless as a means of protection. Because most of the trade was still regulated by quotas the situation did not greatly change after 1949, except for the fact that it would have now fallen on the industry to bear the cost of the tariff. However it was soon agreed that the government would refund that cost, if necessary, by granting yet another subsidy, while in 1952, given that the increase in demand related to the Korean boom was leading to a surge in imports, the government convinced itself that under the circumstances the best solution was simply to suspend the duties. This decision was carried forward by way of successive temporary reprieves of six months each for a number of years.[41]

None of this however eliminated the fact that there was a tariff in existence and that it was the same very high one that had been adopted to fight the continental cartel in the 1930s. The tariff had been conceived as a double-decker one, with a standard rate set on an *ad valorem* basis, averaging around 33 per cent, and specific duties attached to it which were designed to increase the duty to as much as 75 per cent in the case of falling import prices and to reduce it to around 20 per cent if imports were dearer. The rise in prices which had occurred since the 1930s had meant that the tariff rate had been reduced in the upper bracket and further reductions were granted during the GATT negotiations at Annecy and Torquay in 1949 and 1950. The government would have preferred the industry to go further, whereas the industry resisted this, demanding instead that a system akin to that of the pre-war period be reinstated.[42]

The protection issue therefore was one over which some tension was apparent in what otherwise might be regarded as a very close *entente* between the industry's association and government departments. One other element of this understanding related to exports.[43] The first thing to note is that steel exports throughout the years of the reconstruction were kept low, because steel was meant in the first place to contribute to domestic manufacturing. This was made possible up to 1953 by a system of official export licences, which was part of a wider pattern of central allocation of domestic steel deliveries carried over from the war years (and in fact given fresh life during the Korean rearmament cycle). Thereafter licences were replaced in most cases by an informal system of restraints operated by the industry itself, but statutory controls of exports were maintained over many products, such as sheet, tin plate and plates, well into the 1950s.

There are indications that these controls were also used to steer sales in the direction of the sterling and Commonwealth markets, in which, among other things, British steel goods enjoyed preferential tariff treatment. Export prices, on the other hand, were not fixed by the government and were an important element for the industry, since charging a high export premium was essential to raise the meagre profits to which firms were held by low fixed domestic prices. A differential between home and export prices was not something peculiar to British producers, but it could be argued that British firms were less flexible than they might have been under different circumstances. The percentage of British exports going to Commonwealth and Imperial markets was high, amounting to between 50 and 60 per cent in all the years from 1949 to 1953, whereas the share going to the five main continental European markets was a very modest one. It was essentially made up of steel plates and rails shipped to the Netherlands, and to a much lesser extent to the German Federal Republic.[44]

The intimate relation between the industry and the government extended to the field of investment.[45] Most commentators have insisted that the investment plans were drawn up by the single firms, with some guidance and co-ordination on the part of the BISF, and that there was therefore very little long-term planning of a more technocratic, presumably enlightened, nature. Nevertheless, it remains true that the First Plan was drawn up and implemented in close consultation with the government, and that it included ambitious schemes, such as the hot wide-strip mill in Port Talbot, requiring considerable financial assistance from government-sponsored bodies, most notably from the Financial Corporation for Industry. There was, moreover, a considerable amount of concentration and relocation, to which state intervention had also much to contribute. It is likely that substantial inputs to the steel plans were made by foreign policy considerations, such as, for example, predictions of the rate of recovery of the German economy as well as about dismantling in the Ruhr. It is a subject on which little is known. In any case, to come back to the original point, it is clear that the basis on which the industry operated had very little to do with the market: prices were artificial and kept inordinately low; the domestic arrangement allowed for little flexibility; and the impact of competition was, to say the least, blunted. In fact one might argue further that the industry had been put on a defensive footing by the impact of continental competition in the 1930s, whereupon it had proceeded to insulate itself by developing a coherent self-regulation and calling upon the state to enforce it.

To say this is not however to imply that the continental market was in the nature of a free trade paradise. All we have said about it in fact should dispose us to believe the contrary and Monnet showed himself well aware of the problem when he proposed a High Authority which was meant, in the first place, to neutralize cartels by taking upon itself most of their functions on prices, quotas and investment. His venture however was only partially successful, so that the new Community when it started operating at the end of 1952 appeared to be a combination of centralized regulation, traditional business practices and elements of genuine liberalization. The fact that an agreement may be the result of a number of compromises does not necessarily imply that it is a bad one; there were some elements of the new Community which not only were to prove lasting, but which also presented a degree of immediate attraction to the British.

One such possible attraction was the ECSC's basing-point pricing system, which was designed to combine flexibility with a certain amount of stability.[46] According to its rules, firms would have to publish their prices at a chosen basing-point. They were then allowed to align themselves to prices set by other producers at a different point, provided they revealed the amount of price-cutting which this might have involved by publishing their transport costs. Whereas price alignment clearly favoured the most efficient producers and entailed a measure of price leadership, the transparency requirements allowed the High Authority to impose checks to unruly oligopolistic behaviour. National governments, as it proved, also retained a large say in price determination, especially in ensuring that prices would not be pushed up. But ultimate powers to fix prices, as well as to allocate supplies, were vested in the hands of the High Authority in times of scarcity and of surplus. If a scarcity of steel should develop, the High Authority was allowed by the treaty to arrange for maximum prices as well as for eventual quotas inside the Community, while in a situation of surplus it could set minimum prices in order to avoid damaging price wars.

Under normal circumstances, it could be argued, the Community might become little more than a producers' cartel, a fact which prompted the Italians to ask that price alignments should not be allowed on the Italian market. But it was also recognized that a system of basing-points could, if not too conservatively handled, encourage concentration and some degree of competition. To this must be added that inside the Community double pricing for raw materials, such as coking coal, was eliminated, and so were quotas and tariffs – with however a few notable exceptions such as the ones for Belgian coal and Italian steel and coke. Protection against non-Community steel makers was retained in various ways, ranging from a common commercial policy to a number of anti-dumping regulations, which, among other things, allowed Community producers to meet any price, however low, that an external producer might charge inside the common market. Finally, an export cartel was surreptitiously reinstated, although there was some dispute over whether this was not against the Community rules and the High Authority made an ineffectual attempt to stop it.

British steel makers therefore had many reasons to see the Community at the outset as a cartel and, referring to past experience, prepare for a confrontation with it. The question however that was bound to be asked, was if such arm-twisting was not counterproductive. We have already noted that one of the aims of planning in the United Kingdom was the achievement of a greater degree of self-sufficiency. But even granted that this could be achieved – and there was always another argument about the benefit of mutual interchange of steel goods among areas possessing a very similar industrial structure and affected by similar patterns of demand – would it have really been sufficient to insulate the British domestic market?

It might have been so, if it could be shown that British costs and prices were always going to be lower than continental ones. During the post-war years well into the 1950s British domestic prices were in fact considerably lower, both for pig iron and for practically all shapes of open hearth steel, although not for Thomas steel.[47] When the figures however are examined more closely, it appears that the advantage derived mainly from two factors: lower costs at the steelworks of coke and of scrap. Nor was it true that these simply went to offset the burden of higher British wages as had been the case before the war, for continental wage costs, especially when taken together with social charges borne by the employers, had risen to a level comparable to the British ones. It was therefore precisely the most artificial elements of the British price structure which accounted for most, perhaps even for the whole, of the difference between British and continental prices. Moreover, if prices rather than costs were considered, the likelihood was that continental steel makers would not hesitate, if necessary, to sell abroad at well below cost – in fact the Belgians appeared to be doing just that in the period leading up to the Schuman Plan.[48] Of course, this threat of continental 'free-riding', as it was referred to, might well have been construed in the United Kingdom as an argument for protection, but it might also have been taken as an inducement to try to stop these practices by building into the European market permanent rules which would make them impossible, providing at the same time for greater openness and competition. Might such an opportunity be seized? And how?

The debate revolved around the idea of 'association' with the Six. If this word were to mean anything, it would mean that the British steel industry would shed much of its protection against the Six and demand from them a set of guarantees about prices and dumping, such as to avoid price fluctuations and damaging price wars. This implied reaching a common set of rules, minimum prices for example in periods of scarcity, which could be best enforced if British producers themselves were prepared to abide by the Community's pricing mechanism. It was no small step to take: to mention but one consequence it would have immediately carried with it a rise in domestic prices, given that subsidies for raw materials would have had to be abandoned. Double pricing of exports to the Community would, equally, have to be forgone, and this, presumably, would have disrupted the whole structure of export premiums. The opportunity, on the other hand, seemed essentially to lie in the fact that the Treaty of Paris and Monnet's High Authority proclaimed themselves firmly committed to low and stable prices. In other words, what was required was an act of faith, an attempt to make the new institutions abide by their own principles and stated objectives, after which other bonuses might follow: more reciprocal trade with the Six, a healthy degree of liberalization, more competition. Finally there was the question of exports and preferential markets, over which however it was conceivable that some appropriate agreement could be found with the ECSC, whether association was achieved or not, although the question of retaining Commonwealth markets was used during the debate as an argument against joining the Six.

Could the British steel industry and the British government be expected to cast such a full vote of confidence in the Community? The question might seem to be rhetorical; yet the evidence points to the fact that this was not wholly the case. The nature of the choice however deserves a little more attention. Was it possible to envisage a half-way solution, whereby the British steel industry, while not accepting and sharing the Community's rules, would still be able to make a significant gesture towards the Six? Here was a conundrum over which negotiators struggled hard, without being able to produce a viable solution. If trade were to be liberalized, this would mean shedding quotas, since to reduce tariffs – for which, in any case, it would have been necessary to go through the complex and uncertain procedure of securing a waiver from the GATT – without doing away with the quotas, was not a very significant gesture.[49] The OEEC trade liberalization programme in any case implied an eventual widening of the quotas. But to liberalize meant to deregulate the domestic market, thus exposing the industry to the threat of continental price fluctuations. In other words what was in prospect was either a common market, entailing adequate guarantees and institutions, or some kind of repetition of the 1930s, in the form of a bargain over reciprocal trading quotas and on third markets, the British market and the common market remaining otherwise strictly separate.

Many on the continent wanted the British to join with them to counterbalance German industrial might. Certainly this was the message which the British steel makers received from their counterparts in France and elsewhere. On the other hand, the industrialists in the ECSC were themselves extremely uncertain about the Community, often worked against it and tried to flout its regulations. Monnet, for his part, after having played an important part in keeping the United Kingdom out of the Schuman Plan, showed his readiness at a later stage to provide just the kind of framework the British might have relished, had they decided for genuine association. By the end of 1953 however Monnet's influence was already declining. He was under pressure both from industrial cartels and, more importantly, from fellow politicians at home. It would therefore have required a very far-sighted approach on the part of the British government to pursue the matter of integration more explicitly and courageously than some of its original advocates seemed prepared to do. In the event it would have also needed to convince its own steel industrialists that this was in their better interests.

Another possibility would have been for the steel makers themselves to build a new framework for the future, opting for internal competition, lower protection and more trade with Europe. Finally, it is conceivable that some pressure towards Europe might have developed on the part of steel users wishing to have easier access to foreign supplies. From the admittedly scant evidence that we possess, such a pressure does not seem to have developed. It might be that the steel users were satisfied with low steel prices and that they considered domestic steel supplies as being adequate. There were moreover close links between the two sides of the industry which in fact were at the root of the scattered and regional pattern of steel-making, a good example being provided by Sheffield where a few larger vertically integrated companies were loosely linked to a host of small re-rollers specializing in different grades of special steels. Nevertheless the fact remains that the prospect of a less regulated steel market and a more open trade with Europe should have had a stronger appeal for the steel users than it seems to have had.

Which of the two routes, the governmental or the industrial one, was more likely for a possible British *rapprochement* with the Community? We have already discussed the way in which the industry and the state were intricately bound in their operations. To this however must be added that they were not always of the same view and that over the particular issue of nationalization they were locked in bitter contest. In addition it should be remembered that the Schuman Plan was essentially a diplomatic act and that Monnet, in particular, did not wish to negotiate with industrialists. There was ample scope for British governments to pursue their own agenda on the matter. Admittedly the Labour Cabinet of 1950–1 was not in the best position to do so, because of its very small majority and the fact that it had by general recognition run out of steam. The discussions taking place in 1953–4 might provide a better test, given that the Conservative government felt more at home in its relations to the steel industry and might have chosen to take a longer-term view on Europe. In the event its outlook on the European issue, although not entirely negative, proved very unclear and was fraught with fears and anxiety. Ultimately on the particular issue of relations with the ECSC, the Conservatives felt that they could do worse than seek guidance from the industries involved. Because the coal industry never deviated from a protectionist and isolationist stance, had the steel industry decided in favour of joining Europe, in order to carry the day it would have had to do so very forcefully indeed.

One more detail should be added to this picture. The records reveal that a group of civil servants belonging to key government departments – primarily the Treasury followed by the Ministry of Supply and to some extent by the Board of Trade – produced a strong case for the steel industry to associate with the ECSC. This is the remarkable story of the working parties which were set up in 1950, and it is a story whose details have yet fully to emerge.[50] Because however in the following pages the focus is mainly on the debate inside the steel industry proper, it will suffice to underline the existence of considerable pressure on the industry from civil servants to join the Six and face up to the consequences. As far as the industrialists were concerned, the issues were thrashed out in the Executive Committee and in the International Trade Committee of the BISF, an organization manned by a staff of officials many of whom had considerable experience in international negotiations. The final word however rested with the steel companies, whose managers ultimately were to take the matter in their own hands.

We will look at the two crucial moments in the process of the steel industry's decision-making on the question of the ECSC: first, at the response to the Schuman Plan in the course of May and June 1950, and then at the position taken in early 1954 on the eve of direct negotiations between the High Authority and the British government over a Treaty of Association.

The debate on the Schuman Plan revealed the extent to which the question of nationalization dominated the concerns of the steel industrialists. After the Labour government had scraped through the February 1950 election with a majority of six it had immediately stated its intention of nationalizing the industry by carrying out the provisions of the Iron and Steel Act which had been passed on to the statute book in the previous November. The terms of the Act however were such as to maintain the industry in a very strong position, for, whereas the shares of the companies were to be vested in the new Iron and Steel Corporation, their structure and management were to remain, at least for the time being, unaltered and the BISF would still act as the industry's main organ. In any case, the prospect of a return of a Conservative government pledged to denationalize, had the effect of further hardening the industry's opposition to nationalization. As a result the BISF under the leadership of its influential and well-connected chairman Sir Andrew Duncan, who had among other things served as shadow front-bench spokesman up to 1950, and of its president Sir Ellis Hunter, had started adopting an obstructionist tactic, refusing to provide the government with any assistance in appointing the new Iron and Steel Corporation.[51]

Such was the situation on 9 May when the Schuman Plan was cast upon the British steel industry. When the Executive Committee of the BISF convened on 16 May Sir Walter Benton Jones, chairman of United Steel, set the tone: 'The government', he said, 'might use the French proposals as an argument for state ownership of the steel industry . . . '[52] At which Sir Andrew Duncan tried to strike a note of reassurance: 'It should be borne in mind', he said, 'that the French and German steel industries were not nationalized and the Foreign Secretary had failed in his attempt at nationalization of the German industry.' Moreover, he added, Schuman and Monnet were known not to be nationalizers. On the other hand, Sir Andrew declared himself unhappy about the *dirigiste* bent of the Schuman Plan. Nor did he like the talk about implementing anti-cartel measures, which, he thought, was to a great degree directed at assuaging American feeling on the issue. 'The difference between the Federation and the High Authority now envisaged', he observed, 'was that the industry was in fact controlled by the Executive Committee who were themselves members of the industry.'[53] M. Mather of the Skinningrove works, who had been a member of the first ISB, was prepared to recognize however that 'the Schuman Proposals in the international sphere were very similar to the earlier conception of the IDAC control and the later Iron and Steel Board organization and this was therefore a strong argument for the continuation of some similar arrangement of internal control of the Industry'. He also sounded a warning, for although he acknowledged that the British steel industry had 'established a great lead in development' over its neighbours, 'it was unlikely', he added, 'that this would be retained for more than a few years, particularly if the German steel industry were to get going again'.[54]

At this juncture however nationalization loomed larger than the German threat. If it was true that the Schuman proposals were leading away from state ownership, or even in the words of Sir Charles Bruce Gordon, deputy chairman of the Steel Company of Wales, 'might well provide the Labour Party with the "climb-down" which certain of their members demand', then, according to the chairman of Colvilles, Sir John Craig, 'we might do some good by being inside'.[55] There was, in truth, much scepticism about the feasibility of the French proposals and suspicion of the motives behind them. But these doubts could not be openly expressed, for they might have been seized upon by the government, whose position was as yet unclear and who therefore conceivably might have accused the industry of being uncooperative. It was thought that the best course was to show a positive but guarded attitude, and this was expressed in the noncommittal statement issued at the end of the meeting, according to which 'the proposals give the Committee no ground for consternation'.[56]

A more thorough discussion on the Schuman Plan was conducted at a special meeting on 13 June. Had the industry intended to seize the initiative, it would have done so too late, since the government had already decided not to join the negotiations over the plan. As is well known, the split between the British and French governments occurred on the French request for a prior British commitment to the supra-national and binding character of the new organization.[57] The decision appears to have been taken mainly on foreign policy grounds, although among the steel industrialists many believed that Labour's ideological attachment to nationalization had played a large part in it.[58]

The Federation had been asked to contribute to an inter-departmental working party, whose brief it was to work out a set of alternative proposals for a European coal and steel organization which the United Kingdom might have been prepared to join. The idea seemed to be that the French initiative would eventually fail and that the British government would then step in to provide the leadership to which it had felt entitled in the first place.[59] In the event this did not happen. The elaboration of an alternative to the Schuman Plan on the part of the working party was therefore a somewhat futile exercise, but the very fact that it was embarked upon is an indication of the uncertainty which surrounded the issue. It also prompted the steel industry's leadership to state their position more clearly.

When the Executive Committee of the BISF examined the Schuman Plan more closely, the case for increasing interdependence with the Six did not appear to be very clear-cut.[60] There was no interest in obtaining coke from Europe and the only iron ore that was of interest was that of French North Africa, which it was believed, quite rightly as it proved, the French would keep out of the pool. Nor was there much promise in developing exports to the Continent. 'The British industry', it was said in the final statement of the Executive Committee, 'could not contemplate access by Europe to British scrap at British home trading prices, since this would jeopardize the United Kingdom price structure.' It was also thought unacceptable for Europe to have access to the 'limited reserves of Durham coking coal, since these were a vital factor in the further operation of the industry'.[61]

Did this mean that the whole idea of freer trade would have to be shelved? Robert Shone, the Federation's economic director, pointed to the danger of taking a protectionist stance, for, he warned, it would play into the hands of those inside the government who advocated more centralized control, for inside the working party a quite different opinion seemed to be prevailing, that the industry was overprotected and that it could not presume to remain indefinitely sheltered behind tariffs and quotas. Was the BISF prepared to act in response to these sentiments?[62]

The answer which emerged out of the meeting was not wholly negative. It was said that in 'a period in which exchange rates had been fluctuating and costs had not settled down to any stable level, also when countries are still practising dual pricing, dumping and other similar devices, it is unsafe to rely on complete freedom of trade'. A number of preconditions were therefore set out, such as the 'option of a common steel price policy', primarily tailored to make dumping impossible. It was also thought that differences in steel wages might be narrowed and 'special discriminations in the treatment of the steel industry as compared with other industries in the same country', such as cheap state capital or subsidies, might be eliminated.

To implement such measures it was necessary to grant a broad mandate and sufficient powers to a European body, whose powers however were to remain, for the time being, 'almost entirely advisory'.[63] This body was conceived as a projection on the European level of the public agencies which had supervised the industry in Britain.[64] In place of an institution directly thrust into the steel market with the ambition of reshaping it, like the High Authority of the Schuman Plan (though much less so that of the ECSC), the BISF's proposal envisaged a two-tier governance, whereby an institution enjoying some kind of public mandate would act in concert with the industrial associations, offering them supervision, perhaps cajoling them to take certain decisions, but with no power to give them directions.

Hence the 'European Authority' or the 'High Authority', as it was alternatively referred to, would be comprised of independent persons not acting directly as government delegates (this was a last-minute correction to the text expressly meant to avoid any interference on the part of present or future nationalizers), but with a wider view of pursuing the public interest both of producers and consumers. It would have to be informed and approve of any industrial 'international agreement on markets, prices' and the like. It could also initiate some measures on raw material supplies, on the rationalization of production and on price policies, but these should take the form of recommendations upon which the industries would then be called to act. Nor would it have any have any binding powers on development plans. On the British side a 'suitable' representative to it might be 'say, the Chairman of the Iron and Steel Board' assuming the industry were not to be nationalized.[65] In other words there would be the best of all possible worlds: the industry would be made European without any loss of national sovereignty, it would subject itself to international regulation without forgoing the advantage of international cartels, it would endeavour to shed its protection without depriving itself of the advantages of its carefully crafted price structure.

Were these compatible objectives? One note of scepticism was sounded by A. G. Stewart, chairman of Stewart & Lloyd; 'it was possible', he said, 'that the necessary safeguards for the British iron and steel industry might make it unworkable'.[66] But the rest of the industrialists seemed in an optimistic mood. According to Sir John Craig the proposed organization 'should be as near as possible to that which obtained under the Cartel, which was sound in every principle' and Sir Andrew Duncan added that 'had we been free from the threat of nationalization, we would in any case have wanted an understanding with France and Germany'. The final touch was added by Captain Leighton Davies (Steel Company of Wales) who said the industry's new-found enthusiasm for Europe 'would make for a favourable public reaction in the event of an early general election'.[67]

During the following months the industry had a chance to rethink its attitude. Nationalization turned out to be a short-lived affair, albeit one that focused most of the industry's attention throughout 1951 and 1952. By May 1953 a new Iron and Steel Board had been appointed to supervise the industry which was now in the throes of reprivatization. In the meantime the High Authority had embarked upon the laborious operation of setting up a common market for coal and steel with the further view of opening discussions with Britain over a Treaty of Association.

On the British side the issue was considered by a new inter-departmental working party, chaired by the Treasury and comprising officials from various ministries.[68] In July 1953 it produced a report whose main conclusion was that the British steel industry should associate itself closely with the industries of the Six: reciprocal tariffs and quotas should be removed and British producers should be prepared to abide by the ECSC's pricing regulations.[69] The working party's report was then submitted to the Economic Steering Committee (ESC), a body comprising officials of a more senior level and chaired on the occasion by Edwin Plowden of the Treasury.[70] Not only did the ESC endorse the report but it pushed the argument further by relating the creation of a freer market for steel to the trade of metal manufactured goods. More competition in the steel market, it was argued, would 'spur to more efficient production and work to the long-term benefit of steel consumers'; it would also check the tendency for the steel industry 'to slip back into restrictive practices'.[71]

Inside the steel industry opinion was moving in another direction. Already in June 1951, when the ECSC Treaty had been agreed upon by the Six, the Federation's International Trade Committee felt it to be 'undesirable for the UK to join the community as a full member' and hinted instead at 'the possibility of developing trade in steel in third countries to mutual advantage' as well as at a 'long-term agreement' covering a limited share of the UK market for continental products, in exchange for 'a counter concession in respect to at least a part of our traditional markets in Holland and Italy'.[72] It was unmistakably the old language. When the Federation was later asked by the government to contribute its opinion to the new working party, Shone and two others insisted that to participate in the common market was likely to bring exposure to 'widely fluctuating continental prices'. 'What we needed', they insisted, 'was the performance of certain policies and the execution of certain rules', but because that requirement was unlikely to be met, 'a commitment to join even in five years was going too far at this stage'.[73] When, regardless, the working party produced its report, the Federation reserved its position on it, rejecting the whole idea of a common market.[74]

What had moved the industry away from the idea of a closer link with the Six? Possibly the opinions expressed in 1950 had never really reflected the federation's true instincts, so that there was no real change of mind. There is however some indication that part of the answer may lie in the change in market conditions which obtained on each side of the Channel in the wake of the Korean rearmament. Whereas boom conditions were similar, the fall in demand after the boom was more pronounced in continental Europe where in 1953 steel production fell, there was a certain amount of destocking, and export markets tightened. By the summer of 1953 the Community producers were finalizing a so-called 'gentlemen's agreement', about which the High Authority was kept in the dark, to keep up prices of exports, some of which went to the United Kingdom.[75] In the United Kingdom, on the other hand, rearmament had started in the most inauspicious conditions, leading to serious steel shortages and a fall in output. Allocations of steel had had to be reimposed, import duties suspended and exports checked, with all the paraphernalia of controls once again in full display. By 1952 however shortages had been overcome, so that when demand for armament petered off, the industry was well placed to meet civilian domestic commitments which had previously been curtailed and to increase its exports. The prospect therefore seemed better than on the continent and there seemed every reason to be wary about continental behaviour.

The matter of association came to a head at the end of 1953. The initiative came from Monnet, whose main concerns had little to do with steel and much more to do with the shaky architecture of his grand European design. Speaking to Cecil Weir, the head of the UK delegation in Luxemburg, on 21 December he claimed that, were it to be known that the British government intended to associate with the ECSC, twenty more votes would be cast in favour of the European Defence Community in the French Assembly.[76]

The official letter he handed over to Weir was in the nature of practical proposals. It mapped out three possible areas of agreement: an association between the markets, a procedure for common action, and common institutions. Association between the markets referred to the reduction and elimination of barriers followed by the establishment of certain rules, which, it was added with a clear reference to the pricing system, were to reflect the pattern followed in the Community. The second area, procedure for common action, drew attention to a certain number of practical steps which could be taken. Consultation in investment programmes, in export markets, in examining trends in demand, and in measures designed to counter shortages and surpluses were mentioned. Finally the letter envisaged the creation of a Council of Association formed by three representatives for each side, appointed by the High Authority and by the British government. The letter was short and the proposals it contained were fairly open-ended. It did not pose conditions, nor did it raise the contentious issue of sovereignty. But it did point to a framework of progressive liberalization leading to the inclusion of the United Kingdom in the common market.[77]

On the British side, the reaction to Monnet's letter was very laborious. The Foreign Office was keen to respond positively, since it believed that a positive gesture should be made towards the Six.[78] It was decided to reconvene the working party at the beginning of January, to prepare a submission to the Cabinet. As might have been expected, their view was that Monnet's proposals were a reasonable basis for talks.[79] It was thought that associating with the Six would be a step of great political appeal and that it would be consistent with the UK's free trade image. Association would provide 'a wider and freer market in two commodities which are at the foundation of our industrial power and in which we as a great trading nation cannot afford to be uncompetitive'. Not only therefore was it a necessary step, it was also a relatively safe one, considering that enough safeguards could be negotiated to avoid the unrestricted competition of the inter-war years. Admittedly prices in the United Kingdom would have to rise, but this, it was said, was bound to happen anyway because costs were rising too. There was, moreover, no reason to fear the loss of imperial preference for British exports. Abiding by the Community's pricing system would mean that export premiums would have to go, but, it was said, their importance was diminishing. The verdict therefore was wholly favourable, although the officials of the working party seemed conscious of the fact that the steel industry did not share their views and that only firm government action might overcome its reservations.

The submission prepared by the working party was then, as had happened previously, endorsed by the Economic Steering Committee, in which civil servants from the Foreign Office, the Treasury and the Board of Trade strongly put forward the case for association in steel with the ECSC.[80] These views were then presented to the Cabinet on 21 January, in a very positive introduction by the Foreign Secretary, Eden.

The Cabinet seemed to be mildly interested in the subject and decided to initiate consultations with the industries. This presumably would take some time, whereas Monnet was pressing for a positive answer at short notice. Nobody however objected to that procedure being followed. Some comments were made on the effects of a possible association on the Commonwealth (which would also be consulted), but nothing decisive emerged. The mood seems to have been rather positive, if somewhat complacent.[81]

The consultations meant that the steel industry would be, for the first time, asked to give its reasoned opinion on the matter of Europe, and that such an opinion was likely to affect the final decision of the government. It was not clear however who should speak on the industry's behalf. Should it be the Iron and Steel Board or the BISF? The board certainly took the view that it was itself alone which was entitled to speak and tried to withhold the content of Monnet's letter from the officers of the Federation. Only after much difficulty, and some rather bitter exchanges, were they able to secure a copy of it and present it for discussion in front of their Executive Committee.[82] The behaviour of the board certainly is revealing of some tension with the Federation, but events were to prove that there was no fundamental disagreement between them. The fact was that by statute the board was called to advise the government over relations with the ECSC, and had it been seen to engage in too close contacts with the industrialists, it might have brought on itself some unwelcome criticism. Also the board appeared to be under pressure from political quarters to come up with something positive and this may have influenced its behaviour. Finally Monnet's letter calling for an inter-governmental negotiation clearly offered the board an opportunity to stamp its own authority on the whole issue.

The crucial meetings of the Federation's executive were preceded by an extremely interesting meeting held in London at the beginning of February 1954 with Pierre Ricard of the Chambre Syndicale de la Sidérurgie Française.[83] Ricard was a very authoritative spokesman for the French steel industrialists and had been a critic of the Schuman Plan and of the ECSC, especially on the question of prices.[84] On this occasion he found himself questioned by his British counterparts especially as to whether the Community could deliver price stability. Ricard did not try very hard to reassure them. He pointed out that there had recently been, both in France and in the German Federal Republic, a weakening of the steel market and that this was leading to great 'disorder', by which he meant that although 'published prices' had remained the same, customers had succeeded in obtaining rebates ranging from 5 per cent to 7 per cent, depending on their bargaining strength. Prices had therefore become so volatile that many in France had started to call for the return of the good old times, when sales and prices had been controlled centrally by the producers' association. But why, his British interlocutors pressed him, had not the High Authority tried to put an end to the confusion by enforcing minimum prices? It was an illusion, replied Ricard, to expect the High Authority to do so. 'Maximum prices can be safeguarded as the consumer is on your side, but in the case of minimum prices the situation is different.' Moreover, he added maliciously, Monnet did not want to be faced with the responsibility of having to halt a fall in steel prices, since he believed that such a fall would go to the Community's credit.[85]

To the British steel industrialists the picture must have seemed very bleak indeed. Here they were, being asked to join a Community which not only appeared to be failing to enforce its own rules, but was also overtly encouraging price-cutting out of political expediency. At the Executive Committee held on 16 February there was great anxiety as to what the government and the board were really up to. This was clearly an emergency and exceptional procedures were called for. It was therefore decided that the industry should express its own considered view only after full consultation and that a special *ad hoc* committee should be created in which the five main regional groups of the industry – Sheffield, Scotland, the North-East, the Midlands and South Wales – would be represented. This special committee would report its conclusions to the next meeting of the Executive Committee.[86]

Over the next three weeks the special committee held a number of meetings. All the major firms of the industry were represented with the possible exception of Consett.[87] Unfortunately we do not possess the records of the meetings. It is possible however from a number of other papers to trace the different positions that were expressed therein. A minority in the committee wanted to reserve the industry's position until more was known about Monnet's intentions. The majority however agreed that the industry should firmly lay down its negotiating position and that it should be couched in utterly negative terms. Sir Ernest Lever, who was chairman of Richard Thomas & Baldwin and who sat on the board of the Steel Company of Wales, made it clear that he did not agree with the decision and refused to attend the final plenary session of the Executive Committee on 9 March.[88] In other words, the most powerful group within the industry was in favour of a more positive approach towards Europe. It is likely that had that group found but one ally it would have succeeded in having its way. The others therefore must have shared a negative view and the indications of the later evidence are that they did.[89]

It is no surprise, in view of the split inside the industry, that the Executive Committee held on 9 March proved to be no formality.[90] The draft of the letter to the Minister of Supply which members were asked to agree upon proved too harsh for some.[91] The document started out by bluntly declaring that in the view of the industry 'nothing but disadvantage to itself and to the British economy would accrue from full participation in the common market', all the more since the High Authority had failed to secure 'adherence in practice' to the provisions of the treaty in regard to steel prices. Partial participation, moreover, was no less objectionable and the only agreement the industry could contemplate was one in which the British and ECSC markets 'were kept separate, not merged'. This section elicited the protest of Sir Wilfred Eady, who said he was 'seriously perturbed at the effect these sentences may have on our power to influence negotiations' and added that 'it was a serious mistake on our part to assume the failure of the High Authority' and that such an attitude 'would be interpreted as door slamming'.

Sir Wilfred Eady had a seat on the board of Sir Ernest Lever's conglomerate. He was no steel industrialist, as he himself admitted on the occasion, but had moved into the steel industry after having been a civil servant in the Treasury for ten years, the last few of which had been spent preparing the industry for privatization.[92] His objections did not cut much ice. The prevailing view was that the industry should inform the government that it did not like the idea at all. The meeting was chaired by Frederick Grant, QC, who had succeeded Duncan as the Federation's independent chairman. He said that the thrust of the letter was to point out to the politicians that 'from the economic point of view, we don't like the idea' and that, therefore, it was perfectly justified to say that the Community was not working. 'We are drawing attention', insisted Grant, 'to the dangers of both full and partial participation.'

A further spate of objections was raised by Captain Myrddin Morris. He recalled among other things that the Federation in the past had approved of 'all measures towards European Unity, and had welcomed the ECSC'. The captain's company was Briton Ferry, a small South Wales firm in the tin plate trade.[93] 'Keep anything positive out of it,' was the curt remark of Chetwynd Talbot (Cargo Fleet) and the chairman elaborated further, explaining that 'What we're saying is that we may enter into contractual agreement, but not become members in any form.'

The latter statement was perhaps the best summary of the way the industry wanted to proceed in respect to the ECSC. It wanted to strike a bargain with it, possibly from a position of strength. Nor did it have any qualms about saying so. Thus there should be no concessions to the 'common principles' Monnet was asking for, nor to common measures in times of scarcity or surplus, nor indeed to liberalizing reciprocal trade. On the contrary, the British steel industry wanted to preserve its own distinctive mode of operation. It told the government clearly that it wanted to keep a tariff and continue enjoying preferential access to the Commonwealth. In the event that the continentals should seek to undercut British prices, the government should grant its steel makers 'special protection'. Price discrimination was not to be eschewed, as Monnet wanted. It was to be pursued, as it had always been, by allowing an export premium to compensate for the lower fixed domestic prices. Home supplies of coking coals and scrap should be strictly reserved for the industry's use. Investment decisions should continue to be taken exclusively at the national level and any common institution which might be established should firmly remain both temporary and consultative in nature and its proceedings should remain secret.[94] The only area in which some consultation with the Community might prove useful was, according to the Federation, that of reciprocal trade and of exports to third markets.

Such was the outcome of the industry's lively consultation. There was very little to indicate that the Iron and Steel Board would take a very different line. Its chairman, Sir Archibald Forbes, had been associated with the industry between 1946 and 1949 as a member of the first board, while one of its other two full-time members was Robert Shone, who had been for many years in the Federation, where, among other things, he had played a large part in engineering the Industry Fund.[95] Not surprisingly, Forbes's letter to Duncan Sandys, the Minister of Supply, was dismissive of Monnet's proposals.[96] 'We believe', he wrote, 'that from a purely economic point of view, the judgement must be against association with the common market.' Most of the points that followed were the same ones made by the Federation.

There was a difference however, for the board saw itself in the position of having to convince the government. Its submission therefore reads as a comprehensive, rather long-winded attempt to present the current arrangements in the British steel market in a most favourable light.[97] Among other things it proclaimed that domestic price control had 'tended to become common ground in the political disputes which have arisen over the industry in the sense of maintaining some public control of the profits of a highly organized industry basic to the economy'. This was a way of reminding the government that the board embodied whatever consensus was to be found among the political parties on the question of steel. The only sign of good disposition shown by the board was on the subject of institutions. If a treaty were to be negotiated the board wanted to play a major part in the process, considering that the High Authority's role and standing 'does not in fact differ much in principle from ours'.

Two more submissions from the employers' side (the trade unions were also consulted) were received by the government: one from the National Coal Board and one from the Engineering Advisory Council. Both were negative. The engineering employers stated that 'they did not accept the argument that a common market for steel would give better prospects of getting cheap steel' and believed that they would be better served by 'a UK steel industry protected from influences likely to cause fluctuations in prices'.[98] In other words they wholeheartedly endorsed the BISF.

In face of such a spate of denials only a Cabinet thoroughly devoted to the European issue would have wished to pursue integration any further. It was not to be. On 7 April the Cabinet felt unable to accept Eden's call to proceed with talks with the ECSC for the attainment of a 'common market' for steel.[99] Sandys bluntly said that the steel industry 'doesn't like the common market in steel at all', although he suggested that if steel industrialists were to be allowed to discuss matters with the technical experts of the Community, 'they might in the end be brought to accept a contractual association including a common market'. The Cabinet decided that a committee of ministers should take a fresh look at the issue.

Monnet was still waiting for a reply to his letter. If the main thrust of his invitation was to be turned down, on what were the talks to take place? Was there a basis for bringing the United Kingdom and the ECSC steel markets closer together, short of the adoption of common policies and common rules? The lengthy, inconclusive and muddled discussion that took place inside the government in April and May 1954 showed that there was not.[100]

There was a widespread feeling that the British steel industry was overprotected and much feeling against the high steel tariffs was expressed. Apart however from the fact that tariffs were just the outer veneer of protection (they were, at the time, suspended), the Board of Trade pointed out that lowering tariffs was a matter for the government and not for bilateral negotiations and should not be done bearing only steel considerations in mind. It was also very difficult to conceive of tariffs being handled on a discriminatory basis. As for prices, any conceivable understanding with the Community would have implied tinkering with domestic pricing arrangements, something which the industry had said was unacceptable. In whatever direction one turned, the answer was the same: the steel market in the United Kingdom was not amenable to piecemeal liberalization.

It soon appeared that the only possible solution was to remove any substantive issue from the negotiating table. The talks should simply agree on setting up a Council of Association. Thus, of the three points of Monnet's letter only the last one would be taken up.

In many ways, therefore, the position of the Federation had been vindicated. Monnet's negotiating mandate had also been somewhat restricted by pressures from the member states, who did not wish to leave the High Authority a free hand, and by industrialists, who feared the consequences of lowering the Community's external barriers towards the UK.[101] Through the summer and autumn of 1954 talks were held between Monnet and Sandys, of which the board was kept informed. The Federation, on the other hand, knew nothing about them, but it hardly seemed to matter.[102]

In December a Council of Association was finally agreed upon, on which, on the British side, the chairman of the Iron and Steel Board was to sit and which would undertake to open consultations and discussion about almost everything. A commitment to reduce trading barriers and to take joint action during periods of shortage and surplus was also included in the treaty. It was, at most, an agreement to agree in the future.[103] The further course of the relations between the United Kingdom and the ECSC lies outside the scope of this chapter. One thing however is clear: the solution which was reached in 1954 effectively brought to a halt any serious prospect of including the UK in a common market for steel. Over the next few years there were prolonged discussions on tariffs resulting in an agreement signed in November 1957, whereby the United Kingdom undertook to reduce its duties and the Community pledged itself to some action whenever dumping from the continent should take place. The two markets were, in other words, to remain strictly separate.

This story has raised as many questions as it has sought to answer. What would have happened, for example, if Sir Ernest Lever and the Welsh sheet and tin plate producers had prevailed? How far were they prepared to go in their relations with Europe? While the attraction which more trade with Europe might have held for them is obvious at a time when the demand for thin flat products there was surging ahead, was it simply by chance that the group which had undertaken the largest investment projects and had been more closely involved with the state was also the one that was better disposed towards the High Authority and integration? On the whole, the records reveal considerable disquiet about the steel market, primarily inside government departments, but also among politicians and in sections of the industry itself. Reforming it however was a very difficult exercise. The industry's rejection of the common market was fraught with a sense of bitterness towards the politicians and the state and couched in terms of a strong vindication of its own autonomy and methods. In a way, this is quite remarkable when so much of the industry's daily operations depended on the government. Nor was there any real chance that matters could be taken up again, as in the past, by industrial associations. There would always be a minister or a board to represent the industrialists, and the Federation must have been aware of it. Furthermore it had itself very little to offer as an alternative; arm-twisting between private cartels was clearly out of order in the mixed economy. Rejection of Europe on the part of the steel companies was a bid to cling on to isolation, but the dilemma of a common market lingered on.

BRITISH AND ITALIAN ATTITUDES IN PERSPECTIVE

Might any general lessons be drawn from the experience of the attitude of the two industries towards the ECSC, examined under the light of integration and interdependence? In the past interdependence between steel markets had taken the form of cartels. Integration policies, on the other hand, were very much the expression of the will of nation-states to alter the terms previously set by the cartels. This is why they were designed to attack their powers from two opposite directions: by stimulating the emergence of a more competitive market as well as by the interventionist powers of a central technocratic body. The terms offered by the cartel to industries not belonging to the inner core of the continental grouping were stark. As the inter-war period had shown, in the case of Italy they implied virtual submission, whereas for the United Kingdom they had the effect of engendering a damaging price and tariff war.

Presumably, therefore, there was also a large degree of attraction in the idea of integration for the steel industry both in Italy and the United Kingdom. Our account has shown that the opportunities offered by the ECSC were indeed recognized in both countries. The lengthy discussion over a possible common market in the UK is a testimony to this, whereas in Italy integration offered a way to give Cornigliano an international sanction.

Who was able and willing to seize such opportunities? Certainly not the industries themselves, as constituted in the national associations of steel producers. Nor could the choice be left to diplomatic circles, who understood little about the issue. The burden lay entirely on economic policy-makers. The most favourable scenario for integration in this respect was perhaps the French one, with the government taking the necessary steps with little, if any, consultation with the industry. The view taken in the United Kingdom by the working parties, and by others, showed that there was a recognition that something similar was needed. In the end however the intimate relationship which had developed between the government and the industry made the government a hostage to the BISF's view, rather than an active agent of integration.[104] The position of the Minister of Supply in 1954 speaks eloquently of this. Nor was the position of the board strong enough to differentiate it from the BISF.

In Italy part of the industry also held the traditional cartel view and it might be interesting to ask whether any government would have managed to convince the Falck family that the Schuman Plan was a good thing. The section of the industry owned by the state was able however virtually to set itself up as the government and steer the course of integration. The operation was largely defensive, for it was recognized that, at least in the short term, full exposure to the rest of the Community was too great a risk. In view of the Italian experience it is not inconceivable that the British could also have negotiated favourable terms allowing them to take full advantage of a larger market. But this was not put to the test and the British steel industry, abetted by the government, continued to operate a policy expressly designed to curb even interdependence with the continental steel market.

6 Interdependence and integration in American eyes: from the Marshall Plan to currency convertibility

Federico Romero

In the 1950s, the main US assumptions and policy goals concerning Europe inherited from the Marshall Plan's effort at reconstruction, remained paramount. The more successful they had been, the more treasured they were in Washington, but their very success was rapidly changing the terms of the relationship between the USA and western Europe. If the strategic axioms of containment (a revived and united Europe for a strong anti-Soviet alliance) remained crucial, they increasingly came into friction with the economic consequences of the peculiar nature of transatlantic interdependence. The strong return to world markets of European exports and the emerging US payments deficit slowly brought new domestic priorities to bear on a redefinition of the USA's national interest and foreign goals.

The task of devising new policies was to be taken up by the Kennedy and Johnson administrations in the 1960s, but the debate within the Eisenhower administration already shows the uncertainties of the new situation. Its attitude towards the advancement of European integration illustrates the dilemmas the USA had to face with the emergence of its own still limited but growing sensitivity to interdependence. Rather than being, as originally intended, a mere transitory stage towards multilateralism, regionalism, especially in the form of integration, could become a barrier to the pursuit of US foreign economic goals. The debate on European integration in the United States in the 1950s heralds the crucial passage from the unilateral dependence of post-war Europe on the United States to a new era of still uneven but increasingly mutual Atlantic interdependence. Ironically, integration in Europe was a strong force for generating a more genuine interdependence between western Europe and the United States.

AMERICA AND POST-WAR EUROPEAN INTEGRATION

In the post-war years three main ideas motivated the United States' insistence on western European unification. First there was a strategic concept of integration as the way to reconcile Germany's recovery with France's security and build up enough strength to contain the Soviets. Second, the principle of a customs union (derived from the United States' own federal experience) was supposed to spur fast economic growth based on scale, specialization, competition and higher productivity. Finally, it was to satisfy the domestic imperative of achieving tangible results in return for aid – integration was presented to Congress as the means to break Europe's economic nationalisms, to accelerate the closing of the dollar gap, and to make further American aid unnecessary. Different economic visions converged on the importance of integration. New Deal planners saw a large unit regulated by supranational institutions as the appropriate sphere for growth-orientated economic management. To the free traders, on the other hand, a liberalized market seemed the best recipe to defeat nationalism and bilateralism by means of international market discipline. With Marshall Aid European integration in fact became the 'interlocking concept in the American Plan for Western Europe': it was seen as the key to the growth of western economic and political strength, and thus to a favourable balance of power on the continent.[1]

By 1950 however, the scope of US plans had already been considerably narrowed. It had become clear that the United Kingdom would not participate in unification and that the sterling area would not disappear. The OEEC had turned out to be not the much hoped-for instrument of political unification, but an inter-governmental forum for the liberalization of industrial trade. Most importantly, even after the devaluations of 1949, the liberalization of trade and payments proved to be feasible only on a regional basis. With the European Payments Union, established in 1950, recovery found its pivotal institution and a system of settlement built around a limited, rather than worldwide, multilateralism which discriminated against the dollar area. And the European Coal and Steel Community, which began operations in 1952, while achieving the crucial Franco-German pacification, shifted the process of European integration towards a geographically narrower, sectoral dimension that had only a pale resemblance to the American view of a unified Europe. For the State Department and the Economic Cooperation Administration however, these compromises were the best that could be achieved. Under the umbrella of the NATO alliance and with the help of dollar aid a discriminatory but viable system of trade and payments had been put to work and the ECSC at least represented a cherished promise for the future growth of supranationalism. Even the American Treasury, though wary of limitations to worldwide multi-lateral free trade, had to accept the EPU as a realistic stage in a slower progress towards full convertibility. It remained concerned however that EPU might evolve into a soft-currency bloc and that the dollar might in the future be at a disadvantage in world trade.[2]

US acceptance of these modest compromises was due to sound strategic realism in the face of a relatively limited political leverage. It also revealed the weakness of the domestic conservative opposition to bipartisan internationalism. Protectionist concern for a revival of European competition was expressed by the Republican right wing headed by Senator Robert A. Taft. He fought against aid policy not only out of fiscal conservatism and distrust of European nationalism and socialism, but upon the prediction that only large banks and corpora-tions would gain from the expansion of multilateral trade, while small producers and American workers would be put in jeopardy.[3] This populist defence of the least advanced, most vulnerable sectors of American manufacturing however, was quite isolated at the time. In the post-war USA, and for many years to come, there was little public concern for the international competitiveness of the American economy. Even organized labour, led by the powerful unions of the mass-producing sectors, fully participated in the political consensus that considered multilateral free trade as an opportunity for export rather than a potential threat.[4] Temporary trade discrimination against the dollar area could therefore be tolerated. It did not infringe upon any serious interest in a powerful economy that looked almost invulnerable to foreign developments. The concept of economic interdependence was virtually absent from the contemporary American debate, which rested on the assumption of western Europe's unilateral dependence on the USA, the need for dollar aid appearing as its epitome.

In 1952, with the end of Marshall Aid, the State Department and the Mutual Security Agency (MSA) (the successor to ECA) began to study future options. Their diagnosis of Europe's international economic position was bleak. The dollar gap was not going to disappear and could grow even larger because it had structural origins. Europe was importing essential machinery, cotton, wheat and coal, while exporting to the USA only 'unnecessary items'. It was forecast that European productivity could not catch up and that the USA would grow even more relatively competitive.[5] For some of the officials in charge of foreign aid the prospect of a Europe that could not grow to be internationally viable without permanent American financial aid called for drastic responses, which involved fundamental changes in the world position of the USA.

The MSA envisioned an Atlantic Reserve System with the pooling of dollar, sterling and continental monetary reserves: in order to stop the drain on American resources the USA should accept 'an interdependent and organic relationship' with western Europe, and become part of an institutionalized Atlantic Community – a possibility the Treasury Department, not to speak of Congress, would not even consider.[6]

More realistically, the State Department discarded this idea of what in effect would have been a North Atlantic federation and focused on the functional improvement of existing institutions. European integration remained at the centre of this vision, since its strategic and economic importance was deemed 'vital to the security of the United States'. The ECSC, with its principle of supranationality and its crucial integration of the German Federal Republic, was seen as the core of a set of 'mutually reinforcing concentric circles'. Wider economic co-operation within the OEEC and the strategic Atlantic link established by NATO were seen as additionally supportive pillars.[7] With the new concern for defence and the priority given to the rearmament of the Federal Republic, hopes for further, crucial progress of European integration were concentrated on the negotiations for a European Defence Community. The EDC Treaty and the development of the ECSC thus were the new, parallel goals of the American diplomatic effort for integration. The advancement of the Six towards a strong economic federation with increasing political unity had become and remained Washington's preferred path towards European unification.[8]

Strong political support for the ECSC was not too difficult for the State Department to provide. The domestic demand for US steel was so high after summer 1950 as to diminish fears of a European price cartel, while the maintenance of a large export of US coal required the healthy growth of the European market, which the ECSC seemed to promise. When the ECSC High Authority asked for a direct US loan, the State Department and MSA insisted on the political and symbolic relevance of a gesture of support to European integration. The High Authority represented the only instance of supranationalism and the best hope for dismantling protectionist restrictions. The Treasury, wary of regionalism, laid more stress on the danger that the ECSC could become a new steel cartel, the concern advanced by the US steel industry, which obviously disliked the financing of foreign competitors. But the political reasons for the loan prevailed. The strategic argument in favour of European unity had the full backing of the White House, and the State Department managed to override every objection: the $100 million loan was eventually granted in April 1954.[9]

Political support for integration was increasingly motivated by security rather than economic reasons, and almost totally focused on the fate of the EDC Treaty. On issues of high political profile, like the loan to the ECSC, the State Department could therefore have its way. It was quite a different matter however when moves towards integration had a less visible political value and a more direct relevance to the American economy, as in the case of the 'Green Pool' discussions on European agricultural trade. The MSA had initially supported the idea of a Green Pool on the basis of the established principles of the Marshall Plan: integration would break national restrictions and increase European agricultural productivity. As discussions progressed however, it became increasingly clear that social pressures in most European nations would steer the 'Green Pool' not towards market liberalization but rather towards long-term agreements to organize production and intra-European trade. Integrated European agriculture would not be inherently more liberal than national policies and would probably amount to a protectionist cartel discriminating against American farm exports. Thus, it would damage the US programmes of domestic support to agriculture, the only major sector where American national policies showed a marked degree of reliance on foreign trade, and therefore of sensitivity to its shifts. Support for the Green Pool gave way to scepticism and hostility, and in the end even MSA-FOA (the Foreign Operations Administration) was relieved when the Green Pool negotiations failed.[10] This episode did not have political prominence at the time, but it shows the difficulties left unsolved by Marshall Aid and it points to an inherent inconsistency of American policy which would gradually grow through the 1950s. With the recovery of European output and trade US policy would have to find a new balance between the support for European growth through the concept of integration and the upholding of national interests that were to become not only increasingly affected by the emerging Atlantic interdependence but, as in the case of agriculture, even more threatened by integration.

A NEW FOREIGN ECONOMIC POLICY?

Successful as it had been, the Marshall Plan had none the less left the dollar gap still wide open, and its ending saw a growing American concern for the commitment to long-term financial aid. The election of Eisenhower at the end of 1952 signalled a reassertion of fiscal conservatism aimed at balancing the budget and limiting foreign spending. The new President was a convinced Atlanticist who believed in the strengthening and uniting of Europe as the basic tenets of the strategy of containment, which remained unchanged. But he also wanted to check public spending and cut down on foreign aid. The successor agency of MSA, the Foreign Operations Administration, saw its influence severely reduced. The new political outlook emphasized anti-inflationary fiscal moderation and the role of private investment for foreign growth.[11]

Foreign economic policy underwent its first official review since the Marshall Plan. In August 1953 Clarence B. Randall of Inland Steel, a staunch free trader and an early sceptic about the ECSC, was appointed to chair a bipartisan Commission on Foreign Economic Policy (CFEP). Consensus around the pursuit of multilateral free trade was unquestioned: it was seen as the main avenue to international stability and the best trading environment for the highly efficient American producers. Currency convertibility was thus singled out as the main goal, although its attainment was pragmatically postponed to the moment when the persistent world payments imbalance had been reduced. In order to narrow the dollar gap the new approach stressed the role of increased mutual trade rather than aid. The CFEP did not dwell on the issue of regionalism and European integration, but it restated America's support for EPU as a temporary arrangement on the way to full convertibility.[12]

In a message to Congress on 30 March 1954 Eisenhower endorsed the new approach. The negotiation of new tariff cuts in order to expand trade and make the American market more accessible to foreign exports was the main measure to tackle the dollar gap. The administration would try to advance towards convertibility and encourage an outflow of dollars in the form of private investments rather than state aid. But his proposals were rather timid as a result of political compromise. The Treasury insisted on convertibility and immediate cuts in foreign aid; the Department of Commerce opposed deep tariff reductions; the State Department did not want to press for convertibility lest this might endanger EPU, and suggested a more liberal import policy.[13]

From its very beginning trade rather than aid appeared as a wobbly and uncertain strategy. The CFEP discussion had tried to enlarge the range of available options in order to make a reduction of aid possible. But an attack on the dollar gap based on the expansion of trade raised even more difficulties. By calling the Europeans to gain more dollars with import competition on the American market the administration was narrowing the divide between foreign and domestic economic policy. Tariff policy was obviously liable to robust, divergent domestic pressures which brought serious constraints to bear on the administration's autonomy. The trade rather than aid campaign would be hampered by a widespread reluctance to accept the consequences of even a moderate growth of economic interdependence.[14]

The automobile, machinery and, in general, hard-goods exporting sectors with high productivity argued for more liberal tariff policies. The Department of Commerce tried to balance the pressures from these 'Detroit free traders' with the opposite ones coming from low-technology, low-wage, small-scale producers of consumer goods who started to fear the comeback of European competitors. The Secretary of Commerce argued at the White House that tariffs ought to be used to 'equalize the differential in wage rates'. Free trade had to be accompanied by specific protections for those sectors that would suffer from lower-wage competition, 'unless we want a particular industry to go out of the picture'.[15]

At the opposite end, the State Department worked on the assumption that the US economy enjoyed 'a relative invulnerability to changes from abroad', and feared that the international imbalance might become permanent and even deeper. Europe had to be offered larger markets to stimulate its output, reduce unemployment and increase its ability to pay for dollar imports.[16]

The real stumbling-blocks however were to be found in Congress, where the representatives of local and sectoral interests would not give up useful commercial protections for the sake of foreign allies. Congress reluctantly conceded the renewal of the Reciprocal Trade Agreement Act requested by the White House in order to have the authority to negotiate a modest 15 per cent reduction of US tariffs over three years. But the administration did not even try to attack the main instruments for protection enshrined in American trade legislation: the 'escape clause' and the 'peril point clause'. These entitled American producers threatened by foreign competition to request a suspension of tariff reductions. If the Tariff Commission upheld their case – as it usually did – the President had to raise import duties again. Finally, the trade rather than aid campaign did not touch upon controversial agricultural policies of domestic price support, disposal of surplus abroad as aid, and outright import restrictions.[17]

The real issue was not the general level of tariffs but the specific policy instruments that allowed the USA to unilaterally repeal negotiated trade concessions when they affected domestic producers and national policies. The 'peril point' and 'escape clause' made US trade policy unpredictable, and discouraged foreign competitors from entering the American market since this could be shut close again as soon as their efforts were successful. The same applied to agriculture, where the USA maintained the right to impose import restrictions, in violation of

GATT, when imports were threatening domestic price-support policies. Throughout the 1950s Congress maintained the view that no international obligation could override a national interest, often perceived in narrowly sectoral or regional terms, and limit national sovereignty.

This exceptionalist concept of interdependence – which attributed to the USA the unilateral right to reverse its consequences when they hurt national producers – emasculated the administration's trade campaign. While the State Department was preaching the urgency of mutual trade liberalization, its action was undermined by the Tariff Commission accepting several requests for new import duties on items that were beginning to hurt marginal, backward sectors of the American economy. Between 1953 and 1955 tariffs were unilaterally raised on bicycles, pipes, fur hats, watches, garlic, cheese, figs, lead and zinc. The bicycle case assumed an exemplary relevance. In a fast-expanding market the share of American producers was being reduced by new British models. These had been specifically developed for export with Marshall Aid funds in order to improve the British balance of payments. The Tariff Commission request for new import duties thus struck at the heart of the credibility of the USA's trade policy. The Europeans considered it a test case of the administration's consistency. But Eisenhower, in spite of strong opposition from Agriculture and State departments, had to bow to internal pressures, and in August 1955 raised import duties on bicycles by 50 per cent.[18]

A new bold trade policy thus never did really take off. For Atlantic interdependence and European integration, however, the other issue at stake – European currencies' convertibility into dollars – was far more important. The USA's preference for full convertibility had had to be put aside, after Bretton Woods, for the whole period of post-war reconstruction. But when the United Kingdom, in early 1953, came forward with a request for American credit and larger imports to support a move to sterling-dollar convertibility, the issue emerged once again as a matter for policy consideration. Domestic pressures were less relevant than on trade issues, but the administration was deeply divided on essential strategy considerations, and this in the end prevented any dramatic change of policy.

There was a general consensus on the necessity to overcome the separation of currency areas, but almost every department had different ideas on the way to achieve this broad goal. In talks with the British the Americans took time: they favoured an 'orderly transition' to convertibility but did not want a breakdown of EPU, which seemed an inevitable consequence of the British plan. Any move towards freer trade in the Atlantic area had to be reconciled with further progress in

European integration to which the administration saw EPU as a step.[19] US agencies were divided between three different viewpoints. The Treasury and the Federal Reserve deemed convertibility essential: the economic strength of the West had to be based upon full multilateralism and international market discipline. Perhaps more crucially, they thought the American national interest required a rapid end to dollar discrimination in foreign trade by the Europeans. On the other hand, to the foreign policy establishment and particularly to FOA, European unity and integration appeared as more tangible assets to be safeguarded even at the cost of dollar discrimination. They rejected sterling-dollar convertibility since, by breaking EPU, it would endanger the very centrepiece of their post-war policy. Even the State Department, however, was not unanimous in the defence of regionalism and many officials argued for global trade and payment arrangements. But they believed that the low level of reserves and the huge European requirements for dollar imports made convertibility still unsustainable. Thus, convertibility looked futile to them as long as the dollar gap was not reduced by increased trade.[20]

The most radical ideas were harboured in FOA, which however was the least influential among the executive agencies. Its main concern was that a British move to convertibility would unravel the patchy but functional framework for European recovery that had been built over the past five years around OEEC and EPU and wreck any prospect of further European integration. At that point all the major pillars of the United States' European policy would lie in ruin. Instead, FOA advanced once again its view of a deeper American involvement in an institutionalized Atlantic Community, either in the shape of a tripartite Atlantic Reserve System (the USA, the UK and the Six) or by means of a full membership of the USA in a transatlantic OEEC. The latter hypothesis aimed at strengthening American leadership in Europe and preventing a retrenchment of European deficit countries into protectionism and bilateralism. Convertibility should be gradually achieved, they argued, between the dollar and EPU as a unit, thus safeguarding the conditions for deeper continental integration and establishing a framework for 'an expanding trade and payments relationship between EPU area–dollar area'.[21]

At the opposite end the Treasury and the Federal Reserve – which always had reservations on EPU as a soft-currency bloc, seeing it as something to be accepted only as a stop-gap measure – saw in the British proposal the opportunity to begin the dismantling of regionalism. The return to convertibility ought not to be retarded, they argued, by a collective approach, such as that proposed by FOA, which would tie everybody to the pace of the weakest members of EPU. Thus the Treasury suggested giving support not only to the United Kingdom but to every other European country prepared to go convertible. That the deficit nations inside EPU would be forced to deflate was seen as a healthy return to financial discipline. The Federal Reserve and the Treasury thought that the way to overcome dollar discrimination was convertibility, rather than a liberalization of US imports. Interdependence had to be organized not as a privileged access to the American market but as a global, open system of trade and payments where the competition from more efficient American producers would force the Europeans to adjust and increase their productivity.[22]

The State Department stayed clear of these grandiose designs for future interdependence and opted for a middle ground defined by political realism. Even if its economic view leaned towards multilateralism, the department did not share the Treasury's praise of 'the beauties of convertibility'. It rather insisted on 'the problems involved in getting there' and on the importance of 'the US interest in European integration'.[23] Both points carried considerable weight. Outright support of a British move to convertibility would divide the Europeans, tear the OEEC apart and sink the EDC project. Besides, few really believed that convertibility could be sustained given the size of the dollar gap and the trade imbalance. It appeared as a goal for the future to be approached gradually, rather than a practical policy for the present. By allowing European growth the EPU, after all, prevented deeper national restrictions that in many countries would have been inevitable in the case of deflationary pressures. Some hardening of its criteria for settlement was advisable, as a step on the way to convertibility, but EPU had to be preserved and its regional discrimination tolerated, since nothing better could replace it. Along these realist lines a compromise was reached that found its way into the Randall Commission Report, which praised EPU as a temporary arrangement preceding convertibility. Actual decisions about abandoning the current regional framework were *de facto* left to the Europeans themselves.[24]

The UK was not encouraged by the purely formal support it received in Washington and postponed any decision on an official proclamation of sterling convertibility. But because the practical thrust of British policy was still towards effective sterling–dollar convertibility, the American debate dragged on throughout 1954. Whenever an OEEC meeting on the matter required an official US position, the interdepartmental disagreement was rehearsed once again. But between the Treasury's view of a hegemonic interdependence defined by free multilateral trade and payments, and FOA's dream of currency blocs linked together by transatlantic institutions and upheld by dollar reserves, there could be no convergence. And both approaches were unsustainable in view of European politics and economic conditions.[25] The State Department's conservative stance avoided the dangers of a leap in the dark and built upon the results so far achieved. Regional integration, OEEC trade liberalization and dollar discrimination had been the pillars of post-war European stability. The strategic importance of Europe required that this equilibrium be maintained and improved only with cautious, *ad hoc* steps. The rewards of regionalism could not be sacrificed to fancy blueprints for greater interdependence or a dogmatic, nationalistic assertion of US hegemony.

THE EUROPEAN COMMON MARKET

The failure of the EDC project in 1954 did not induce Washington to abandon its desire for European integration, but it certainly brought some disillusionment and a cautious scepticism about future prospects. In principle, a 'steady progress towards integration' remained a key US strategic objective, now motivated by the need to reconcile France with the forthcoming inclusion of the German Federal Republic in NATO. American diplomats also kept arguing that only a larger integrated market could assure Europe's survival in the economic competition with the USA and the USSR on the world market. But they had little confidence that the impasse could be overcome, and were even concerned that the defeat of EDC might indicate a new trend back towards nationalism.[26]

Thus the State Department paid only superficial attention to the May 1955 meeting of the Six in Messina. It expressed 'friendly interest and support' for further supranational integration in other sectors, like transport, but it was quite sceptical on the feasibility of the new plans. The deepest scepticism was reserved for the common market plan, which was dismissed as 'a pretty nebulous project' with little possibility of success. On the other hand, American diplomacy was attracted by the Euratom project and began to watch the negotiations for it with optimism. In the top echelons of the State Department, and at the White House as well, a European community for the non-military use of atomic energy appeared as a highly promising development. Not only would it enhance European unity and strength and enlarge the successful supranational experience of the ECSC on a new crucial ground, but Euratom was attributed a high strategic value as an instrument for allowing US control over the national nuclear programmes. By providing a central European agency to which the USA could release fissile materials and nuclear technology it could prevent their transformation into military ventures with nationalist overtones. Most importantly, it could securely tie the German Federal Republic to its allies on the most sensitive of all issues. The economic side was also enticing: Europe was in great need of new energy sources, and American industry would naturally be the main supplier of nuclear technologies. Thus, Euratom immediately received strong diplomatic and, later on, technical support from the USA, which sustained the project with keen interest throughout its development.[27]

Other agencies were even more dismissive about the common market. FOA (about to be renamed the International Cooperation Administration [ICA]) still praised the key importance of European integration for faster growth, trade expansion and the gradual liberalization of payments. Regional arrangements were essential in order to promote trade liberalization and narrow the dollar gap. But it simply meant that the USA had to keep supporting, and possibly lead, the OEEC's process of inter-governmental co-operation, which was hailed as the only functional framework for the advancement of intra-European trade liberalization. In fact, by the term integration FOA-ICA was by now referring only to the removal of national restrictions and the mutual opening of markets, no more than what we have defined in this book as interdependence. Tighter arrangements conducive to political unification were deemed improbable, while sectoral integration along the ECSC pattern was seen with ill-concealed concern as potentially conducive to restrictive cartels. The project for a common market was conspicuously absent from FOA-ICA's analysis of current European trends.[28]

The administration's economic departments also took little notice of the common market project, and remained officially silent for quite some time. The Treasury and the Federal Reserve maintained their view that international trade and payments, and Europe's own economic performance, could be improved only by currency convertibility. But they had resolved to wait for the next opportunity and appeared momentarily satisfied by the gradual hardening of EPU's internal payment system. Their leading officials however did not conceal their distaste for Europe's regionalism and anticipated a harsh American reaction if the common market led to increased commercial discrimination. In their opinion 'US interest in an economically united Europe' was 'ill considered' and no longer appropriate.[29]

This economic disregard for integration left the strategic and political aspects of American interest in a unified Europe unchallenged. At a National Security Council meeting in November 1955 the President himself emphasized 'the desirability of developing in WE [western

Europe] a third great power bloc' by means of further progress towards 'the unity of Western Europe'. With such a powerful backing, Secretary of State Dulles articulated the US strategic priority for 'the closer community of interests that Europe can build'. The most urgent goal was still the irreversible integration of the German Federal Republic in the West, and to this end 'the greatest hope' lay in 'the six-nation grouping approach', even if this might entail some protectionism.[30] OEEC co-operation was useful, but only the effort by the Six to enhance their supranational integration was deemed capable of cementing the crucial Franco-German alliance. Dulles even believed that the Six could open the way to 'a genuine United States of Europe': thus, their new initiatives were worthy of the strongest US support. Euratom in particular – for its deepest strategic relevance and its promise of technological modernization – became the new State Department's pet project. In its wake the common market started to be seen as a positive development, even though with less 'security and political significance'.[31]

In December 1955 the State Department then began to assess the economic implications of the common market project and stated appreciatively that no sign of protectionist leanings had yet emerged from the Brussels discussions. A few criteria were set upon which to evaluate the treaty. Its commercial regulations had to respect GATT article XXIV which accepted customs unions only if they embraced the whole economy and were no more restrictive than the constituent countries. Thus the scope of the common market and the level of its external tariff were to be the crucial yardsticks. US interest also required that the common market be provided with anti-cartel measures and provisions for the encouragement of free trade with third countries. It was clearly stated however that the political priority of integrative progress made commercial issues 'necessarily subordinate'. The department was already prepared to accept a certain degree of discrimination for the sake of its broader political goals.[32]

The discussion on the common market remained dormant for a few months (while US attention focused on Euratom) but acquired urgency after the meeting between the Foreign Ministers of the Six, held in May 1956 in Venice, made clear that the project was actually taking off. Besides, the UK was about to table its proposal for an OEEC-wide Free Trade Area. The future of Europe's economic institutions suddenly seemed open again, and both the strategic and commercial aspects of integration took once more the centre stage.

In July, a set of instructions prepared by the State Department gave shape to the future pattern of US policy. Regional trade arrangements could be accepted if they contributed to the attainment of US political objectives in the area and to an overall expansion of international trade. The common market received a positive evaluation upon the first criterion, since it enhanced the integration of western Europe. But the idea of a Free Trade Area was less welcome: its discriminatory effects would not be matched by clear political advantages on the grounds of European unity. The State Department bias in favour of the Six was reinforced by the early outlines of the common market project. The inclusion of agriculture, the possibility of admitting new countries and the 'attention given to the international obligations' of the participating countries 'gratified' the department. The USA was prepared to support the project but three issues needed further clarification: the strength of supranational institutions capable of guaranteeing an irreversible dismantling of trade barriers; the effectiveness of provisions against export cartels and other private restrictive arrangements; the degree of external protection granted to agriculture.[33]

Little was said however about the impact of either scheme on the US economy and foreign trade. This moved the White House to review the long-term effects of European integration, initiated in August by the inter-departmental Council on Foreign Economic Policy (CFEP). A strong consensus emerged on the desirability of further European integration, not only for political reasons but in an economic perspective as well. It was expected that the common market by accelerating Europe's internal growth, would become 'a better market for US exports'; external tariff discrimination would be moderate and could be negotiated away in GATT without 'net adverse effects upon US trade'. Besides, supranational institutions were deemed more malleable to international pressures for a liberal trade policy. The common market would restrain and eventually abolish national protectionism and this appeared the primary, most welcome effect of integration. The CFEP chairman, Clarence Randall, declared that the common market could be 'the most significant economic event in [his] generation', and argued for unreserved US support.[34]

Such optimism was grounded in current economic conditions and trade flows, which bore out the view of a highly competitive US economy that could only benefit from European growth. The trade balance with western Europe was not only positive but rapidly improving, with a strong growth of exports. The US trade surplus with the Six had risen from $908 million in 1954 to $980 million in 1955 and then again to $1,463 million in 1956. It would further grow to $1,636 in 1957. The protectionist sectors of American industry were temporarily silent, and no major domestic voice was raised against the potential for trade discrimination and increased international competition represented by the common market.[35] As long as the American economy remained buoyant, and foreign trade growing, the US positive attitude towards European integration was not vulnerable to domestic pressures for an assertion of the USA's immediate commercial interest.

Even the emerging concern with the balance of payments did not alter this view. The Treasury worried about the yearly accumulation of payments deficits and the corresponding rise in foreign – mostly European – liquid dollar claims. But the solution sought by the Treasury was the reduction of foreign aid and military spending abroad. With a healthy trade surplus, which partially offset the large deficit incurred by public expenditures abroad, concern for the payments deficit simply did not translate into a call for new trade policies and a reassessment of US attitudes towards European regionalism. Besides, there were no serious anxieties about the competitiveness of American products; with its prospect of internal growth the common market appeared primarily as an opportunity for a further increase in US exports, and the Department of Commerce sided with State in support. The Treasury and the Federal Reserve, wary of regionalism as always, expressed reservations but did not engage in a struggle to prevent US endorsement of the common market project.[36]

Amidst the internal debate Eisenhower publicly praised the importance of further European economic unity, and this set the tone for the CFEP decisions. In November it concluded that integration appeared 'desirable on political and economic grounds' provided that it did not lead to 'an inward-looking regional bloc'. The USA was prepared to support both common market and Free Trade Area in so far as the new arrangements did not hamper the advance towards multilateral trade and currency convertibility and did not bring increased discrimination against dollar goods, in the form either of higher tariffs or tighter quantitative restrictions, or of further discrimination on agricultural imports. On these conditions the treaties were to be evaluated later on in GATT, when their details were known. The CFEP emphasized the US interest in seeing the UK more closely linked with the Six through a free trade area, but it also expressed a preference for the deeper integrative approach represented by the common market by stressing that trade liberalization should be accompanied by the liberalization of capital and labour movements as well.[37]

The CFEP debate thus settled the issue and inaugurated a policy of official support for the common market. The State Department could now enter into friendly diplomacy with the Brussels negotiators with no major restraint. Its post-Marshall Plan view of a Europe integrated around the Six and behind the shelter of dollar discrimination remained at the core of US foreign economic policy. The march towards multilateral trade and convertibility was still subordinated to the priority of European unity. The alternative concepts of interdependence were not taken into consideration. When the hypothesis of a more integrated Atlantic economic community was voiced in NATO, the State Department did not just reply that Congress would not allow any US participation in supranational institutions, it stated quite clearly that there was no need for Atlantic interdependence to become more tightly knit because integration in Europe together with existing co-operation across the Atlantic was quite satisfactory as a framework.[38]

The negotiations for the Treaty of Rome were entering their final stage. The Treasury and the Department of Agriculture recommended exerting pressures in order to ensure that US commercial interests were given due consideration. The State Department issued a public statement of support to the common market (and to the Free Trade Area project) and submitted to the Six an *aide-mémoire* which detailed the issues of major concern. The USA, though prepared to accept the trade diversion resulting from the formation of a customs union, hoped that common market tariffs and commercial policy would not increase the current level of discrimination, particularly on agricultural products. Furthermore, the Six were asked not to prevent a member country from liberalizing its dollar imports and to discourage the use of quantitative restrictions against third countries in response to national payment imbalances arising from the removal of internal trade barriers.[39]

Even though the replies were largely noncommittal, particularly in respect to agricultural policy, the State Department saw no reason for pessimism. It was thought that by its very nature the common market would stimulate the growth of competitive internal pressures for freer trade, and economic expansion would be such as to accommodate increasing imports from third countries. The political priority of seeing the treaty safely completed induced American diplomats to shelve their queries on commercial issues. The common market had to be solidly and irreversibly established before the USA would negotiate on its more controversial issues. The State Department went even as far as proposing to postpone the GATT debate on the new customs union to the moment when the Treaty of Rome had been ratified by the parliaments of the Six. The Treasury and the Department of Agriculture pointed out that after ratification the treaty would be unchangeable and the negotiating position of the Six certainly less flexible. But the State Department had the political weight of the CFEP decisions on its side and was handling relations with the Six almost totally on its own, and its proposal was not contested.[40]

Secretary Dulles had by now lifted the integrative effort of the Six to a central role in the USA's world-view. Their economic unification was seen as a step in the building of a powerful bloc that was to become 'one of [the] cornerstones in Atlantic construction'. The State Department was committed 'to safeguard [the] integrity, cohesion and growth potential' of the new Community of the Six in GATT and in every other international forum. Even the association of French overseas territories to the common market, though commercially damaging to the USA and its Latin American allies, was praised as the basis for the emergence of 'Eurafrica', a geopolitical entity that Dulles fancied would open 'immense possibilities' for future world stability.[41]

In April 1957 the department triumphantly reported to the CFEP that the Treaty of Rome was 'in accord with the US policy objectives' and deserved US support. Some of the American concerns had been taken into consideration and the treaty contained 'a broad recognition of the interests of third countries'. Future GATT negotiations would take care of the remaining problems, which the department indicated might lie in the height of the common market's external tariff, in the long-term contract and minimum prices for agricultural products, in the tariff preference resulting from the association of overseas territories, and in the possibility that member countries might impose import restrictions on third countries for balance of payments reasons. From a commercial point of view these issues were substantial and could very well be crucial. But it was argued that the common market was no more restrictive than any customs union would be by its very nature, that protectionism would be weaker than at national level, and that the growth of a large free market would benefit everyone's trade. The Treasury complained once again that the State Department was underestimating the economic consequences of the common market. But it felt it could not override the essentially political approach and did not amend the report, which the CFEP then approved as the official US position.[42]

The European common market was now well protected against any attempt to alter or water down its provisions by means of a hostile GATT review. The United Kingdom pressed for such a critical review by GATT, but without the concurrence of the USA no other country could lead an effort to impose modifications to the treaty before it was ratified. In the international arena the State Department actively smoothed out frictions arising from the widespread criticism of the common market's protectionist features and assured the USA's acceptance in GATT. Thus this new, crucial advancement of European integration was allowed to entrench and strengthen itself behind the shelter of the USA's friendly diplomacy.[43]

THE END OF THE POST-WAR ERA

That US support for integration through the new European Economic Community originated primarily in considerations of strategic interdependence is unquestionable. It is also evident that the persistent concern for the strengthening of western Europe could have justified a further, partial sacrifice of the USA's short-term commercial interest. Yet these overriding strategic motives – which had already been applied in the case of the ECSC and the EDC – do not entirely explain why such an eventful economic initiative as the EEC was not assessed primarily for its long-term economic consequences. One does not need retrospective wisdom on the world impact of the EEC to see that the CFEP review fell far short of a proper evaluation of long-term US interest in the matter. The debate remained anchored to the axioms that had guided US policy in the decade of post-war recovery, each agency stuck to its own long-held views on transatlantic economic relations and little attention was devoted to the changing terms of interdependence. Even outside the government, proper analyses of the economic significance of the common market began to appear only a couple of years later, when the structure of the European Economic Community was in place and could no longer be modified. By that time, in 1959–60, economic leaders and policy-makers were looking at the international position of the USA with very different eyes: foreign economic policy had indeed become a matter of serious concern. And in the 1960s the relationship with the Community became a major political issue.

The profound changes that intervened in the brief period between 1957 and 1960 provide, by way of contrast, a few answers to the previous questions. To begin with, during the negotiations for the Treaty of Rome the US policy-making process remained singularly unaffected by private domestic pressures. In a period of buoyant exports to western Europe the news that a common market was being contemplated did not hit raw nerves. The protectionist, inward-looking sectors did not raise their voices; the common market did not appear as an immediate threat of increased competition on the American market and no explicit linkage with a further round of mutual tariff reductions was publicly suggested by the administration until 1958.

The competitive sectors, on the other hand, began to voice their opinions only in the aftermath of the treaty's signature and, even though aware that US exports were in for short-term displacement and tougher competition, they generally welcomed the common market. Surprising European and even American officials, big business saw in the EEC a 'juicy opportunity' for massive direct investment. To big automobile, machinery and chemical corporations a large, booming market with rising productivity offered the profitable prospect of replicating abroad their experience of large-scale production with advanced technologies. They shared the State Department's optimism on the long-run growth of international trade resulting from the common market and decided for an internationalization of their productive cycle.[44] Obviously not all industries went for investment in Europe and there were exporters who feared that the common tariff would cut down their sales. The aircraft industry for instance asked the administration to intervene against trade discrimination by the EEC, and so did Chrysler. But this did not amount to a generalized, pressing effort by a powerful export lobby, which in 1956–7 simply did not materialize. The farming sector, surely the best organized and most cohesive export lobby, exerted strong pressures through the Department of Agriculture, foreseeing quite clearly how the Community would be an 'organized' agricultural market with a high level of discrimination. Agricultural issues were, indeed, at the centre of US diplomatic representations with Brussels. But the very nature of the Treaty of Rome, which postponed most economically crucial decisions, and particularly the formation of the Common Agricultural Policy, to a later stage, obliged the USA to give a political recognition first and engage only later in hard bargaining on specific economic issues. In early 1957 the US strategic goal of European integration certainly could not be sacrificed for agricultural policies that the EEC had not yet finalized.[45]

Thus, the real economic issues between the USA and the Six were to be dealt with only later on, when the EEC was established. Then the USA proposed a new GATT round of mutual tariff reductions in order to negotiate down the external tariff which surrounded the common market. It was only in 1959 that a domestic debate on the economic significance of the common market for the USA was started, in conjunction with the 'Dillon round'. And any new American political response to the new configuration of Atlantic interdependence determined by European economic integration was postponed to the Kennedy presidency.[46]

A second factor, again related to timing, was the dilemma on the Free Trade Area proposal advanced by the UK in 1956. The proposal would have been very welcome in Washington if it had healed the split between the United Kingdom and the Six by establishing a multilateral framework of association between them and other OEEC members. It was hoped that it could deepen the OEEC experience of Europe-wide trade liberalization, accelerate growth and thus expedite convertibility and reinforce the liberal elements within the Six. At the same time it raised serious concerns. A larger preferential area would entail a bigger commercial disadvantage to the USA without the political reward of progressing towards European institutional unification. And it seemed likely that the UK and the Six could strike a compromise only on highly discriminatory terms. More importantly, the Free Trade Area proposal was perceived as a threat to the unity of the Six and the success of the common market whose supranational dimension had the highest priority for the State Department. This hardened Washington's view that the most urgent goal was to have the Treaty of Rome signed and the EEC supranational institutions established in order for the Six to negotiate with the Free Trade Area group as a solid, cohesive unit. Thus a proposal that might have induced a thorough evaluation of US foreign economic goals in fact further precipitated Washington's rush to support the birth of the EEC on political grounds.[47]

A third, important element was the attitude of the Treasury and of Washington's economic establishment in general. Their outlook for international trade and payments revolved around the attainment of convertibility, and they welcomed every development which could bring financial discipline and fiscal orthodoxy nearer, especially in France. Thus, they hoped that further internal liberalization would force the Europeans to 'put their own house in order' and abandon inflationary policies. If the opening of the common market was to have such an effect – by making the consequences of France's trade deficit inescapable and by bringing the pressure of surplus countries like the German Federal Republic to bear on French policies – this would certainly be a positive step.[48] On the other hand, it was possible that in order to accommodate French policies the common market would grow into a protectionist and internally restrictive institution, as was becoming apparent for agriculture. But the United States did not have much clout to directly influence these alternative choices, aside from supporting the most liberal elements among the Six; and this was precisely the State Department's strategy.

The adoption of a hostile posture against the strengthening of European integration would have entailed a radical departure from the established interpretation of world economic problems that had guided Washington's policies ever since the Marshall Plan. And even though the Treasury's concern for the US balance of payments was growing, the payments deficit did not yet amount to a major national policy issue. Its domestic consequences were simply not large and serious enough to trigger a whole rethinking of foreign economic policies. The current interpretation of US payments problems was not focused on trade, where the US maintained a healthy surplus, and the persistence of an American payments deficit could well be read as a function of the success of US policy for European recovery and international growth.

As late as October 1957 the constant rise of foreign liquid dollar holdings – which had doubled from 8 to 16.5 billion dollars in the period 1949–56 and exceeded the US gold reserves available for conversion by 6.5 billions – was still welcomed in Washington as evidence that American policy had helped the Allies to 'get back on their feet'. Thanks to US government grants, military expenditures and private investments abroad, 'the old bogey of the dollar gap' that had marked the post-war era had finally been overcome. The Treasury and Congress obviously thought that the time had come to scale down American financial commitments, and proposals were made for a cut-back on military expenses and general budgetary restraint. Besides, pressures began to be exerted on the European countries that had built up surpluses and large reserves – primarily the German Federal Republic – to take upon themselves part of the financial burden of providing aid to less developed countries. These measures, coupled with further progress on the liberalization of dollar imports in Europe, were deemed sufficient to redress a situation that caused concern, but no alarm as yet.[49]

It was only a matter of months however before the US deficit started to be seen in an entirely different light. In 1958 the payments deficit jumped to $3.5 billion from the yearly average of $1 billion registered over the period 1951–7. This rise was almost entirely due to a sudden, large drop in the trade surplus from $6.1 to $3.3 billion. More than half of this worsening of the US trade balance was related to trade with western Europe, even though the latter accounted for only 23 per cent of US total imports and exports. In a recession year, when overall US imports decreased by 1.4 per cent, imports from western Europe increased by 10.6 per cent, while US exports to western Europe went down by 23.6 per cent. As a result, the US trade surplus with western Europe dropped from the $2.3 billion reached in 1957 to $844 million. The first consequence of this abrupt change was to focus political attention on the international role of the dollar and its relation to gold, which became the central issue in the following decade. With a drop of $2 billion in just one year, US gold reserves were for the first time under the level of foreign liabilities to official dollar holders. A run on the dollar still seemed unlikely, but it was evident that a new era of uncertainties about the American currency had begun. The Treasury renewed its demand for anti-inflationary restraints on public spending, but fears also emerged about the trade performance of the American economy. For the first time since the war, and quite unexpectedly, policy-makers found themselves facing a 'weakening of [the USA's] ability to compete with other countries in world markets'.[50]

By the end of the year western Europe was ready to move into a new system of liberalized currency transactions: the EPU was disbanded, France devalued the franc and adopted a plan of strict financial stabilization, and non-resident convertibility among most western European currencies and the dollar was established on 29 December 1958. Both the State Department and the US Treasury supported and welcomed the European move – which signalled the end of a decade of post-war recovery and could only be helpful to American trade – but made clear that convertibility ought to be followed by swift action against import restrictions based on balance of payments considerations.[51] At the State Department the arrival of convertibility in conjunction with French stabilization was seen as a vindication of its support for a liberal-minded EEC. Integration was not only the product of 'the major political, technological and economic currents created by the ground swells of our time'; it could also be an effective, outward-looking force for the enhancement of worldwide free trade. For political and economic reasons its supranational institutions deserved continued support. But convertibility had also raised the stakes. The degree of regional discrimination that used to be accepted in view of the dollar gap could no longer be tolerated. Even though the Free Trade Area proposal was already moribund, the USA wanted to make clear that OEEC-wide trade agreements would not be welcome. The era of US commercial sacrifices for the sake of European growth and stability was over.[52]

The new mood, spurred by a worsening trade performance that could revive domestic protectionism, was decidedly assertive. The Treasury required rapid action to prevent the Europeans from preserving a 'deeply embedded' discrimination against dollar goods, still substantial in France and the UK. The State Department too focused on long-term US commercial interest and circulated a proposal that would alter even its policy towards the common market. The Six were to be told that import quotas discriminating against dollar goods had to be eliminated. It was unacceptable that a 'quota regime instituted to conserve hard currency before European convertibility should be used for commercial differentiation between Member and non-Member countries' of the common market. Several embassies in Europe replied that the USA had previously accepted a more rapid removal of common market internal quotas than quotas with the rest of the world. They warned that since the differential treatment between the Six and the rest of the world was a 'symbol of [the] integrity of [the] common market', the proposal would be interpreted as a 'major shift away from US support for European integration'.[53]

The idea of attacking the EEC on quotas was shelved, but that it had emerged at all signals a deep change of priorities in US attitudes. By mid-1959 the paramount concern was for the balance of payments, and a cabinet-level group headed by the Secretary of the Treasury was set up in order to formulate new policies. In 1959 the trade surplus dropped further to $1 billion, the lowest level in the decade. The administration excluded a devaluation of the dollar and concentrated on measures to relieve the burden of foreign aid: the other industrialized countries were to be pressured into giving more aid to the less developed world, and new development loans would be tied to procurement in the USA. The new policies for an assertive defence of the national interest extended also to trade matters. In May the USA explained its new approach at the GATT. Convertibility had created a new setting, it claimed, and trade discrimination no longer responded to any 'financial logic' and had to be superseded by non-discrimination and multilateralism. 'The period of postwar adjustment is behind us. The old arguments about "dollar shortage" . . . have lost their relevance.' At the OEEC as well the USA made clear that it expected European allies to take action – on aid and increased imports from the USA – to help redress the American deficit.[54] Interdependence had now reached the USA as well, and it carried a price. An entirely new game had begun.

In the second half of 1959 the new attitude brought noticeable policy changes. First and foremost was an explicit hostility towards regional arrangements in the OEEC to compose the contrasts between the Six, the UK and other member states. A European Free Trade Association (EFTA) was about to be established between the UK, Austria, Switzerland, Portugal, Norway, Sweden and Denmark. The USA did not encourage the new grouping, and expressed its aversion to any discriminatory arrangement between the EEC and EFTA. Trade liberalization had from now on, in American eyes, to proceed in a multilateral, worldwide dimension within GATT's larger framework.[55]

The State Department then came up with a plan for disposing of the OEEC as a regional organization. In order to exercise direct American leadership, the USA (and Canada) would become full members of a reorganized OEEC, no longer entrusted with the task of trade liberalization but transformed into a 'forum' for directing an increased flow of European capital aid to less developed countries, co-ordinating the relations between the EEC and EFTA 'in a manner beneficial to US trade and GATT objectives', eliminating 'all quantitative trade restrictions' still maintained by western Europe and discussing economic policies.[56] In short, the new OEEC, or the OECD (Organization for Economic Co-operation and Development) as it became, was to be an instrument for pursuing those policies the USA thought could solve its payments deficit. As a vision for interdependence, it was focused on the hegemonic assertion of US national policy.

The Treasury concurred with the plan's aims but objected to the sacrifice of the USA's 'freedom of action in the economic and financial field' entailed by full membership. US national autonomy would be endangered by belonging to an organization where 'the Europeans would have a large voice'. In particular, the prospect that US policies on the balance of payments and the management of business cycle fluctuations could be 'reviewed and hampered by the new group', was utterly unacceptable. Co-ordination of specific policies, like financial aid, would be better left to global institutions like the International Bank for Reconstruction and Development, with no infringement of US independence.[57]

The new strategy was submitted to the Europeans on the trip which Undersecretary of State Douglas Dillon made around the major capitals in December. The USA, he said, had supported the EEC for the political urgency of advancing the process of integration. But now it was securely established and American priorities had shifted as a result of balance of payments difficulties. Even though the USA still had a strong interest in 'maintaining the political cohesion of the Six', American commercial interests were now paramount and discriminatory policies would not be accepted either from the EEC or, even less, from EFTA. Differences between the two blocs should be solved according to GATT rules, and Dillon asked the Europeans to extend to all GATT members their planned reductions of quotas and tariffs. He also stressed the urgency of a financial commitment for the less developed countries. For the first time since the war an American statesman was not touring Europe to organize recovery, strengthen NATO or preach integration, but, as Dillon said, was 'promoting US exports and removing discrimination'.[58]

As a result of his trip Dillon asked the President to 'launch a new initiative to find [a] constructive solution to the growing trade rivalries in WE [western Europe] and to mobilize the energies of industrialized countries in a concerted effort to help the less developed areas'.[59] The USA was now directly committed to ensuring that the rivalry between the Six and the UK was not solved at the expense of American trade and that European trade arrangements would rapidly evolve towards multilateral liberalization. Interdependence had grown and required, in the American interpretation, new arrangements to cement the international community around the solution of US national priorities in the sphere of trade *and* payments. Within six months the OEEC was replaced by an OECD, with much-diluted powers of reviewing national policies, and the USA joined without infringement of its national policy-making autonomy. With the 'Dillon round' in GATT the USA then began the bargaining down of commercial tariffs with the EEC and EFTA that in the 1960s, with President Kennedy, would become the centrepiece of US international economic policy.

CONCLUSION

US support for the Treaty of Rome was the last chapter of Marshall Plan strategy determined by the dollar gap. Until 1956 dollar shortage and Europe's productivity gap were seen as unchangeable realities. Against the background of a healthy American commercial surplus the rapid growth of European exports, even into the US market, was still welcomed as a way out of the dollar gap. Even though integration gave rise to discriminatory European regionalism, it could be accepted as a half-way step towards a future of multilateral liberalization that enjoyed the support of a large domestic consensus. Meanwhile, limited protectionist interests could take advantage of US hegemonic strength to wring out *ad hoc* privileges from the general principles. Then in 1958 the first big drop in the US trade surplus, the worsening of its payments deficit, and the convertibility of European currencies into the dollar suddenly brought the post-war world to an end. Interdependence had grown far beyond what US policy-makers had envisioned a few years earlier, and it was not just the rosy, theoretical world of multilateral free trade. It carried a price for the USA as well. The defence of the United States' commercial and financial position took the centre stage. Thus timing was crucial: if it had come about just two years later the common market would have certainly received very different treatment in Washington. In a few years trade patterns showed that US support for the common market was not in fact harmful to the American economy. Between 1958 and 1965 the US share of EEC imports underwent a slight decrease. But the EEC's rapid economic growth enlarged the volume of its total imports. In absolute terms, and as a share of total US exports, overall US sales to the EEC steadily increased. The loss of market share was concentrated on farm products, even though US agricultural exports to the EEC grew by 80 per cent over the years 1958–65. Even more relevant than exports was the boom of US direct investment in many of the EEC's fastest-growing manufacturing sectors.[60]

But this did not solve the difficulties of the USA's international position. European integration certainly did not help to achieve the expanding trade surplus that the USA needed in order to contain the payments deficit. Above all, US power to determine the framework of international economic relations was significantly reduced. As the 'Kennedy round' of GATT negotiations in the 1960s made clear, the EEC represented a great trading power and a new major actor that could force the USA to concessions. On commercial matters, multilateral interdependence did not simply mean freer trade, but the emergence of stronger regional blocs.

In the US post-war vision of interdependence, multilateral free trade promised to safeguard the USA's own national autonomy and economic growth by maximizing the advantage of its higher productivity while avoiding compromises of its political and economic independence. The hegemonic strength of the USA and its relatively closed economy were the foundations of such a view. An unchallenged power to organize the international framework of the western economy seemed to warrant the success of this unilateral approach to interdependence. Its potential rewards shaped a durable domestic consensus centred not on a large export-orientated manufacturing sector but rather on the expansion of foreign investments and a consequent multinationalization of production. European integration, originally conceived as a strategic necessity, could then be accepted even in its own discriminatory terms as a temporary deviation on the route to multilateralism.

In Europe, on the other hand, the integrative process that led to the EEC developed along different lines. It aimed at the creation of a limited and protected regional space within which national programmes for industrial expansion could find their markets, while simultaneously controlling the pace and effects of larger, worldwide interdependence. This segmentation of the international framework allowed the Six to pursue parallel domestic strategies based on the gradual readjustment of national output to international markets by means of industrial policies and welfare measures co-ordinated by the state.

The post-war era thus saw two concepts of interdependence, compatible but diverse and sometimes conflicting, which stemmed from different responses to the increasing internationalization of economic relations. As a result, the return of Europe to world markets and the growth of international trade took place throughout the 1950s and 1960s within a contradictory mixture of regional discrimination, multilateral liberalization (in most manufacturing sectors) and managed protectionism (primarily in agriculture). Post-war European discrimination cannot be considered merely as a temporary exception to a historical process of unfettered multilateralization: it actually was one of the pillars of a more complex architecture of global interdependence. Regional integration probably allowed for a deeper, more sustainable trade liberalization than was otherwise feasible, because it allowed nation-states to control the consequences of the removal of protectionist barriers.

For the USA this turned out to be a mixed blessing. On the one hand European integration helped to make the overcoming of the dollar gap possible, thus accomplishing – even though by a different route – the major goal of the USA's post-war strategy. At the same time this segmented interdependence strengthened the competitive role of the USA's allies, facilitated the outflow of multinational investments (which would gradually dilute the US domestic manufacturing base), and accelerated the erosion of the international role of the dollar. The increasing rivalries and tensions of the 1960s, up to the dollar devaluation in 1971, would gradually bring the coexistence of these different approaches to interdependence to a breaking-point.

7 Conclusions: the value of history

Alan S. Milward

The hypothesis with which we started was set out in its most simplified form in the first chapter. Nation-states since the late nineteenth century have been increasingly held together not by traditional symbols of allegiance nor by repressive force but by national policies designed to secure material benefits for large social groups. As these policies have evolved, the reality has had to be faced that to be fully effective many need some form of international agreement, or occasionally even depend absolutely on the international framework, for their effectiveness. Integration, the surrender of some limited measure of national sovereignty, is, we suggested, a new form of agreed international framework created by the nation-states to advance particular sets of national domestic policies which could not be pursued, or not be pursued so successfully, through the already existing international framework of co-operation between interdependent states, nor by renouncing international interdependence.

Our reason for selecting this hypothesis was that it seemed to correspond to the results of recent historical research on the origins of the European Community. How well has it stood up to the further historical research which was designed to test it?

Properly to answer this question something must first be said about the strengths and limitations of historical research. All national governments in western Europe, as well as that of the United States of America, have granted themselves the power to keep their written materials secret for at least thirty years after their date and in most cases for much longer. It follows therefore that a full knowledge of what governments intended when they set out in 1950–2 along the road of European integration could only begin to be acquired in 1982 and is at present severely limited after the year 1962. Of all the limitations on the value of history as a medium for understanding European integration this is the most obvious. We have not accepted however that it is a finite limitation. Having constructed our hypothesis from a selection of the historical writing published over the last decade, in some cases we extrapolated it to interpret developments in Europe since that time. We did this in the first chapter to show that our hypothesis could explain the signing of the Maastricht Treaty of European Union, and in chapter 4 to show that it could explain Danish attitudes both to the European Community and to the idea of a nordic association in the 1960s, as well as presenting the outcome of the 1992 referendum in Denmark as the logical continuation of events.

In deriving a hypothesis from the recent historical literature we confined ourselves to those works which relied on archival research and in doing this set aside the great body of popular, semi-popular and synthetic literature about the development of the European Community. How far was this a limitation, and one which was likely to bias our hypothesis? There are in fact surprisingly few works which do rely fundamentally on research to explain the Community. There are only three monographs and one collection of miscellaneous essays which rely almost entirely on government records to try to interpret the collective motives of the signatories of the Treaties of Rome.[1] There is one essay in a collective volume which uses archival records to elucidate the Dutch motives.[2] And some light is shed by historians using the British records, although very little since the United Kingdom was a non-signatory.[3] There is a much longer list of works which explain the Treaty of Paris from government records and several others which trace the evolution of government policies on integration between the two treaties. These are referred to throughout the text. It has been suggested that this valuing of archival research above other types of history imposes an additional limitation on history's value as an explanatory tool. We do not think so.

It is true that most of the archives on which we have placed such weight consist of the papers of government ministries. It is also true that it has become a common feature of western European government records that politicians leave few traces in them. National bureaucrats are still forced by their working practices to commit their opinions and the records of their discussions to paper. Politicians are more reluctant and when they do so their opinions and attitudes are less methodically filed and preserved. What else, it has been frequently asked of the type of research we are preferring, can be expected of national bureaucrats other than a resolute defence of the interests of the nation-state, which not only employs them but is the very reason for their existence? Their memoranda are the last place where the evidence of the changing tide of opinion against the nation-state and in favour of other forms of governance will be found.

This cannot be gainsaid. But we have not solely relied on works whose evidence is culled from government archives. We have taken into account also systematic research into business archives, the archives of international organizations and those of pressure groups, and this reinforced our argument.[4] Indeed, for this reason our own studies to test our hypothesis specifically included a study of business opinion in a large industry, steel, in two countries. As Ranieri shows there, opinion in the industry, although strongly divided, was on balance at least as national in its emphasis as that of the machinery of national government.

The claim that national bureaucratic records are misleading because they disguise the reality of a continuing swing of opinion away from national government seems to us to have no basis unless this swing of opinion can be demonstrated from historical sources, which no one has yet managed to do. It will surely not surprise readers, knowing little of the history of the subject and picking up this book out of curiosity, that much of the history of European integration has been written in a propagandistic spirit by various enthusiasts of a united Europe. Works of this kind seize on a tiny part of the historical evidence as a small germ of truth, the seed of the future Europe, and ignore all the rest as irrelevant.[5] We have done the opposite, using the greater mass of evidence from which to build our theory. We are not, as we pointed out in chapter 1, in any way implying that the concepts of united Europe and supranational government have not become more popular. We are simply pointing out that national government has not become less popular. In our view traditional methods of archival research from which we have derived our hypothesis explain both tendencies.

There are other reasons too, beyond the preference for rational enquiry and assessment based on the weight of evidence, for valuing archival research above the assertions of propagandists that a united Europe has become over the last fifty years the will of the people and that national bureaucracies represent the last dam which stops that will breaking through and flooding over the whole continent. Opinions of that kind, which cannot be supported from evidence, are not, it seems to us, any more likely to bring an epoch of peace and harmony to Europe than the ill-founded universalist constitutionalism – and nationalism – of those who overthrew state governments in 1848. In resting our case on recorded historical evidence we are by no means coming to conclusions which are necessarily adverse to the vision of a united Europe. We are arguing that if it did come to pass it would be for the national reasons set out in this book and would therefore be far better founded than on the fantasy that national government has become perceived by its citizens as inappropriate, incapable and unwanted, however much it might justify such reproaches.

We have not excluded from our hypothesis the personalities and ideas of that small group of men now revered inside the Community as the fathers of united Europe: Konrad Adenauer, Alcide de Gasperi, Walter Hallstein, Robert Schuman, Paul-Henri Spaak and, first among his peers, Jean Monnet. For their admirers they are men who in the cause of a great idea burst the conventions of the European state system. But very little that we could treat as historical evidence is known about their opinions, as opposed to their actions.[6] Confining ourselves to the evidence we see these individuals, not as going against the trend of their times, but as exemplars of our argument, politicians who understood more clearly than their fellows that the post-war reconstruction and survival of the nation-state reposed on policies which might well require a certain surrender of national sovereignty for their effectiveness. Some, Monnet and Schuman for example, do seem to have eventually reached the conclusion that the day of the nation-state was closing, but only when they had fallen from all political power.

In general we have not seen the belief that a united Europe is in itself a desirable ideal as having any strong explanatory force outside its capacity to help in consensus-building in the post-war nation-state. For that reason we have not used as the basis for our hypothesis the intellectual history of this idea in earlier periods. There is, revealingly, virtually no serious intellectual history of the idea after 1945. Neither did we take into account the repeated assertions that western Europe has been moving towards some form of cultural and social uniformity since 1945 and that this is the real underlying force behind European integration. There has been no serious historical exploration of those themes either. This may be a more serious limitation on our hypothesis. But if the hypothesis stands the tests we have applied to it, we would argue that it could also serve as a framework for a more systematic historical exploration of the social (and cultural) trends in western Europe since 1945 to see whether they have in fact contributed towards the process of integration.

Belief in the ultimate value of a united Europe appears in our hypothesis merely as one possible element in national policy formulation. It establishes an interest group in each country which the nation-state can mobilize behind any policy choice which seems better advanced by means of integration. After all, to believe in a united Europe above any other cause, whatever it might mean in domestic politics, is a belief so risky as to appeal only to a restricted number of citizens at any time, and probably mainly to those with millenarian tendencies, a dangerous political constituency. Once allied to desired specific domestic objectives however, or, more strongly, once it becomes the thing that makes those objectives attainable, then the idea of a united Europe does become a more powerful explanation for much of western Europe's recent history.

Lest the reader should think this is a Bismarckian preference for state power over popular will, we should point out that the only defence for national government since 1945 which we have offered in the book is that it has better represented popular will than in the past, even if still only partially and imperfectly. That is, for us, the historical reason why it has survived. As our studies show, that survival has been finely balanced. In so far as they support our hypothesis, as in its essential outlines they do, they also imply that the balance would be no less fine and no less difficult to preserve for a supranational government, but also not impossible. Because it is on the positions taken by governments and political parties that our theory depends for its explanatory power, it makes sense that we should put such emphasis on government records both in the value we attribute to the existing literature and in our own research.

So much for the type of historical evidence we valued in establishing our views and in testing them by our own research. It does not seem to us to be unduly limited, other than by the problem that governments do succeed in keeping things secret. We do not exclude other kinds of evidence, if they can be discovered. Far from it, we are concerned to establish a more operative intellectual base from which they may be explored. If the theory we derive from that method could do that, it would not only demonstrate the superior strength of history as a vehicle for understanding modern political trends but would also serve as a powerful incentive to further systematic historical research on a broader front which might make that understanding still greater.

An overall conclusion from our historical studies is that the hypothesis from which we started is strengthened by the additional research presented here and does appear as the best foundation for a theory of European integration, but that it is also too simple. In defining the way national policy has been formulated since 1945, and taking that policy as a national interest pursued through the international system, we relied too heavily on the vote as the determinant of consensus-building. What our research shows is that in reality the consensus-building out of which national policy is formulated is not merely a matter of political parties competing for votes in a more democratic post-war state. The political coalitions which formulate the national interest are more complicated than that.

The national bureaucracy – the state machine – appears to play a big part too. This was strikingly the case in France and Italy where it had its own agenda; in the first case, the modernization and greater international competitiveness of industry, in the second, emigration. Popular support for this long-run programme in France was, to judge from the hesitations of French politicians about the common market, variable and sometimes tenuous. As for Italy no issue could have been more ambivalent than to strengthen allegiance to the state by making it easier for the population to leave. The ambiguities were less risky if such a policy remained strictly bureaucratic; it was too dangerous for the hustings. Organized interests, not necessarily democratic, played their role too. In the guise of the British steel industry they can be seen in chapter 5 thwarting the will of the state apparatus in a struggle which was not allowed to disturb voters, although it closely concerned European integration.

The hypothesis from which we started does not set an agenda for research into the process of integration alone, because the process of integration is not separable from the evolution of domestic politics. If we see policy formulation as a production process, in defining and pursuing the national interest the coalitions that formulate a national policy to be advanced through the international system reach the production frontier of national sovereignty. It is for that reason that one of the central debates about the Treaty of European Union is also the debate about how to inject further measures of democracy into the operations of complex modern societies. In our studies, where integration proves the best method for advancing the national interest, as it did in France, that national interest was not defined in the simple democratic way which our initial hypothesis implied. Citizens do not only change domestic priorities by voting, they change them in other ways too. And sometimes the priorities are changed, although perhaps not radically, in opposition to presumed majority opinion.

When we set out to test our hypothesis the choice of one topic was unavoidable: why did France sign the Treaties of Rome? There was no clear explanation of this in the existing literature, although there were certain suggestions, as Lynch points out, that it was actually the weakness of the French state that forced it into integration, or that it was a decision made as a result of the British withdrawal from the Suez invasion. The French government has delayed releasing the Foreign Ministry papers which might have gone some way to answering the question. Küsters, for example, is obliged to rely for the French side of the story of the negotiations for the common market treaty on speeches, memoirs and articles by politicians and on certain insights into the French negotiating position offered by those miscellaneous German archives, excluding the Foreign Ministry archives, to which he had access.[7] In the period between 1945 and 1952 France was the driving force behind the idea of European integration, as has been the case in many subsequent periods, yet it was also known that its attitude to the proposed common market treaty was for long a reticent one. This was a central problem for our hypotheses. From the little that was known from historical research in the archives of other countries, it was evident that in 1955 at the Messina conference, which is popularly regarded as the 'relaunch' of European integration, it was the French government which was the most reluctant to support the idea of a common market. It was evident too that this was still the case as late as summer 1956.

On the occasion of a special conference called by the Italian government in Rome in March 1987 to commemorate the signing of the treaties thirty years before, this gave rise to a sharp public dispute.[8] The one historian whose detailed work in French archives had brought him nearest to being able to resolve the conundrum of why France changed its position, Pierre Guillen, suggested that in all probability it was the sudden British termination under American pressure of the invasion of Egypt in November 1956 that led the French government to seek security in the alliance with the German Federal Republic and so abandon its objections to the common market treaty.[9] He was publicly and harshly repudiated in the conference by the French Foreign Minister at the time of the Suez invasion, Christian Pineau, and by Emile Noël, the *chef de cabinet* of Guy Mollet, the French Prime Minister of the time. Both asserted publicly that it had been the government's wish to adhere to the common market treaty from a much earlier date than the Suez invasion. The fierceness of their attacks led to protests from the assembled historians, on the grounds that the only worthwhile historical evidence was that assembled by Guillen and that it did seem to point to his conclusion.

Lynch however on the basis of new research confirms the memories of MM. Pineau and Noël. The diplomatic archives remain closed, but her evidence is drawn from other sources, the records of economic ministries, of the planning commissariat and of the inter-ministerial committee for European co-operation. By 1956 France, she argues, could go no further along the chosen path of national reconstruction without reshaping the international framework to make its domestic policy choices feasible. There was by then an irreconcilable clash of interests between the co-operative interdependence which OEEC represented and the national objectives of the French state apparatus, just as there was certain also to be if the Bretton Woods vision of one worldwide multilateral commercial and payments system were to be brought into reality, as the United Kingdom wished, and OEEC and EPU to be wound up leaving no special commercial and political arrangements in western Europe. Once the Dutch, and then Benelux, proposals for a common market had been accepted as a possible arrangement by the Federal Republic they offered France an economic way out of this trap, and one in accordance with the foreign policy objectives originally so boldly put into practice in 1950 with the Schuman proposals. The problem for France was to make sure that the common market proposals were adapted to meet its own policies: that they left some scope for national industrial policy, that they did not penalize French industry for the relatively high wage and social security costs it bore, and that they preserved the economic relationship between metropolitan France and its empire. When this did prove possible European integration was the logical way forward, whereas interdependence would have required drastic policy changes.

This conclusion is a particularly strong justification of our approach. The French Foreign Office was indeed on balance, as Guillen had perfectly correctly construed, opposed to the common market. So much for another frequently expressed critique of our approach, that the causes of European integration were primarily political, to be found in foreign policy narrowly defined and especially in France's foreign policy towards Germany. What drove France forward once more in 1956 down the path of European integration was the need to adjust the international framework to the long-run requirements of its economy, to find a way of persisting with economic planning whose primary objectives were wholly domestic, avoiding too abrupt a withdrawal of protection from some economic sectors and yet finding a way of increasing exports without having to adjust prices too violently. Foreign policy bowed to those economic imperatives. The ultimate goal of course remained an increase in French national power and influence in Europe and to that extent was a foreign policy objective too. But in this case foreign policy was first and foremost formed by the possibilities of domestic economic and social development. At the crucial moment it was not even made by the diplomats.

We now have the first account based on good evidence of why France signed the Treaties of Rome and thus of why the common market came into being. It not only shows how the formulation of the national interest was more complex than in our original simplified hypothesis, it shows also that the national interests which have underlain the process of integration are made up of positions taken by interest groups which are themselves compromises in consensus-building at a micro level before they become part of the greater compromise represented by a national policy. Not only was the French state apparatus divided on what the national interest in respect of the common market treaty was, the sectional interest groups who sought to affect its decisions were also divided.

For example, the modernization of France as conceived by the national bureaucracy involved an attempt to overcome the vested interests which had secured agricultural protection since the 1890s. This however was abandoned in the face of the severe dollar shortage in 1947; any food grown in France was effectively dollar-saving because it substituted for imports from North America. Agricultural modernization remained the objective, but it was to be carried out within the existing politico-economic structure. Prices set to protect the least efficient meant that surpluses might be produced which, if they were not going to be a drain on the public purse, would have to be exported. Initially this could be done through export contracts which were also dollar-saving for France's trade partners. But by 1956 a more secure international framework for modernizing the agricultural sector while not radically disturbing its existing politico-economic structure had to be found. It cannot be said that this was in the interests of all French agriculture. Not disturbing the politico-economic structure meant continuing with subsidized surpluses of grain and sugar, the products of the arable farming sector and its larger farms, the sector to which protection since 1892 had diverted resources, and where France stood the least chance of producing export surpluses at prices genuinely competitive with world prices. The rural riots of 1951 and 1953, the revolt of smaller farmers whose cash crops came from the livestock sector, show that not only did the state bureaucracy have to compromise its idea of modernization to accommodate the political importance of agricultural voters, but that agriculture was also able to get its way as a corporate vested interest without using the ballot box (French farmers in fact spread their vote widely among all political parties), and that when it did so it was at first because of the greater weight in policy formulation of one particular sector of French agriculture which was not the most numerous in terms of votes. Agricultural modernization was, further-more, only one aspect, and not the most important, of what the state apparatus meant by modernization. Evidently, in exploring the origins of integration along these lines we are also exploring the nature of post-war national democratic states as a whole.

The original hypothesis still stands; it is the nature of domestic social and economic choice which pushed France down the path of integration. But research now should concentrate on more detailed investigations of the political economy of that choice. It should be noted that one development that tends to confirm Lynch's view of the importance of agricultural modernization to the story was France's resolute resistance to any modification of the Treaty of Rome which would have weakened the initial provision it made for medium-term export contracts as a way of venting agricultural surpluses before a common agricultural policy could be devised. This was a strong French objection to the first British attempts to merge the common market into a wider free trade area.

If France has been conventionally regarded as the driving force behind further European integration, Denmark became fixed in the public eye in 1992 as the chief barrier to it. It was for this reason that we sought to test our hypothesis by a study of Danish attitudes to both interdependence and integration in Europe since the end of the Second World War. The method is the same, an attempt to relate foreign policy positions to the political economy of domestic consensus building. Sørensen's study reveals three things which were not widely known or understood.

One part of the Danish agricultural interest, which in its totality still in 1956 outweighed the industrial interest electorally as well as finding a greater sympathy in the public consciousness because of its central role in the Danish national myth, was ready even before the Treaties of Rome to consider membership of the common market as economically advantageous under certain circumstances. The story in most narrative accounts of European integration, that because of the importance of the British market to Danish agricultural exports the opinions of Danish agriculture were solely determined by British foreign policy positions, and that Denmark was a solid British ally against integration, is not true. It was, rather, the other sectors of the economy, manufacturing industry in particular, management and unions alike, which feared inclusion in a common market with the German Federal Republic.

For those who feared that common market there was always a substitute, or so they hoped, in some form or other of a Nordic Union. The persistent appearance since 1947 of proposals for some form of customs union between Denmark, Norway and Sweden has been treated in an offhand way by historians as an idea that was manifestly impractical because so small a proportion of the total trade of the Scandinavian countries was with each other. Sørensen shows that this observation has only restricted value; in the trade in those modern manufactures which Denmark was striving to develop, and protect from German competition, the nordic market might have sufficed. Denmark thus appeared to have more ways of shaping the international framework to accommodate its national policy choices than France.

This raises the whole issue of the relationship of agriculture to the other sectors in post-war Denmark. Here the convention has been to explain Danish attitudes to Europe on the basis that agriculture remained the dominant political interest there in the 1950s and that this only began to change in the 1960s. Sørensen argues that this is a misconception and that from 1945 onwards Danish governments, especially when they had a Social Democratic component, were deeply anxious that so predominant an agricultural sector, even though it had a high level of productivity and a low level of export prices, was not a satisfactory basis for the survival of the state. All attempts to create a more viable national economic balance for the future exposed however the lack of a clear political consensus about what was to be done. The relatively low rates of growth of national income, which could well have had as one of their causes this inability to construct a coherent long-run national policy, exacerbated the problem.

The conclusions from our study of Denmark not only support our hypothesis, they even seem to bear out the restricted predictive capacity of our theory. But as in the case of France they direct us towards a closer study of the micro-level compromises and consensuses that go towards making up the national policies that competed with each other at the macro level for acceptance as the prime expression of national interest. The political parties in Sørensen's story, which throughout are the main actors, making and remaking coalitions and so continually readjusting Denmark's policies in Europe, over so long a spell of time do not consistently represent the same socio-economic interest groups. The nature of those groups will itself change over that period, even if their party loyalties do not. Political parties might receive consistent support from the same socio-economic interest groups over a long period of time, but opinion in those groups changes because of changing economic circumstances. Danish agriculture was not, Sørensen shows, a monolith; it was divided. The same could be shown to prove true of manufacturing: some industries believed that a Nordic Union would suit their purposes while others had less fear of the common market of the Six. In this light opinions within the political parties might have been potentially more volatile than our simplified hypothesis allows. The same of course would be true for other countries. French governments did carry out detailed enquiries into the ability of each major industrial sector to compete in a common market of the Six, but did not entirely believe the results. Their most credible aspect was that opinion inside French manufacturing was deeply divided. The clear policy positions taken by political parties and governments which in our theory propel nations towards integration or interdependence, or even away from both, actually rest on divided and inconclusive opinions in many, perhaps most, of the groups for whose political loyalty parties and governments bid.

This is confirmed by Ranieri's study of the attitudes of the Italian and British steel industries. In fact, once we descend to the level of a single industry the simplifications which our approach imposes stand even more revealed. The divisions over adherence to the Treaty of Paris inside the Italian steel industry, and over the proposed 'association' with the Coal, Iron and Steel Community inside the British steel industry, were as wide as divisions within the national parliaments. As Ranieri shows, the divisions were most usually, although no doubt not invariably, related to the exact nature of the business the firm was in. But they were also related to the attitude of individual firms to the intricate relationship with government which had developed. Some thought that integration under the High Authority would prevent a return to the arrangements of the pre-war International Steel Export Cartel. Others thought that this problem could be partly circumvented and that the sacrifice of some advantages of that cartel might be recompensed by the advantages of the common market. Some thought the High Authority the final intolerable example of the tendency of post-war government to impose its will on industry. Others thought there might be some reinforcement of their position from this association.

The state-owned sector of the Italian steel industry was able in this uncertainty to use the Italian government to make the common market mean what it wanted it to mean, a satisfactory international framework for the expansion of domestic 'integral-cycle' steel production. Ranieri implies that important sectors of the British steel industry, had they accepted 'association' with the Community in the meaningful sense in which it was first entertained by the British government, might have been able also to use that framework to advance their own objectives. They chose instead a strictly national path, rejecting not only integration but even a closer interdependence with the continental market. They did so against the wishes of government, whose economic policy-makers, unlike those of France or the German Federal Republic, gave in before the opposition of management and unions alike to any 'association' that was not merely cosmetic. In both France and the Federal Republic government used the divisions of opinion inside the steel industry to find allies for the policy of integration. In the event the arrangements were highly beneficial, at least in the 1950s, to French steel exports, while German steel makers were so busy struggling to meet the surge of domestic demand that some of their more vehement objections to the Treaty of Paris between 1950 and 1952 seemed irrelevant between 1953 and 1958. The implication of Ranieri's work is that the British government too could have exploited the divisions in the industry had 'association' been a high policy priority, but it did not really try.

Nevertheless, complex though the formulation of national interest at lower levels than government undoubtedly is, our studies seem to show that the preponderant influence on the formulation of national policy and the national interest was always a response to demands from electors. Even in the case of France where the state bureaucracy imposed its concepts of modernization from above, the common market treaty had to incorporate an additional international guarantee of national policies which had welled up from below: high industrial wages, high social security benefits of which a larger part than elsewhere was contributed by the employer, a shorter official working week than elsewhere, equal pay for the sexes. Integration could not be imposed from above by a minority. The view, of which many in Britain are fond, that it was in some way a semi-secret conspiracy of like-minded politicians is an absurdity. Such a view could only be held by those who believe the foreign policy of a modern state can be a secret and élitist choice which can ignore the national consensuses on which post-war states have been refounded. When it failed to appreciate in time that France would indeed sign the common market treaty the British Foreign Office was itself a victim of that mistaken belief.

Most accounts of the growing interdependence between developed economies after 1945 put heavy emphasis on the facts that commodity trade between the more industrialized economies grew in value more rapidly than other categories of international trade, that this was accompanied by continuous reductions in barriers to trade, and that it was followed by a great increase in capital flows between those countries, so reversing the trend of the 1930s. Yet a phenomenon even more striking is the increase in flows of people between them, for this does not merely indicate a return to an earlier trend, but its dimensions suggest we should consider it as a wholly new development. This phenomenon is often seen as a profound underlying cause of integration. Yet, as Romero argues, it was the outcome of national policy choices rather than a cause of them.

Tourists, because of the foreign exchange and additional employment they brought, were overtly encouraged by the receiving countries, and, for the same reason in reverse, sometimes restricted by the sending countries, some of which maintained tight controls on the amount of currency which a tourist could export. As the ideology of economic growth became more pervasive and increases in labour inputs were seen as essential in conditions close to full employment to increases in overall national output, policies, at first very selectively, turned towards encouraging immigration. When the huge internal migration from agriculture to the other sectors began to slow down in the early 1960s, and when unemployment in the German Federal Republic also fell, an inflow of foreign workers was seen as even more necessary. But the fact that policy and national interest were ultimately shaped by pressures from below was never seen more starkly than in 1967 with the return of unemployment and with the violent social protests against immigrants. The striking phenomenon that western Europe for a decade and a half replaced the United States as the main recipient area for immigrants was policy-induced. So was the drastic and sudden reduction in immigration which brought that period to an end. In both cases it could well be, to repeat Romero's phrase, the most striking of all attempts 'to shape the terms of continental interdependence in accordance with the perceived national interest'.

From the end of the war it seemed imperative to the centrist coalitions which governed Italy to export people. Yet the clash of Italian policy with that of the other five member states of the European Community meant that integration was of no significant help in advancing this national priority. Even when at the start of the 1960s immigrants were actively sought, member states retained complete national sovereignty over immigration policies, which were indeed widely different between them. The perceived necessities of national policy were co-ordinated, but no more than that. There was no spillover from the establishment of the Community machinery to effect technical solutions into the concession of greater political powers over the labour market to the Community itself. The riots against immigrants in Copenhagen, London, Marseilles and elsewhere as the European labour market began to slacken perhaps showed that this was well judged by governments. There was a consensus in favour of economic growth, but economic growth remained a national, not to say nationalist, conception. One element in the support for it was that it promised high employment. It was the national labour market that mattered, a message which trade unions were quick to deliver to the parliamentary centre and to which politicians were equally quick to respond. Shifts in migration policy were only what governments found to be possible and Italy was left to solve its problems within the older pre-integrationist framework. In explaining integration from above, from the standpoint of domestic policies formulated, decided and put into action, we only learn that the frontier of national sovereignty is determined from below, even if votes and voters are less important than our original hypothesis suggested.

If British government in the 1950s, usually regarded as firmly seated in power, so soon abandoned any attempt to shape an international policy towards a steel industry which it half controlled when that policy was opposed, the role of government initiative in policy selection becomes a difficult one to assess. How far a government is willing to impose a choice of international framework on any domestic interest-group is a function of how many different, and in its own eyes important, policy objectives it can attain if it goes into battle against vocal and energetic opposition. There is all the difference in the world, in this perspective, between a United Kingdom government, which was opposed to integration in western Europe but might have found some closer interdependence between its steel industry and those of the Six mildly favourable to its other diplomatic initiatives, and a Federal German government whose need for integration to bestow full sovereignty and equality of rights with other western European governments was so compelling that it could not allow the opposition of much of the German steel industry to prevent the ratification of the Treaty of Paris. The Belgian government, because the long-run dangers of staying out of the Community were so various and great, faced down an even noisier opposition from its own coal industry.[10]

These studies, then, while confirming the value of a historically based theory of integration as a key to the accurate understanding of post-war European developments, also suggest that it would be dangerous to use it as a basis for prediction without much more detailed research into the way that national policy choices emerge. If we take a view of opinion about interdependence and integration from the top, the political parties having already decided the domestic policies attempt to put them into practice and secure support for them at the international level. But if we take a view from the bottom, the socio-economic interest groups which support these parties appear as themselves divided, and opinion within them may be finely balanced. Small shifts of opinion at the micro level might thus become decisive shifts at the macro level. It is only necessary to consider the waverings of the two major British political parties on the question of the Maastricht Treaty since the Danish referendum to see the point.

We argued in chapter 1 that the theory we were proposing could have no predictive value, even if when historically tested it proved robust, unless it could be coupled with a further theory which could predict the choice of national domestic policies, but that if these choices could be predicted our theory could then predict whether the outcome would be integration or not. The whole difficulty of predicting national choices of domestic policy lies however in understanding the detail of the choices made by an almost infinite complexity of interest groups, activated by a complicated set of socio-economic, cultural and political motives at the lower level. This might seem a pompous way of saying that more facts are always valuable. But it is more than that, because it elaborates our claim that the historical approach we have taken is not merely a way of analysing the relations between western European states since 1945.

In identifying the particular changes which it would be necessary to analyse to understand why countries sacrifice a measure of national sovereignty we are also identifying those currents of change which are most central to the evolution of the nation-state, which determine its capacity to survive. What was it that made the different groups of Danish agricultural producers change their opinions about the optimum international framework for their country? The answer implicit in Sørensen's analysis is markets, together perhaps with changes in the overall status of agriculture in the Danish polity. Or, to ask a counterfactual question, what might have shifted opinion in German trade unions against integration, which might in turn have meant that the Treaty of Paris would not have been ratified by the Bundestag? One answer is offered by Romero in chapter 2: a genuine common market in labour of the kind the Italian government wished. To put another counterfactual; if Italy had not been granted the exemptions from the common market in steel for which it negotiated in the Treaty of Paris, would the industrial modernizers who made policy for the state steel sector have joined the private sector opponents of the treaty? The implication of Ranieri's argument is that they would.

To take but one example of how our approach could be used to identify changes which were crucial both to the post-war reassertion of the nation-state and to the choice of integration, we need only point to the still unexplained mystery of French farmers' support for the Treaty of Rome. They had been deeply suspicious of government plans to expand agricultural output after the war, fearing these would only culminate in the same glut of produce that had held down prices in the early 1930s. They had stayed aloof from and hostile to discussions between the French and Dutch ministries of agriculture between 1950 and 1952 on the possibility of a common market for agricultural produce in western Europe, leaving the plans which had been formulated in that part of the French state bureaucracy to collapse.[11] Their professional representatives still opposed as late as 1955 proposals for any common European organization for agriculture. Could the decision for integration have been made if French farmers had persisted in their public hostility to it? They and their dependants were still more than a quarter of the electorate. Why did they change their attitude?

Ultimately the explanation of both integration and the evolution of the post-war nation must be a complex social history. But we need to know first what it is we want to find out about society, and since our theory seems to give an accurate guide to which shifts of opinion take on political importance as far as the choice of integration (or not) is concerned, it defines the questions we should ask. This seems to us an essential agenda. Whether the nation-state will survive is now a matter of almost daily discussion in the newspapers. A history which could help to provide the answer seems to us more useful than the observation of sexual exoticism or the semantic discussion of the trivia of daily life to which social history has now mostly turned. The capacity of historical analysis to explain the course of European integration, and perhaps even to predict it, is surely far from exhausted and the high value we are claiming for history as a medium for understanding present international trends might eventually prove an underestimate.

Obviously we see European integration as something made in Europe springing from the evolution of the European nation-state. For that reason there was one further question about the frontier of national sovereignty that we could not avoid. Virtually all scholars accept that in the capitalist world the rules of the international order have been set since 1945 by the United States, and particularly so for the first two post-war decades. It is well known that the foreign policy of the United States from 1947 onwards was ardently in favour of European 'integration', without being entirely clear what was intended by this word.[12] It has even been maintained that the European Community would not have been born without the support which the US government gave to it, and also that it was continuing American support for an 'integrated' Europe which ultimately led to the Treaties of Rome.[13] By definition we see the role of the United States in the story as much less important than this. But did its early support for European 'integration' create a unique circumstance? What happens when in one region of the world the domestic evolution of nation-states requires so drastic a change in international relations? Can a group of relatively rich and powerful nation-states decide to adjust the frontier of national sovereignty in certain areas to their own powerful advantage, on commodity trade for example where together the EC countries are the world's most important trading bloc, without normally encountering destructive opposition?

Very recently, as historians have managed to win access to hitherto unreleased archives, the extent of the opposition in the US government to a foreign policy which so favoured European integration has been revealed. Some economic agencies of government, the Treasury Department, the Federal Reserve Board, the Department of Commerce and the Export-Import Bank, were sceptical throughout the 1950s of the value to the United States of a policy which encouraged an integrated bloc of countries in western Europe allowed to operate within their own international settlements mechanism, the European Payments Union, and with their own commercial rules, which for example permitted widespread discrimination against American exports. This, they thought, was no way back to the USA's primary international objective, proclaimed and established at Bretton Woods, of a worldwide multilateral trade and settlements mechanism. The Department of State had to rely on the successor agencies of the Economic Cooperation Administration for support for its commitment to integration. In the circumstance where the President himself was a firm believer in European integration, this was enough. But as Romero shows, it was this powerful questioning within the US government of whether European integration actually was in the USA's national interest that eventually altered the American stance.

As soon as it became obvious that a common market of the Six would institutionalize their individual systems of agricultural protection at the international level the US Department of Agriculture added its weight to the protests against the established foreign policy. In fact the American government's attitude to the common market treaty was detached and distant compared to its active intervention in certain details of the Treaty of Paris and its energetic support for that treaty as a whole. The majority of economic departments clearly preferred the interdependence of OEEC as a European framework and saw continued American interest in an integrated Europe as ill considered. With the Euratom treaty it was another matter; this seemed to offer the United States the possibility of controlling the spread of nuclear technology while remaining the technological leader and principal exporter in the field. But that, of course, was one reason why the Euratom treaty proved so insignificant; France wanted independent nuclear weapons and German industry wanted technological independence.

The grounds for American support of the European Economic Community were strategic, and when the Cold War dominated, that was decisive. The circumstances in which the European nation-states were able partially to adjust the frontier of national sovereignty in their own interest without incurring too severe an opposition from the international system as a whole were therefore more favourable than might normally be the case. Furthermore, as Romero argues, policy formulation in the United States did not take sufficient account of the USA's own increasing interdependence with the rest of the capitalist world. This attitude changed only when the US balance of payments deficit increased by a factor of about 350 per cent in the recession year 1958. The cause was almost entirely the increased deficit in the balance of commodity trade. And within this increased trade deficit the most striking aspect was that in a recession year, contrary to all experience since 1918, the value of manufactured imports from western Europe rose steeply. From 1958 onwards awareness of the USA's interdependence with the international system began to replace the sentiment of hegemony which had allowed such uncritical support for European integration.

The European states were perhaps lucky in another sense too. The ideal of a united Europe was appealing at many levels in the United States. All sorts of false analogies could be drawn with the grand march of American history. A far-flung liberal market in which ideals of freedom and democracy happily combined with material prosperity was part of the USA's own self-image, and would therefore have been a painful target for criticism, especially when that self-image served to bind American society closer in the task of winning the Cold War. If the reality of an integrated Europe was quite different, there was an understandable reluctance at first to listen too attentively to those US government departments which said so.

But this does not exclude the possibility that similarly powerful domestic forces in other sets of countries could also adjust the established frontier of national sovereignty, if they are strong enough. If only one proof were needed of the strength of the forces in national policy leading to integration, it could be found in the fact that it has taken almost twenty-five years of pressure from the USA to change the Common Agricultural Policy of the European Community, and that that change has only come because there are no longer enough European farm families to make it worthwhile for politicians to defend their interests to the same degree as before. Fortunate though the circumstances of the 1950s were for the integration of western European states, there does not seem any theoretical ground for arguing that the international order cannot be again changed by integration as well as by the disintegration which has added nine new national frontiers to the European map in two years.

We close our book at what looks a decisive moment. The banner of European Union, the Treaty of Maastricht, still flies, too tattered to be distinguishable. If Denmark marches under it, that is only because it is so tattered. The United Kingdom, responsible for the initial damage, but forced to march in order because it could find no other international framework which would support its future development, displays all the bitterness and spite springing from that situation. Its government announces repeated plans to lead Europe in directions in which it manifestly does not wish to be led, while demands for a referendum become more insistent. Opinion is strong in Germany against the monetary union and sometimes takes the form of demands for a referendum on that sole issue. As this book goes to press, France has confirmed by a majority of only 51.7 to 48.3 per cent in a national referendum its pursuit, however wavering, for forty-five years of the same European objectives.

But this sudden taste for referendums cannot mark a new stage in the history and theory of integration. Even though it submits the policies emerging from complex alliances and consensuses to the test of a single vote on the one issue of national sovereignty, the national interest will continue to be defined within more systematic constitutional procedures. It is by their votes in those systematic procedures that citizens will continue to exercise the preponderant influence in defining the national interest by shaping national policy. Those systematic procedures and the way citizens choose within them are defined by history. By their choices about what the nation-state is for, it is they who will continue to define the frontier of national sovereignty.

Notes

1 INTERDEPENDENCE OR INTEGRATION? A NATIONAL CHOICE

Alan S. Milward and Vibeke Sørensen

1 'It is quite true that societies caught up in the process of translating industrial potential into satisfaction of consumers' wants and diffusing the new goods and services on a widening basis are likely to generate powerful checks against aggression and increased willingness to accept dilutions of sovereignty to preserve a reasonably comfortable *status quo.*' W. W. Rostow, *The Stages of Economic Growth. A Non-Communist Manifesto* (Cambridge, 1960), p. 136.

2 K. W. Deutsch *et al., Political Community and the North Atlantic Area* (Princeton, 1957).

3 For a fuller account of the evolution of such theories, A. J. R. Groom and P. Taylor (eds), *Functionalism, Theory and Practice in International Relations* (London, 1975).

4 E. B. Haas, *Uniting of Europe* (Stanford, 1968).

5 E. B. Haas, 'The Uniting of Europe and the Uniting of Latin America', *Journal of Common Market Studies*, 5, 1967; E. B. Haas and P. Schmitter, 'Economic and Differential Patterns of Political Integration: Projections about Unity in Latin America', *International Organisation*, 18, 1964.

6 This circle consisted mainly of Ernst B. Haas and some of his most influential students, Philippe Schmitter, Leon S. Lindberg and Joseph S. Nye, and was centred in California, the World Peace Foundation and the influential journal *International Organisation.*

7 Even in retrospect neo-functionalists have rejected any connection between their theory and cold war politics. See for example E. B. Haas, *The Obsolescence of Regional Integration Theory* (Berkeley, 1975). For an unusually frank self-criticism see Joseph S. Nye's introduction to J. S. Nye, *Peace in Parts. Integration and Conflict in Regional Organization* (New York, 1987).

8 P. Taylor, 'The New Dynamics of EC Integration in the 1980s', in J. Lodge (ed.), *The European Community and the Challenge of the Future* (London, 1989); S. George, *Politics and Policy in the European Community* (Oxford, 1991); R. O. Keohane and S. Hoffmann, 'Conclusion: Community Politics and Institutional Change', in W. Wallace (ed.), *The Dynamics of European Integration* (London, 1990).

9   T. Parsons, *The Social System* (Glencoe, 1951); D. Easton, *The Political System* (New York, 1953); D. Bell, *The End of Ideology* (New York, 1960).

10 'Political integration is the process whereby political actors in several distinct national settings are persuaded to shift their loyalties, expectations and political activities towards a new centre, whose institutions possess or demand jurisdiction over pre-existing national states.' Haas, *Uniting of Europe*, op. cit., p. 16.

11 For works relying on historical evidence which take that point of view, J. Gillingham, *Coal, Steel, and the Rebirth of Europe, 1945–1955. The Germans and French from Ruhr Conflict to Economic Community* (Cambridge, 1991); A. S. Milward, *The Reconstruction of Western Europe, 1945–1951* (London, 1984); R. Poidevin, *Robert Schuman, Homme d'état, 1886–1963* (Paris, 1986).

12 For a discussion of the influence of private foundations and the US government in promoting behavioural research during the Cold War, T. Ball, 'The Politics of Social Science in Postwar America', in L. May (ed.), *Recasting America. Culture and Politics in the Age of the Cold War* (Chicago, 1987).

13 'Spillover depends on prior inter-governmental bargains. When those bargains are fresh and viable, pressures appear for intensified co-operation in sectors where the bargains were made, and for extended co-operation in related sectors. But these pressures by no means automatically lead to common policies, and they certainly do not necessarily create new centralized institutions. Indeed for the latter to happen, a new set of inter-governmental bargains – perhaps generated in part by prior spillover pressures but by no means preordained by them – must be consummated. Until the end of 1992 spillover pressures are likely to be evident in the European Community, as the bargain of the Single European Act works itself out.' Keohane and Hoffmann, 'Conclusion', op. cit., p. 293. Although the pressures are indeed evident, their outcome as yet is not.

14 The most general discussion, although exaggerated and in parts incorrect, remains that of A. Shonfield, *Modern Capitalism: The Changing Balance of Public and Private Power* (Oxford, 1965). For a more specific study in the case of France, B. Cazès and P. Mioche (eds), *Modernisation ou décadence: études, témoignages et documents sur la planification française* (Aix-en-Provence, 1990); in the case of the Netherlands, H. de Liagre Böhl, J. Nekkers and L. Slot (eds), *Nederland industrialiseert!: politieke en ideologiese strijd rondom het naoorlogse industrialisatiebeleid 1945–1955* (Nijmegen, 1981).

15 J. J. Kaplan and G. Schleiminger, *The European Payments Union: Financial Diplomacy in the 1950s* (Oxford, 1989); R. Triffin, *Europe and the Money Muddle* (New Haven, 1957).

16 The issues are discussed in A. S. Milward, *The European Rescue of the Nation-State* (London, 1992), pp. 119 ff.

17 J. E. Meade, H. H. Liesner and S. J. Wells, *Case Studies in European Economic Union. The Mechanics of Integration* (London, 1962); Milward, *European Rescue*, op. cit., p. 46.

18 B. E. Hill, *The Common Agricultural Policy; Past, Present and Future* (London, 1984); for a more detailed historical account, Milward, *European Rescue*, op. cit., pp. 228 ff.

19 We here refer to the distinction conveyed by the concepts 'traité-loi' and 'traité de procédure'. R. Reuter, *Organisations Européennes* (2nd edn, Paris, 1970), p. 188.

20 See for example P. Taylor, *The Limits of European Integration* (London, 1983), pp. 21–2.

21 'This Treaty marks a new stage in the process creating an ever closer union ...' Treaty on European Union, 9–10 December 1991.

22 On the priorities determined by the Interlaken principles, F. Laursen (ed.), *EFTA and the EC: Implications of 1992* (Maastricht, 1988).

23 For an interesting discussion of the convergence–diversity dilemma which supports our hypothesis, H. Kastendiek, 'Convergence or a Persistent Diversity of National Politics', in C. Crouch and D. Marquand (eds), *The Politics of 1992* (Oxford, 1990).

24 R. Aron, 'Old Nations, New Europe', in S. R. Graubard (ed.), *A New Europe?* (Boston, 1964); S. Hoffmann, 'Obstinate or Obsolete? The Fate of the Nation State and the Case of Western Europe', *Daedalus*, 95, 1966.

25 S. Bulmer and W. Wessels, *The European Council. Decision-making in European Politics* (London, 1987).

26 T. Pedersen, 'Political Change in the European Community. The Single European Act as a Case of System Transformation', *Cooperation and Conflict*, 27, 1992; J. Tranholm-Mikkelsen, 'Neo-functionalism: Obstinate or Obsolete? A Reappraisal in the Light of the New Dynamism of the EC', *Millenium*, 20, 1991.

27 The most detailed investigation so far of the negotiations leading up to the Single European Act rejects the neo-functionalist interpretation and emphasizes the role of national governments, especially of the large member states, and the convergence of national policies. A. Moravcsik, 'Negotiating the Single European Act: National Interests and Conventional Statecraft in the European Community', *International Organisation*, 45, 1991.

28 P. Cecchini, *The European Challenge: The Benefits of a Single Market* (Aldershot, 1988); M. Emerson (ed.), *The Economics of 1992: An Assessment of the Potential Economic Effects of Completing the Internal Market of the European Community* (Luxemburg, 1988).

29 L. Tsoukalis, *The New European Economy: The Politics and Economics of Integration* (Oxford, 1991) gives as good a historical account of these manoeuvres as is possible on present evidence.

30 George, *Politics and Policy*, op. cit., p. 188. Economists disagree over this issue. Some find that the EMS as it exists will be able to 'function smoothly even after liberalization of capital controls': D. Gros and N. Thygesen, *The EMS: Achievements, Current Issues and Directions for the Future*, Centre for European Policy Studies Paper, no. 35 (Brussels, 1988). Others believe that liberalization will require monetary integration: T. Padoa-Schioppa, 'The European Monetary System: A Long-Term View', in F. Giavazzi *et al.*, *The European Monetary System* (Cambridge, 1988).

2 MIGRATION AS AN ISSUE IN EUROPEAN INTERDEPENDENCE AND INTEGRATION: THE CASE OF ITALY

Federico Romero

1 For an overview of the still scarce theoretical approaches to the relationship between migrations and international relations see C. Mitchell, 'International Migration, International Relations and Foreign Policy', *International Migration Review*, XXIII, 3, 1989, pp. 681–708.

2 See United Nations, *Labour Supply and Migration in Europe. Demographic Dimensions 1950–1975 and Prospects* (New York, 1979); International Labour Office, 'Recent Developments in the Clearance of Manpower between Western European Countries', *International Labour Review*, LXXIX, 2, 1959, pp. 173–88.

3 The literature on post-war migration from southern to western Europe is very large. Among the most significant analyses and interpretations see: W. R. Böhning, *The Migration of Workers in the United Kingdom and the European Community* (London, 1972); W. R. Böhning and D. Maillat, *The Effects of the Employment of Foreign Workers* (Paris, 1974); S. Castles and G. Kosack, *Immigrant Workers and Class Structure in Western Europe* (London, 1973); M. Livi-Bacci (ed.), *The Demographic and Social Patterns of Emigration from the Southern European Countries* (Florence, 1972); S. Paine, *Exporting Workers: the Turkish Case* (Cambridge, 1974); E. Reyneri, *La catena migratoria. Il ruolo dell'emigrazione nel mercato del lavoro di arrivo e di esodo* (Bologna, 1979); R. Rogers (ed.), *Guests Come to Stay. The Effects of European Labor Migration on Sending and Receiving Countries* (Boulder, 1985).

4 Democrazia Cristiana, *I Congressi nazionali della Democrazia Cristiana* (Rome, 1959), pp. 222–31, 248–57, 315.

5 'Programma economico italiano a lungo termine 1948–49, 1952–53 presentato dal Governo italiano all'OECE nell'ottobre 1948', in the Ministry of the Budget, *La programmazione economica in Italia* (Rome, 1966), vol. I, pp. 3–100.

6 Ministry of Foreign Affairs (Direzione Generale dell'Emigrazione), *Emigrazione italiana (Situazione, prospettive, problemi) 31 marzo 1949* (Rome, 1949).

7 For an extensive discussion of this argument see F. Romero, *Emigrazione e integrazione europea 1945–1973* (Rome, 1991), ch. 2.

8 See M. Weiner, 'On International Migration and International Relations', *Population and Development Review*, XI, 3, 1985, pp. 411–55, on the theoretical and political relevance of immigration controls for the exertion of sovereignty.

9 On the main features of these agreements see: International Labour Office, 'Postwar Manpower Problems in Europe', *International Labour Review*, LV, 6, 1947, pp. 485–511; International Labour Office, 'Recent Developments in the Clearance of Manpower', op. cit.; D. Silletti, *Libera circolazione della manodopera fra gli stati membri della CEE* (Milan, 1962).

10 See Public Records Office, London, Ministry of Labour (hereafter PRO-LAB), 13/722 and 13/817.

11 'Memorandum italiano sul "surplus" della manodopera', submitted to OEEC in 1950, annexe 1 to *Documentazione sul problema della*

sovrapopolazione presentata al Consiglio d'Europa, Archivio Storico del Ministero degli Esteri (Italy), Dir. Gen. Affari Politici (hereafter AS MAE-DGAP), 1950–7, b. 333, f. Consiglio d'Europa'.

12 See Romero, *Emigrazione*, op. cit., pp. 43–7 for a more detailed account of these events.

13 European Coal and Steel Community, *Traité instituant la Communauté Européenne du Charbon et de l'Acier* (Brussels, 1958). The figures on Italian coal-miners in Belgium are from the Belgian *Bulletin de Statistique*, July–December 1951.

14 Dir. Gen. Emigrazione, Rome, circular instructions of 29 May 1953 and 21 June 1954, b. 256, f. 'CECA 1953' and b. 334, f. 'CECA 1954' respectively, in AS MAE-DGAP, 1950–57; Archives Générales C.C.E., Florence, CEAB 1/1649, 1/1653, 1/1660, and CM 1/1954/194–9.

15 European Coal and Steel Community, *Obstacles à la mobilité des travailleurs et problèmes sociaux de réadaptation* (Luxemburg, 1957); European Coal and Steel Community (Commission des Affaires Sociales), *Rapport sur la migration et la libre circulation des travailleurs dans la Communauté, par A. Bertrand* (Luxemburg, 1957); R. Ranieri, 'L'espansione alla prova del negoziato. L'industria italiana e la Comunità del carbone e dell'acciaio 1945–1955' (unpublished PhD dissertation, European University Institute, Florence, 1988), pp. 282–7.

16 For the discussion in the Commission for the European Political Community, Paris 12 December 1953 – 8 March 1954, see 'Rapporto ai Ministri degli affari esteri. Seconda parte, questioni economiche', AS MAE-DGAP, 1950–7, b. 333 f. 'CPE'. Also M. Dumoulin, 'L'émergence du facteur Europe dans la politique de l'immigration de la Belgique à l'égard des italiens au début des années cinquante', in M. Dumoulin (ed.), *Mouvements et politiques migratoires en Europe depuis 1945: le cas italien* (Brussels, 1989), pp. 53–64.

17 On trade unions' attitudes see International Confederation of Free Trade Unions, *Report of the Third World Congress* (Brussels, 1953), pp. 494–501; B. Barnouin, *The European Labour Movement and European Integration* (London, 1986), pp. 4–5; C. R. Beever, *European Unity and the Trade Union Movements* (Leiden, 1960), p. 59.

18 See US Department of State, *Foreign Relations of the United States (hereafter FRUS)*, 1952–4, vol. V, 1, p. 107 and vol. VI, 1, p. 10.

19 OEEC, *Europe. The Way Ahead* (Paris, 1952), p. 191.

20 See OEEC, Groupe de Travail sur la liberalisation des mouvements de main-d'oeuvre, 'Projet de rapport établi par le Secretariat, Première Révision', Paris, 12 August 1952, in AS MAE-Verbali OECE, 1952, b. 60; telegram n. 8923 from Cattani to the Ministry of Foreign Affairs, Paris, 22 July 1952 in AS MAE-DGAP, 1950–7, 'Fondo cassaforte', f. 530, 'OECE 1952'; Public Records Office, Foreign Office (hereafter PRO-FO), 371/100286/M4914-3.

21 See PRO-FO, 371/100286/M4914-6, -9, -13, -14, -15, -19; OEEC, Groupe de Travail, 'Projet', op. cit. G. Malagodi to A. de Gasperi, Paris, 28 July 1952, in AS MAE-DGAP, 1950–7, b. 167, f. 'OECE 1952.'

22 Telegram 65/53041/c from Giusti to various embassies, Rome, 23 July 1953, and telegram 65/80172/c from the Dir. Gen. Emigrazione to various embassies, Rome, 20 October 1953, both in AS MAE-DGAP, 1950–7, b. 256, f. 'OECE 1953'. Also OECD, *The OECD and International Migration* (Paris, 1975), pp. 7–12.

23 See 'Notiziario sulle attività dell'OECE. Gennaio–febbraio 1956', p. 28, in AS MAE-DGAP, 1950–7, b. 480, f. 'OECE 1956'. *First Report*, Paris, 3 March 1953 and *General Report*, Paris, 4 June 1956 by the OEEC Manpower Liberalization Group, in PRO-LAB, 13/990.

24 OEEC Sixth Report, *From Recovery Towards Economic Strength* (Paris, 1955), vol. I, p. 19. France alone represented a partial exception due to the hospitable tradition of its constitutional system and its concern for a limited demographic growth; the ensuing liberal policy on residence and natural- ization, together with the freedom of movement for the Algerians and, above all, a considerable unregistered immigration, pre-empted any strict planning strategy. None the less, in terms of intentions and instruments France too relied quite rigidly on an immigration policy based on governmental control of the national labour market, and it was always adamant in defending its sovereign prerogatives.

25 For the German-Italian agreement see *Rassegna del lavoro*, vol. II, n. 5–6 (1956), pp. 879–910. On German migration policy see K. J. Bade, 'Transatlantic Emigration and Continental Immigration: the German Experience', in K. J. Bade (ed.), *Population, Labour and Migration in 19th- and 20th-Century Germany* (Leamington, 1987), pp. 135–62; G. Baratta *et al.*, *L'emigrazione nell'Europa del MEC* (Rome, 1974); H. Korte, 'Labor Migration and the Employment of Foreigners in the Federal Republic of Germany since 1950', in Rogers (ed.), *Guests Come to Stay*, op. cit., pp. 30– 49. On Italian migration to Germany in the 1960s, in the context of the common market, see Romero, *Emigrazione*, op. cit., ch. 5.

26 Underneath the heavy idealistic rhetoric which surrounded Italy's European policy, all its initiators and pilots were quite explicit about its eminently national function. See Adstans, *Alcide de Gasperi nella politica estera italiana 1944–1953* (Milan, 1953), p. 129; G. Pella, 'European Economic Inte- gration', *Banco di Roma – Review of the Economic Conditions in Italy*, V, 5, 1951, pp. 363–73; P. Taviani, *Il superamento dello Stato nazionale e la Comunità europea*, in G. P. Orsello (ed.), *L'Italia e l'Europa* (Rome, 1965), vol. I, pp. 319–23; M. Ferrari-Aggradi, *Europa. Tappe e prospettive di unificazione* (Rome, 1958), pp. 41–2.

27 'Procès-verbal de la réunion des Ministres des Affaires Etrangères, Messina 2/6/1955', Archives of the Dutch Ministry of Foreign Affairs, The Hague (hereafter AMBZ), 913.000/21 EEG.

28 See 'Rapport présenté par M. J. Doublet au nom de la sous-commission des problèmes sociaux à la Commission du Marché Commun, des Investis- sements et des Problèmes Sociaux', doc. n. 146, 22 August 1955, in AMBZ, 913.100/48 EEG. Also the documents n. 117 and n. 137 in AMBZ, 913.100/ 61 EEG.

29 'Procès-verbal de la Conférence des Ministres des Affaires Etrangères, Bruxelles 11–12/2/1956', in AMBZ, 913.100/24 EEG; 'Projet de rapport aux Ministres des Affaires Etrangères', tome I, MAE 80, Brussels, 8 April 1956, in AMBZ 913.100/42 EEG, pp. 90–101; 'Procès-verbal de la Conférence des Ministres des Affaires Etrangères, Venezia 29–30/5/1956', in AMBZ, 913.100/25 EEG.

30 'Projet du procès-verbal des réunions du groupe du marché commun tenues à Bruxelles les 8 et 10 octobre 1956', (Mar. Com. 84), Brussels, 18 October 1956; 'Tableau synoptique des projets d'articles concernant la libre circu- lation des travailleurs', Brussels, 25 October 1956: both in AMBZ, 913.100/

83 EEG. 'Note sur les dispositions du Traité relatives à la libre circulation des travailleurs', (Mar. Com. 122), Brussels, 3 December 1956, in AMBZ, 913.100/85 EEG. 'Projet d'articles'. Titre III', (Ch. Del. 156), Brussels, 10 January 1957, in AMBZ, 913.100/7 EEG.

31 For the conceptual debate on social and labour market issues that accompanied the treaty see M. Heilperin, 'Freer Trade and Social Welfare', *International Labour Review*, LXXV, 3, 1957, pp. 173–92; A. Philip, 'Social Aspects of European Economic Cooperation', *International Labour Review*, LXXVI, 3, 1957, pp. 244–56; M. Byé, 'Freer Trade and Social Welfare. Comments on Mr Heilperin's Article', *International Labour Review*, LXXVII, 1, 1958, pp. 38–47.

32 Specifically on this matter a bitter controversy arose in the early 1970s between Italy and the Commission: see Ministry of Labour and Social Security, *La politica dell'impiego nella CEE* (Roma, 1971) and the response in Commission of the European Communities, *Memorandum del Governo italiano sulla politica dell'occupazione nella Comunità* (Brussels, 1972).

33 See K. A. Dahlberg, 'The EEC Commission and the Politics of the Free Movement of Labour', *Journal of Common Market Studies*, VI, 4, 1968, pp. 310–33; European Economic Community, *La libre circulation de la main d'oeuvre et le marché du travail dans la CEE*, CEE, Brussels, issues of 1964, 1966 and 1970.

34 I have analysed and discussed in detail the process of implementation of the common market in the 1960s, its consequences and its interpretative implications in Romero, *Emigrazione*, op. cit., chs 5 and 6.

35 A rather precocious and completely unfulfilled forecast that EC regulations on migration would grow – in a truly neo-functionalist fashion – into high levels of social and political supranational integration was advanced by H. S. Feldstein, 'A Study of Transaction and Political Integration: Transnational Labour Flow within the European Economic Community', *Journal of Common Market Studies*, VI, 1, 1967, pp. 24–55.

3 RESTORING FRANCE: THE ROAD TO INTEGRATION

Frances M. B. Lynch

1 P. Guillen, 'La France et la négociation des Traités de Rome: l'Euratom', in Enrico Serra (ed.), *The Relaunching of Europe and the Treaties of Rome* (Brussels, 1989).

2 François Caron, *An Economic History of Modern France* (London, 1979), p. 327.

3 William James Adams, *Restructuring the French Economy. Government and the Rise of Market Competition since World War II* (Washington DC, 1989), p. 122.

4 One of the main concerns of this 'plan' was to safeguard the value of official reserves in the event of a devaluation of sterling against the dollar, but this was not taken into consideration by either the Americans or the British.

5 French Ministry of Foreign Affairs (hereafter MAE) DE-CE, 1945–60. Service de Coopération Economique, 'Effet de la libéralisation des échanges sur les territoires d'outre-mer', 16 July 1949.

6 MAE, DE-CE, 1945–60, 351 Conseil Economique, 26 January 1950.

7 French Ministry of Finance, the Budget and Economic Affairs, *Inventaire de la situation financière* (Paris, 1951).

8 A. S. Milward, *The Reconstruction of Western Europe, 1945–1951* (London, 1984).

9 French Ministry of Industry (hereafter Min. IND) 830587 Ind 11, report by Bellier, January 1950.

10 MAE, DE-CE, 1945–60, 351 Conseil Economique, 26 January 1950.

11 French national archives (hereafter AN), Interministerial Committee for Questions of European Integration (hereafter F^{60ter}) 474, 12 May 1950, Schweitzer to Filippi.

12 AN, French Ministry of Agriculture (hereafter F^{10}) 5628. French Ministry of Finance and Economic Affairs, Comité des Importations, 'Compte rendu de la séance', 24 August 1950.

13 MAE, 1945–60, 353, Comité de direction des échanges, 3 April 1954.

14 French Ministry of Finance and Economic Affairs, *Commission créée par arrêté du 6 janvier 1954 pour l'étude des disparités entre les prix français et étrangers* (Paris, 1954).

15 AN, Commissariat au Plan (hereafter 80AJ) 71, Deuxième Plan de Modernisation.

16 The franc area included metropolitan France, Algeria, Tunisia and Morocco, as well as the territories and departments overseas. The French Union excluded Tunisia and Morocco.

17 S. Moos, 'The Foreign Trade of West-European Countries', *Bulletin of the Oxford Institute of Statistics*, 7, 1 and 3, 1945.

18 MAE, Gatt A-10–13, dossier 1, Direction des Affaires Economiques, 22 October 1946.

19 Commissariat Général au Plan, *Rapport sur la réalisation du plan de modernisation et d'équipement de l'Union française* (Paris, 1953), p. 84.

20 French Ministry of Finance (hereafter Min. Fin.) B24947, Relations de trésorerie, 'Note au sujet du financement des dépenses d'équipement en Afrique du Nord', 22 October 1952.

21 Min. Fin. B24929, Fangent to Bissonnet, 17 November 1954.

22 AN, 80AJ 71, Commissariat Général au Plan, document from Ministry of Foreign Affairs.

23 MAE, DE-CE, 1945–60, 197, note from Service de Coopération Economique, 12 June 1954.

24 AN, 80AJ 72, 'L'integration de l'Union française dans l'Europe des Six', 9 February 1955.

25 AN, F^{10} 5620, 'Rapport au sujet de la quatrième session du Conseil International du BIE', 24–7 October 1950.

26 Food and Agriculture Organisation, *Commodity Policy Studies*, no. 2, April 1953.

27 AN, 80AJ 54, CGP, 'Projet de rapport général des Commissions de la production agricole et de l'équipement rural', 22 September 1953.

28 MAE, Accords Bilatéraux, France: Allemagne, note, 28 April 1955.

29 Gilbert was the joint author of an official study which compared national products and the purchasing power of currencies in OEEC countries and the United States. M. Gilbert and B. Kravis, *An International Comparison of National Products and the Purchasing Power of Currencies* (OEEC, Paris, 1954).

30 MAE, DE-CE, 1945–60, 613, note, Service de Coopération Economique, 30 August 1956.

31 Quai Branly, Interministerial Committee for Questions of European Integration (thereafter SGG1), 122.22A, note from the High Authority of ECSC, 27 June 1956.
32 SGG1, 122.21, 'Réunion du Comité interministériel', September 1956.
33 SGG1, 122.13(b), 'Réunion Mollet, Adenauer', 6 November 1956.
34 MAE, DE-CE, 1945–60, A-30–6 Marché Commun, Bousquet to Pineau, 21 Febraury 1957.

4 BETWEEN INTERDEPENDENCE AND INTEGRATION: DENMARK'S SHIFTING STRATEGIES

Vibeke Sørensen

1 For a discussion of the particular development of Scandinavian social democracy in the 1930s, G. Esping Andersen, *Politics against Markets* (Princeton, 1985).
2 H. C. Johansen, *The Danish Economy in the Twentieth Century*, (London, 1987), p. 45.
3 See for instance the Social Democratic post-war programme, *Fremtidens Danmark* (Copenhagen, 1945).
4 The 205,000 agricultural units were divided almost equally between smallholdings (under 10 hectares) and farms (between 10 and 60 hectares). Both units achieved high yields per hectare via the co-operative processing and marketing system. The smallholdings produced only butter and bacon especially for the British market and were highly dependent on cheap feeding-stuff imports, while the farms had a more diversified production structure including grain. Both smallholders and farmers were advocates of free trade, but the smallholders have historically been more positive towards corporatist arrangements with state and industry because of their more vulnerable position in the economy. As an interest group the smallholders were organized separately from the farmers, in the Federation of Danish Smallholders, but as a rule agricultural policy was defined by the farmers' organization, the Agricultural Council. While the farmers politically were represented by the Liberal Party, the smallholders worked closely with the Radical Party and, intermittently, with the Social Democratic Party.
5 L. Dalgas Jensen, 'Denmark and the Marshall Plan, 1947–48: the Decision to Participate', *Scandinavian Journal of History*, 14, 1989, p. 59.
6 P. Gersman, A. Therkildsen and O. Tobiesen Meyer, 'Fra importregulering til moms 1945–1986', in their *Dansk Toldhistorie* (Copenhagen, 1987), vol. V, p. 77.
7 The government also clashed with the opposition over the use of the Marshall Aid counterpart funds for productive purposes. After persistent political pressure from the Economic Co-operation Agency, about one-third of the counterpart funds was eventually used for such purposes; see V. Sørensen, 'The Politics of Closed Markets: Denmark, the Marshall Plan and European Integration, 1948–63', *International History Review*, 14, 1, 1993.
8 For a discussion of these contracts, see B. Nilson, 'Butter, Bacon and Coal: Anglo-Danish Commercial Relations, 1947–51', *Scandinavian Journal of History*, 13, 1988, pp. 257–78 and V. Sørensen, 'Social Democratic Government in Denmark under the Marshall Plan, 1947–50' (unpublished PhD dissertation, European University Institute, Florence, 1987).

9 V. Sørensen, 'Danish Economic Policy and European Cooperation on Trade and Currencies (1948–59)', EUI Working Paper 86/251 (Florence, 1986).

10 Denmark attempted to limit the effects of the OEEC programme by liberalizing finished goods which represented a large share of total imports but only a relatively small share of domestic industrial production. In 1959 the liberalization percentage for the former was 79; it was only 36 for the latter. Gersman, Therkildsen, Tobiensen Meyer, 'Fra importregulering', op. cit., p. 21.

11 International borrowing led to rapid growth of the foreign debt, equivalent to 36 per cent of annual exports and 13 per cent of GNP in 1972. Johansen, *The Danish Economy*, op. cit., p. 131.

12 For a more detailed discussion of the negotiations with the ECSC and the Green Pool see V. Sørensen, 'How to Become a Member of a Club without Joining. Danish Policy with respect to European Sector Integration Schemes, 1950–1957', *Scandinavian Journal of History*, 16, 1992, pp. 105–25.

13 Ministry of Foreign Affairs Archive (hereafter MFAA), 73C13g, 'Notat 6/10–53 fra Direktoratet for Vareforsyning'.

14 Johansen, *The Danish Economy*, op. cit., p. 119, and Nordisk Økonomisk Samarbeidsudvalg (hereafter NECC), *Nordisk Økonomisk Samarbejde* (speciel del: Vareområderne) (Oslo, 1957).

15 De Samvirkende Fagforbund, *Nordisk Økonomisk Samarbejde* (Copenhagen, 1952).

16 B. Stråth, *Industry and Nordic Economic Cooperation* (Stockholm, 1978) shows that the Danish Industrial Council in the beginning of the 1950s was very positive towards a customs union.

17 It was estimated that a Nordic Customs Union would take a larger share of British exports than the USA or Australia. F. Wendt, *The Nordic Council and Co-operation in Scandinavia* (Copenhagen, 1959), p. 222.

18 B. Haskel, *The Scandinavian Option* (Oslo, 1976); G. P. Nielsson, 'The Nordic and the Continental European Dimensions in Scandinavian Integration: NORDEK as a case study', *Cooperation and Conflict*, VI, 1971, pp. 173–8; N. Amstrup, 'Nordisk samarbejde – myte eller realitet?', in *Nær og Fjern. Samspillet om den indre og ydre politik. Studier tilegenet dr. phil. S. Henningsen* (Copenhagen, 1980); B. Stråth, 'The Illusory Nordic Alternative to Europe', *Cooperation and Conflict*, XV, 1980, pp. 102–14; N. Andren, 'Nordic Integration and Cooperation – Illusion and Reality', *Cooperation and Conflict*, XIX, 1984, pp. 251–62. For a more varied analysis see: C. Stålvant, 'Nordic Policy towards International Economic Cooperation', in B. Sundelius (ed.), *Foreign Policies of Northern Europe* (Boulder, 1982); B. Turner and G. Nordquist, *The Other European Community: Integration and Cooperation in Nordic Europe* (London, 1982).

19 NECC (Det Fælles nordiske udvalg for Økonomisk samarbejde), *Nordisk Økonomisk Samarbejde* (Copenhagen, 1950); NECC (Det Fælles nordiske udvalg for Økonomisk samarbejde), *Et Fælles Nordisk Marked* (Copenhagen, 1954); NECC (Det nordiske Økonomisk samarbeidsudvalg), *Nordisk Økonomisk Samarbejde*, vols 1–5 (Oslo, 1957). The argument and results of these reports are summed up by Wendt, *The Nordic Council*, op. cit., 1959, pp. 165–233.

20 Stråth, 'The Illusory Alternative', op. cit., p. 111.

21 In 1980 these products still made up 30 per cent of total Swedish exports. K. Samuelsson, 'The Swedish Model and Western Europe', *Journal of*

International Affairs, 41, 2, 1988, p. 376. L. Mjøset, 'Nordic Economic Policies in the 1970s', *International Organization*, 43, 1987, pp. 403–56.

22 See for example MFAA, 73B66c, 'De foreliggende fællesmarkedsplaner og Danmarks stilling hertil', 4 November 1957.

23 Distribution of Danish exports, 1950–90 (percentages)

Year	German Fed. Rep.	UK	Sweden	Norway	Rest of EC
1950	17	42	6	4	–
1953	11	40	5	3	–
1959	21	25	7	5	11
1967	12	23	14	7	11
1971	12	19	16	7	10
1980	19	14	13	6	16
1985	16	12	12	7	16
1990	20	11	13	7	22

Source: H. C. Johansen, *Dansk Økonomisk Statistik 1814–1980* (Copenhagen, 1985); *OECD Statistics of Foreign Trade* (Paris, 1985 and 1990).

24 H. C. Johansen, 'A Century of Nordic Cooperation', *EUI Colloquium Papers*, 135/89 (Florence), p .8.

25 J. Fagerberg, 'Diffusion of Technology, Structural Change and Intra-Industry Trade: The Case of the Nordic Countries 1961–1983', in J. O. Andersson (ed.), *Nordic Studies on Intra-Industry Trade* (Åbo, 1986); J. Fagerberg, 'Norden og strukturendringene på verdensmarkedet. En analyse av de nordiska lands handel med hverandre og de øvrige OECD-landene 1961–1983', *Statistisk Sentralbyro*, no. 18, 1986 (Oslo).

26 NECC, *Rapport fra det Nordiske Økonomiske Samarbeidsudvalg* (speciel del: Vareområderne) (Oslo, 1957).

27 MFAA, 74C13f, 'Notat ang. Minister Bartels besøg i CECA 24–25 november 1952'.

28 See the minutes from the committee meetings of 1953–6 in MFAA, 73C13g.

29 Sørensen, 'How to Become a Member', op. cit., p. 16.

30 NECC, *Nordisk Økonomisk Samarbeid*, op. cit.

31 MFAA, 74C13g, 'Referat fra ekspertgruppen i jern og stål 21–22 oktober 1955'; MFAA, 73C13g, 'Notat om det fælles nordiske marked for jern og stål 17 november 1955'.

32 NECC, *Nordisk Økonomisk Samarbeid*, op. cit.

33 The belief that the Six, without stringent conditions, would open the door for the largest agricultural exporter in Europe seems overly optimistic and was more likely an attempt to bind Denmark to a united front against the United Kingdom. For the government however it was sufficient to pacify the opposition. See MFAA, 73B66a, 'Resume af samtaler i Bruxelles 10–17 marts 1957'; MFAA, 73B66c, 'Referat af møde med i statsministeriet med erhvervsorganisationerne om Danmarks forhandlinger med de Seks'.

34 The coalition also included a small Georgeist party, the Justice Party, which, apart from its support for land nationalization, generally favoured liberal economic and commercial policies.

35 Ministry of Foreign Affairs, *Economic Survey of Denmark* (Copenhagen, 1961).

36 See H. Rasmussen and M. Rüdiger, 'Tiden efter 1945', in S. Mørch (ed.), *Danmarks Historie* (Copenhagen, 1990), vol. 8, p. 155 and J. Engberg, *I Minefeltet. Træk af Arbejderbevægelsens Historie siden 1936* (Copenhagen, 1986).

37 Between 1951 and 1956, 10,000 jobs were lost in the textile industry. See Gersman, Therkildsen and Tobiesen Meyer, 'Fra Importregulering', op. cit., p. 59.

38 *Danmark og De Europæiske Markedsplaner*, 1–5 (Copenhagen, 1958).

39 It pointed out that Danish industrial exports to the Six had increased by 500 per cent between 1949 and 1957, while the growth of exports to the Seven had been at a much lower rate. 'Markedsplaner og Erhversudviklingen inden for Industrivareområdet', *Danmark og De Europæiske Markedsplaner* (Copenhagen, 1958), pp. 78–9.

40 MFAA, 73B66c/3, Direktoratet for vareforsyning, 'Fællesmarkedernes indhold og plan', 29 May 1958.

41 See Wendt, *The Nordic Council*, op. cit., p. 187.

42 NEEC, *Nordisk Økonomisk Samarbeid*; Wendt, *The Nordic Council*, op. cit., p. 216.

43 Paper and pulp accounted for more than 10 per cent by value of Sweden's and Norway's exports, while aluminium and iron alone accounted for 10 per cent of Norwegian exports. MFAA, 73B66f, 'Undenrigsministerens redgørelse i Tinget 17 februar 1959 for situationen vdr. de europæiske markedsplaner'.

44 In October such a proposal was presented in Paris. MFAA, 73B66f, 'Referat af Udenrigsministerens møde med Erhvervsorganisationerne 5 november 1958'.

45 Even so the Danish Industrial Council remained hesitant with respect to EFTA and never fully supported the government's decision to participate. Stråth, *Industry and Nordic,* op. cit., pp. 224–5.

46 Switzerland was already in October 1958 invited unofficially to participate in a UNISCAN meeting to discuss the free trade negotiations. MFAA, 73B66f, 'Referat af UNISCAN møde i London 15 og 16 februar 1958'.

47 Germany wished to maintain its exports of manufactures to Denmark and was therefore willing to compensate for German discrimination against Danish agricultural exports. MFAA, 73B66f, 'Notat om drøftelserne med DR. Sonneman 30 januar 1959'.

48 Gersman, Therkilsen and Tobiesen Meyer, 'Fra importregulering til moms', op. cit., p. 66.

49 J. O. Krag and K. B. Andersen, *Kamp og Fornyelse* (Copenhagen, 1971), p. 347.

50 For a discussion of the debate with the trade unions see Engberg, *I Minefeltet*, op. cit.

51 For a discussion of the difference between the welfare systems in Scandinavia and in the rest of western Europe see: P. Flora (ed.), *Growth to Limits. The Western European Welfare State since World War II* (Berlin, 1987) and G.

Esping Andersen, *The Three Worlds of Welfare Capitalism* (Cambridge, 1990).

52 P. Crosby, 'Denmark, EFTA and the EC', *The International Journal*, 21, 1966, pp. 508–20.

53 Fagerberg, 'Norden og strukurendringene', op. cit.

54 C. Wiklund, 'The Zig Zag Course of the NORDEK Negotiations', *Scandinavian Political Studies*, 5, 1970, pp. 307–36; Stålvant, 'Nordic Policy', op. cit.

55 Wiklund, op. cit., pp. 120–1. In the entry negotiations Denmark was forced to accept certain administrative limitations on its participation in the nordic labour market.

5 INSIDE OR OUTSIDE THE MAGIC CIRCLE? The Italian and British steel industries face to face with the Schuman Plan and the European Coal Iron and Steel Community

Ruggero Ranieri

1 I would like to thank Andy Burns for his assistance at British Steel's Records Centre, Irthlingborough.

2 D. L. Burn, *The Economic History of Steelmaking 1867–1939. A Study in Competition* (London, 1940); N. J. G. Pounds, *The Ruhr. A Study in Historical and Economic Geography* (London, 1952).

3 N. J. G. Pounds and W. N. Parker, *Coal and Steel in Western Europe. The Influences of Resources and Techniques on Production* (London, 1957), pp. 334–5.

4 D. Barbezat, 'A Price for Every Product, Every Place: The International Steel Export Cartel, 1933–1939', *Business History*, 33, 4, October 1991, p. 69. J. Gillingham, 'Coal and Steel Diplomacy in Interwar Europe', in C. A. Wurm (ed.), *Internationale Kartelle und Aussenpolitik/International Cartels and Foreign Policy* (Stuttgart, 1989).

5 E. Bussière, 'The Evolution of Structures in the Iron and Steel Industry in France, Belgium and Luxembourg, National and International Aspects, 1900–1939', in E. Abe and Y. Suzuki (eds), *Changing Patterns of International Rivalry – Some Lessons from the Steel Industry* (Tokyo, 1991).

6 J. Gillingham, *Coal, Steel and the Rebirth of Europe, 1945–1955. The Germans and French from Ruhr Conflict to Economic Community* (Cambridge, 1991).

7 A. S. Milward, *The Reconstruction of Western Europe, 1945–51* (London, 1984).

8 K. Schwabe (ed.), *Die Anfänge des Schuman Planes 1950–1/The Beginnings of the Schuman Plan* (Baden-Baden, 1988).

9 British Steel East Midlands Regional Record Centre, Irthlingborough (hereafter BSEMRRC), co. 1790, cons. 1, b. 10 (011634); files quoted belong to the BISF secretariat.

10 R. Ranieri, 'La siderurgia italiana e gli inizi dell'integrazione europea', *Passato e presente*, 7, January–April 1985.

11 P. Guillen, 'L'échec des tentatives d'entente économique avec l'Italie (1922–1929)', *Relations internationales*, 13, 1978; E. Falck, 'Il cartello del ferro', *Metallurgia*, xviii, 1926, pp. 10–12.

12 J. C. Carr and W. Taplin, *History of the British Steel Industry* (Oxford, 1962), pp. 483 ff.

13 F. Bonelli (ed.), *Acciaio per l'industrializzazione. Contributi allo studio del problema siderurgico italiano* (Turin, 1982); G. Toniolo, 'Oscar Sinigaglia (1877–1953)', in A. Mortara (ed.), *I protagonisti dell'intervento pubblico in Italia* (Milan, 1984), pp. 405–30.

14 Ministry for the Constitution, *Rapporto della Commissione Economica Presentato all'Assemblea Costituente*, part ii, *Industria*, vol. ii, *Appendice alla Relazione (interrogatori)* (Rome, Istituto Poligrafico dello Stato, 1947), 'Interrogatorio dell'ing. Oscar Sinigaglia', pp. 5–20; O. Sinigaglia, 'The Future of the Italian Iron and Steel Industry', *Banca Nazionale del Lavoro Quarterly Review*, 4, January 1948; R. Ranieri, 'Factores nacionales e internacionales en la Reconstrucción industrial: la siderurgia italiana en una perspectiva a largo plazo', in L. Prados de la Escosura and V. Zamagni (eds), *El desarrollo económico en la Europa del Sur – España e Italia en perspectiva historica* (Madrid, 1992), pp. 396–420.

15 Ministry for the Constitution, op. cit., 'Interrogatorio dell'ing. Giovanni Falck', pp. 195–203; E. Decleva, 'Gli ambienti economici milanesi e il Piano Schuman (1950–1952)', *Archivio Storico Lombardo*, CXII, 1986.

16 M. Pelaja, 'Ricostruzione e politica siderurgica', *Italia Contemporanea*, 148, September 1982; E. Rossi, 'La grande parassitaria', *Il Mondo*, 1, 9, 16 April 1949.

17 M. Balconi, *La siderurgia italiana (1945–1990). Tra controllo pubblico e incentivi di mercato* (Bologna, 1991), p. 96; P. Bairati, *Vittorio Valletta* (Turin, 1983).

18 G. H. Hildebrand, *Growth and Structure in the Economy of Modern Italy* (Cambridge, Mass., 1965).

19 M. De Cecco, 'Economic Policy in the Reconstruction Period, 1945–1951', in S. J. Woolf (ed.), *The Rebirth of Italy, 1943–1950* (London, 1972).

20 V. Zamagni, 'Betting on the Future – The Reconstruction of Italian Industry 1946–1952', in J. Becker and F. Knipping (eds), *Power in Europe? Great Britain, France, Italy and Germany in the Postwar World, 1945–1950* (Berlin, 1986).

21 C. Spagnolo, 'L'IRI e la Ricostruzione. Ipotesi di lettura', *Annali Della Facolta' Di Lettere e Filosofia Universita' Degli Studi Di Bari*, XXIX, 1986; M. Salvati, *Stato e industria nella ricostruzione. Alle origini del potere democristiano 1944–1949* (Milan, 1982).

22 Archivio Luigi Einaudi, Fondazione Einaudi, Turin (hereafter ALE), 1. 2, b. Ferrari Aggradi: Campilli a Sforza, Paris, 16 July 1947, telex n. ce–30.

23 Archivio privato di Paolo Emilio Taviani, Rome (hereafter CT), Piano Schuman 1950–2, Sinigaglia a Taviani, Rome, 25 November 1950.

24 R. Ranieri, 'The Marshall Plan and the Reconstruction of the Italian Steel Industry (1947–1954)', in French Ministry of the Economy, Finance and the Budget, *Le Plan Marshall et le relèvement économique de l'Europe* (Paris, 1993); F. Amatori, 'Cicli produttivi, tecnologie, organizzazione del lavoro. La siderurgia a ciclo continuo integrale dal piano autarchico alla Italsider (1937–1961)', *Ricerche Storiche*, X, 3, September–December 1980; J. L. Harper, *America and the Reconstruction of Italy, 1945–1948* (Cambridge, 1986).

25 Ranieri, 'La siderurgia italiana', op. cit., p. 77.

26 Archivio Storico del Ministero degli Affari Esteri, Rome (hereafter AMDAE), Ambasciata di Parigi, b. 478, fasc. 1, verbale della riunione tenuta al Ministero dell'Industria, 25 May 1950.

27 A. Varsori, 'Italy and the European Defence Community: 1950–1954', in P. M. Stirk and D. Willis (eds), *Shaping Postwar Europe. European Unity and Disunity, 1945–1957* (London, 1991).

28 R. Ranieri, 'L'Italia e i negoziati del Piano Schuman', in E. Di Nolfo, R. H. Rainero and B. Vigezzi, *L'Italia e la politica di potenza in Europa (1945–1950)* (Milan, 1988).

29 For Monnet's plans: Archives de Jean Monnet, Fondation Jean Monnet pour l'Europe, Lausanne (hereafter AJM), AMG 6/5/3, 'Bilan des conséquences économiques et financières du Plan Schuman', 9 September 1950. For Sinigaglia's reaction, *CT,* Piano Schuman 1950–2, Sinigaglia a Taviani, Rome, 25 July 1950.

30 R. Ranieri, 'The Italian Steel Industry and the Schuman Plan negotiations', in Schwabe (ed.), *Die Anfänge,* op. cit.

31 R. Ranieri, 'L'espansione alla prova del negoziato: L'industria italiana e la Comunità del Carbone e dell'Acciaio' (unpublished PhD dissertation, European University Institute, Florence, 1988), chs 6 and 7.

32 Archives Historiques des Communautés Européenes, Florence (hereafter AHCE), CEAB 8, n. 50, 'Capanna a Rollman', 10 October 1953; M. Lungonelli, *La Magona d'Italia. Impresa, lavoro e tecnologia in un secolo di siderurgia toscana (1865–1975)* (Milan, 1991), pp. 119–20.

33 AHCE, CEAB 4, n. 404, Division des Problèmes du Travail, Luxembourg, 'Rapport annexé à l'exposé de la mission envoyée en Italie pour l'enquête sur les licenciements dans l'industrie sidérurgique', 20 November 1953; W. Diebold Jr, *The Schuman Plan. A Study in Economic Cooperation 1950–1959* (New York, 1959), pp. 415–18.

34 D. L. Burn, *The Steel Industry 1939–1959. A Study in Competition and Planning* (Cambridge, 1961) contains the best analysis. Also B. S. Keeling and A. E. G. Wright, *The Development of the Modern British Steel Industry* (London, 1964), pp. 99 ff.

35 D. L. Burn, 'Steel', in D. L. Burn (ed.), *The Structure of British Industry. A Symposium* (Cambridge, 1958), vol. 1.

36 Keeling and Wright, *Development,* op. cit., p. 90; S. Pollard, *The Development of the British Economy, 1914–1980* (London, 1983), pp. 237 ff.; G. D. N. Worswick and P. H. Ady, *The British Economy 1945–1950* (Oxford, 1952), pp. 493 ff.

37 BSEMRRC, co. 1790, cons. 2, b. 1d-2 (00463), 'Control of Iron and Steel Prices in the United Kingdom'; G. C. Allen, *British Industries and Their Organization* (4th edn, London, 1959), pp. 120–6; S. Tolliday, *Business, Banking and Politics. The Case of British Steel 1918–1939* (Cambridge, 1987), pp. 328 ff.

38 Burn, *Steel Industry,* op. cit., pp. 228 ff. and 339 ff.

39 BSEMRCC, co. 1790, cons. 1, b. 8 (011619), Edward Senior (BISF) to J. C. Carr (Min. of Supply), 19 November 1949.

40 BSEMRRC, co. 1790, cons. 1, b. 8 (011619), 'Torquay Tariff Negotiations. Note of a Preliminary Meeting with the BISF', October 1950.

41 BSEMRRC, co. 1790, cons. 1, b. 8 (011619), BISF, 'U.K. Iron and Steel Tariff', 3 July 1953.

42 Public Record Office, London (hereafter PRO), CAB 134/1179, SPC (N), 54/6, 'Association Between the UK and the ECSC – Possible Arrangements Relating to the Iron and Steel Tariff', 29 April 1954.

43 P. D. Henderson, 'Government and Industry', in G. D. N. Worswick and P. H. Ady (eds.), *The British Economy in the Nineteen-Fifties* (Oxford, 1962), pp. 329 ff.

44 PRO, CAB 134/1177, SPC (E) (53) 14-BISF, 'Imperial Preferences and Commonwealth Trade in Steel Products' and 'A Preliminary Steel Industry View on the Development of Association with the ECSC', 11 May 1953.

45 Keeling and Wright, *Development*, op. cit.; J. Vaizey, *A History of British Steel* (London, 1974), ch. 8; W. E. Minchinton, *The British Tinplate Industry. A History* (Oxford, 1957), pp. 235 ff.

46 Burn, *Steel Industry*, op. cit., pp. 377 ff.; papers and correspondence of Duncan Burn, LSE (hereafter BP), C/36 (75), 'Comments on the Chapter on the Community of the new edition of Mr. Duncan Burn's book on "steel"', High Authority Information Service, 30 January 1956; K. Stegemann, 'Three Functions of Basing-Point Pricing and article 60 of the ECSC Treaty', *The Antitrust Bulletin*, XIII, Summer 1968.

47 BSEMRRC, co. 1790, cons. 2, b. 1d (00463), Schuman Plan, 'Western European Iron and Steel Costs', Intelligence, 12 February 1953; Burn, *Steel Industry*, op. cit., p. 355.

48 BSEMRRC, co. 1790, cons. 1, b. 8 (011619), Senior (BISF) to Carr (Min. of Supply), 17 March 1950.

49 PRO, CAB 134/1177, SPC (E) 53/29, 15th meeting.

50 R. Ranieri, 'Attempting an Unlikely Union: the British Steel Industry and the European Coal and Steel Community, 1950–1954', in Stirk and Willis (eds), *Shaping*, op. cit.

51 G. W. Ross, *The Nationalization of Steel. One Step Forward, Two Steps Back* (London, 1965); K. Burke, *The First Privatization. The Politicians, the City and the Denationalization of Steel* (London, 1988), pp. 21 ff.; A. J. Youngson, *The British Economy 1920–1957* (London, 1960), pp. 190–2.

52 BSEMRRC, co. 1790, cons. 1, b. 19 (011635), 'Note on Discussion of French Proposal for International Control of Steel and Coal', 16 May 1950, p. 2.

53 ibid., p. 3.

54 ibid., p. 7.

55 ibid., pp. 3, 4.

56 ibid., p. 8. Sir Andrew also feared that the leader of the opposition, in one of his uncontrollable fits of Europhilia, might seize on them too enthusiastically, thus putting the steel industry at a disadvantage.

57 R. Bullen (ed.), 'Preface', in Foreign Office, *Documents on British Policy Overseas*, series ii, vol. 1, *The Schuman Plan, the Council of Europe and Western European Integration, May 1950–December 1952* (London, 1986), p. xiii.

58 A good discussion of the issue is in A. Bullock, *Ernest Bevin: Foreign Secretary 1945–1951* (London, 1989), pp. 781 ff. For the opinions of the steel industrialists there are many indications in the BISF's correspondence; see also Burke, *First Privatization*, op. cit., p. 28.

59 Foreign Office, *Documents on British Policy Overseas*, op. cit., documents n. 109 and 109.i.

60 BSEMRRC, co. 1790, cons. 1, b. 10 (011635), 'French Proposals for International Control of Steel and Coal', 13 June 1950.
61 BSEMRRC, co. 1790, cons. 1, b. 10 (011634), 'Minutes of the Special Meeting of the Executive Committee', 13 June 1950, p. 3.
62 BSEMRRC, co. 1790, cons. 1, b. 10 (011635), 'French Proposals for International Control of Steel and Coal', 13 June 1950, p. 7.
63 BSEMRRC, co. 1790, cons. 1, b. 10 (011635), 'Note on Discussion of French Proposal for International Control of Steel and Coal', 13 June 1950, 'The Schuman Plan'.
64 Burn, *Steel Industry*, op. cit., pp. 392 ff.
65 BSEMRRC, co. 1790, cons. 1, b. 10 (011634), 'Minutes of the Special Meeting of the Ex. Committee', 13 June 1950, p. 3.
66 BSEMRRC, co. 1790, cons. 1, b. 10 (011635), 'French Proposals for International Control of Steel and Coal', 13 June 1950, p. 3.
67 ibid., pp. 3–4.
68 The ministries represented were the Foreign Office, the Ministry of Supply, the Ministry of Fuel and Power, the Board of Trade, the UK official delegation to the ECSC in Luxemburg, and the Ministry of Labour. In the first working party appointed in 1950 the Ministry of Defence was also represented.
69 PRO, CAB 134/1177, SPC (E) 53/29, 'Report by a Working Party of Officials on the Economic Implications of an Association between the UK and the ECSC', July 1953.
70 On Sir Edwin Plowden's position on the ECSC see A. Cairncross (ed.), *The Robert Hall Diaries 1947–1953* (London, 1989), pp. 112 ff. and 42, with some indication of the Treasury's dislike for the steel industry's protectionism.
71 PRO, FO 371, 105956, 11604/136, Sir E. Plowden (FO) to Sir P. Dixon, 'United Kingdom's Association with the European Coal and Steel Community', memorandum by the Economic Steering Committee, 14 October 1953
72 BSEMRRC, co. 1790, cons. 1, b. 7 (011612), 'Preliminary Report of the International Trade Relations Committee on the Schuman Plan', 16 June 1951.
73 BSEMRRC, co. 1790, cons. 1, b. 7 (011614), 'Relations with the Schuman Committee'.
74 PRO, CAB 134/1177, SPC (E) 53/29, 'Report by a Working Party of Officials on the Economic Implications of an Association between the UK and the ECSC'.
75 Burn, *Steel Industry*, op. cit., pp. 146 ff. and 445.
76 PRO, FO 371, 105957, M604/175, Sir Cecil Weir (UK Del., Lux.) to Sir P. Dixon (FO), 21 December 1953.
77 PRO, FO 371, 105957, M604/160, J. Monnet to Sir C. Weir, 24 December 1953.
78 PRO, FO 371, 111250/25, FO minute by R. S. Crawford, 18 January 1954; J. W. Young, 'The Schuman Plan and British Association', in J. W. Young (ed.), *The Foreign Policy of Churchill's Peacetime Administration 1951–1957* (Leicester, 1988), pp. 123 ff.
79 PRO, CAB 134/1178, SPC (E) (54), 2, draft of working party submission.
80 PRO, CAB 134/888, ES (54), 1st meeting. Mr Strath from the Treasury, who had chaired the working party's sessions, admitted that joining with

the ECSC, which 'maintained restrictions against the outside world was inconsistent with our one world approach to a system of free trade', but on the other hand, he added, it was still better than keeping a tightly protected home market.

81 PRO, CAB 128/27, c.c.(56), and c.c.(54), 4th conclusions (2).
82 BSEMRRC, co. 1790, cons. 1, b. 10, 'Note of a Meeting Held at the Iron and Steel Board on Wednesday 10th of February, 1954'.
83 BSEMRRC, co. 1790, cons. 1, b. 18, UK Liaison – Iron and Steel Board, 'Notes of a Meeting at the Iron and Steel Board . . . on Wednesday 3rd February 1954 to meet Monsieur P. Ricard'. At the meeting the officers of the BISF and the members of the board were present.
84 P. Mioche, 'Le patronat de la sidérurgie française et le Plan Schuman en 1950–52: les apparences d'un combat et la réalité d'une mutation', in Schwabe (ed.), *Die Anfänge*, op. cit.
85 The High Authority had just decided to allow firms a possibility of a 2.5 per cent rebate on published prices in any 60 consecutive days. Both Ricard and the British were aware of it, but they thought it would not work. Burn, *Steel Industry*, op. cit., p. 437; Diebold, *The Schuman Plan*, op. cit., pp. 258–60.
86 BSEMRRC, co. 1790, cons. 1, b. 10, Executive Committee, 16 February 1954, manuscript notes. During the meeting Lord Dudley, owner of Round Oaks, said that Ricard 'had given those present little encouragement to be closely associated with the Community'. The question was also raised as to whether the City institutions, who were the actual owners of the industry pending privatization, should also be consulted. Should 'the advice of Peats' be sought, it was asked – referring to the independent accountants Peat Marwick Mitchell, who acted on behalf of the consortium of City institutions in charge of the flotation of the companies' shares. The general feeling however was that they shouldn't be involved. On the subject see Burke, *The First Privatization*, op. cit., p. 104.
87 BSEMRRC, co. 1790, cons. 1, b. 10 (011635), B. S. Keeling to members of the Executive Committee, 17 February 1954. Members of the committee were: the managing director of Jessops in Sheffield, Lewis Chapman; C. E. Holmstrom, manager of Firth Vickers Stainless Steel (a company belonging to English Steel Corporation & to Firth & John Brown), Sir Ernest Lever, Captain Leighton Davies and E. J. Pode, all belonging to the board of the Steel Company of Wales, Lever also being the chairman of Richard Thomas & Baldwin; C. R. Wheeler of Guest Keen Baldwin; J. C. Lloyd of Stewart & Lloyd's; Sir Andrew McCance, chairman of Colvilles; G. Steel who was managing director of United Steel, and R. F. Summers, chairman of John Summers & Son. The meeting was chaired by the BISF's past president Sir Ellis Hunter, who was chairman of Dorman Longs, and by the current president G. H. Latham, whose affiliation was South Wales since he was also a director of Richard Thomas & Baldwin of which he became in 1955 deputy chairman. Thus there were five spokesmen for South Wales, four of whom belonged to the same group, one each for Scotland and the North-East respectively, and two for special steel producers in Sheffield. United Steel had two members, three if John Summers, who also sat on United Steel's board, was added, and finally the Midlands and North Wales were also represented. For information on the members and on the firms see Burn, 'Steel', op. cit., p. 287 and BISF, *Iron and Steel Trade Directory* (7th edn, London, 1953).

88 BSEMRRC, co. 1790, cons. 1, b. 10 (011635), Executive Committee correspondence, Sir Ernest Lever (Richard Thomas & Baldwin) to Sir Ellis Hunter (Howden Gate, Northallerton, Yorkshire), 5 March 1954. The indications are that the other members of the South Wales group shared his position.

89 Chapman, who was director of Jessops, a firm in Sheffield, expressed himself most forcefully against association during the plenary session. McCance and Benton, chairmen respectively of Colvilles and United Steel, are on record as having been pleased about the committee's result. So was Ellis Hunter, who, being chairman of Dorman Longs, represented the views of the North-East. This leaves us with a question mark about Corby, but J. C. Lloyd of Stewart & Lloyd's sat on the federation's International Trade Committee and there is every indication that he favoured the majority view. See BSEMRRC, co. 1790, cons. 1, b. 10 (011635), Executive Committee correspondence, A. J. Benton (United Steel Companies, Sheffield) to Keeling (BISF, London), 5 March 1954; A. McCance (Colvilles, Glasgow) to Keeling (BISF, London), 5 March 1954. Ellis Hunter stated his position during the plenary meeting of 9 March.

90 BSEMRRC, co. 1790, cons. 1, b. 10 (011640), Special Executive, 9 March 1954, manuscript notes. The text of the letter to the minister which the executive discussed, as well as the final submission, only minor amendments having been made, is in BSEMRRC, co. 1790, cons. 1, b. 10 (011635), F. Grant (BISF) to Duncan Sandys, Minister of Supply, 9 March 1954.

91 BSEMRRC, co. 1790, cons. 1, b. 10 (011640), Executive Committee, 9 March 1954, manuscript notes.

92 Burke, *The First Privatization*, op. cit., pp. 46, 48. At the meeting of the Executive Committee Eady openly referred to the fact that his ideas reflected the thinking of Sir Ernest Lever.

93 Briton Ferry was partly owned by Guest Keen Baldwin Iron and Steel Co. The chairman of the company, Colonel J. M. Bevan, was also present at the meeting. He tried to reassure Morris that the letter was simply staking out the position for future negotiation. The evidence is that that was an unduly optimistic interpretation.

94 Monnet's letter had suggested that there should be a public forum, other than the Council of Association proper, in which to debate the common issues.

95 Burn, *Steel Industry*, op. cit, pp. 537–8, 615; Burke, *The First Privatization*, op. cit., also discusses the political significance of the board's creation.

96 PRO, FO 371, 111252, 601/51, Sir A. Forbes (ISB) to Duncan Sandys (Min. of Supply), 23 February 1954.

97 The industrialists had detected a desire on the part of the board to give away something on a common minimum price, to be set in conjunction with the High Authority in times of scarcity. There was no sign of such a disposition in the board's letter.

98 PRO, CAB 134/1178, SPC (E) (54), 5th meeting.

99 PRO, CAB 128/7, c.c. 54, 27 (3)-(214), 'Meeting of the 7th of April'. Sandys was Churchill's son-in-law. He had a reputation as a committed 'European', having been chairman of the International Executive of the European Movement. On this occasion, he was keener to represent the views of the industry of which he was in charge.

100 The discussions of the Ministerial Committee are in PRO, CAB 130/101, Gen 462.

101 Ranieri, 'Attempting an Unlikely Union', op. cit., pp. 121–2.

102 BSEMRRC, co. 1790, cons. 1, b. 10 (011634), minutes of the Executive Committee, 19 October 1954. On the talks between Monnet and Sandys, R. Mayne, *The Recovery of Europe from Devastation to Unity* (London, 1970), p. 217.

103 Diebold, *The Schuman Plan*, op. cit., pp. 507 ff.; Burn, *Steel Industry*, op. cit., pp. 469 ff.

104 My conclusion therefore bears out the concept of the industry's 'self-government', which the most recent literature expounds (Tolliday, *Business, Banking*, op. cit., pp. 335 ff.). On the other hand, the board which came into power after 1953 appears to have been not devoid of ambitions, and the very concept of a board was fraught with ambiguities from the industry's point of view, reflecting the uneasy balance of power during the phase of denationalization. Arguably the successful opposition to nationalization had strengthened the BISF's leverage and planning had perhaps been pushed out of the front door. But it was always bound to come back through the window.

6 INTERDEPENDENCE AND INTEGRATION IN AMERICAN EYES: FROM THE MARSHALL PLAN TO CURRENCY CONVERTIBILITY

Federico Romero

1 M. Hogan, *The Marshall Plan. America, Britain and the Reconstruction of Western Europe 1947–1952* (Cambridge, 1987), p. 294.

2 A. Milward, *The Reconstruction of Western Europe, 1945–1951* (London, 1984), pp. 284–334.

3 Hogan, *The Marshall Plan*, op. cit., p. 190.

4 F. Romero, *The United States and the European Trade Union Movement, 1944–1951* (Chapel Hill, forthcoming in 1993).

5 Emerson Ross to Miriam Camp, memo, 'Structure of Free World Production', 23 October 1952, in US National Archives (hereafter NA), State Department lot file 55 D 105 (hereafter Miriam Camp Files), b. 1, f. 'Economic Foreign Policy 1952'.

6 The proposal in a memo from H. Cleveland to L. Gordon and E. Martin, 17 July 1952, NA, Miriam Camp Files, b. 2, f. '1954 Green Book'. For FOA internal debate and for the Treasury's opposition see NA, RG 469 Records of the US Foreign Assistance Agencies 1946–1961, Regional Organizations Staff Subject Files 1948–1957 (hereafter RG 469 ROS), b. 15, f. 'Integration: Atlantic Reserve System' and b. 20, f. 'Integration: Memoranda'.

7 Memo, 'European Integration', 11 July 1951, NA, Miriam Camp Files, b. 1, f. 'Briefing Papers'.

8 See T. Tannenwald to D. Bruce, 17 October 1952 and Bonbright to D. Bruce (draft for circular telegram), 15 November 1952, in NA, Miriam Camp Files, b. 1, f. 'EPC 1952'. US Department of State, *Foreign Relations of the United States* (hereafter FRUS), 1952–4, vol. VI, pp. 104–5, 129–31,

224–8 and 261–4. On US support for the EDC and on the defence aspects of the American effort for European integration see P. Melandri, *Les Etats-Unis face à l'unification de l'Europe 1945–1954* (Paris, 1980); E. H. van der Beugel, *From Marshall Aid to Atlantic Partnership. European Integration as a Concern of American Foreign Policy* (Amsterdam, 1966), pp. 249–301.

9   The American debate on the loan in FRUS, 1952–4, vol. VI, pp. 311–80. For the industrialists' positions see the minutes, 'Special Meeting on Coal-Steel Community Loan', 2 April 1954, in NA, RG 469 Office of the Director Subject Files 1948–1955 (hereafter RG 469 OD), b. 21, f. 'ECSC'. On the ECSC in general and on its relationship with the USA see W. Diebold, *The Schuman Plan: a Study in Economic Cooperation 1950–1959* (New York, 1959) and the more recent J. Gillingham, *Coal, Steel and the Rebirth of Europe, 1945–1955. The Germans and French from Ruhr Conflict to Economic Community* (Cambridge, 1991).

10 For the change in American attitudes compare the 'U.S. Statement on Establishment of a Single European Market for Agricultural Products' of 18 March 1952 with the documents of an inter-departmental discussion in June–July 1955: all in RG 469 ROS, respectively b. 21, f. 'Green Pool' and b. 60, f. 'Green Pool'. See also C. P. Boccia, 'L'amministrazione Eisenhower e l'integrazione economica dell'Europa occidentale 1953–1961' (PhD dissertation, University of Genoa, 1992), ch. 1.

11 See S. A. Ambrose, *Eisenhower. The President* (London, 1984).

12 See Commission on Foreign Economic Policy, *Report to the President and the Congress* (Washington DC, USGPO, 1954).

13 Eisenhower's message in *Department of State Bulletin*, 19 April 1954, pp. 602–7. For the State Department's comments on Randall's proposals see FRUS, 1952–4, vol. I, pp. 55–8.

14 A good example of the conservative opposition to the policy of foreign aid and to US tariff reductions is the *Randall Commission Minority Final Report* by Daniel Reed and Richard Simpson, 30 January 1954, copy in RG 469 OD, b. 13, f. 'Randall Commission'.

15 See Craig R. Sheaffer to Secretary S. Weeks, 5 February 1953, and Craig R. Sheaffer to Samuel W. Anderson, 3 March 1953, both in NA, Record Group 40, Records of the Office of the Secretary of Commerce, Central Files 1950–5 (hereafter RG 40), f. 'Finance, Public Duties and Tariffs'. William M. Rand to Harold E. Stassen, memo, 'Discussion of the RTAA at the White House', 16 March 1953, in RG 469 OD, b. 33, f. 'Trade'. Sinclair Weeks to Ward LaFrance, 1 June 1953, in RG 40, f. 'Finance, Public Duties and Tariffs'.

16 FRUS 1952–4, vol. I, p. 74. Also Rand to Stassen, memo, 'Discussion of the RTAA', 16 March 1953, op. cit.

17 For a detailed reconstruction of the debate see B. I. Kaufman, *Trade and Aid. Eisenhower's Foreign Economic Policy 1953–1961* (Baltimore, 1982), pp. 18–29.

18 See FRUS, 1955–7, vol. XI, pp. 110–51. For the other cases the administration's internal debate can be followed in the series 441.003 of the Decimal File of the State Department, NA, Record Group 59 (hereafter RG 59). See also Kaufman, *Trade and Aid*, op. cit., pp. 30–45.

19 Tel. from Dulles–Stassen–Humphrey to Draper, 840.00/3-2053, RG 59. For the March 1953 discussion with the UK see FRUS, 1952–4, vol. VI, pp. 921–63, 1028–9.

20 Memo, 'A New Payment System for Europe', 23 March 1953, in NA, Records of the Office of International Finance (Treasury Dept), Europe (EUR) 1941–59, FRC accession no. 68A2809 (hereafter OIF-EUR), b. 28, EUR/3/11. Memo from Ben T. Moore to R. Perkins, 'The Dollar Problem', 840.00/1-653, RG 59.

21 Memo by H. Stassen, 'The Next Session of OEEC in March 1954', 3 November 1953; also memo from D. A. Fitzgerald to H. Stassen, 22 October 1953 and memo from R. M. Bissell to H. Stassen, 30 April 1953: all in RG 469 OD, b. 21, f. 'EPU 1953'. And J. Hulley to H. Cleveland, 23 January 1953, in RG 469 ROS, b. 2, f. 'Economics: European and Commonwealth, Trade and Exchange Policies'.

22 Memo, 'Next Steps in Free-World Monetary and Trade Arrangements', 21 May 1953; memo from L. Widman to Mr Curtis, 15 December 1953: both in OIF-EUR, b. 28, EUR/3/11. A. Marget to Chairman Martin, 'FOA Memorandum on Relations between EPU and the Dollar Area', 15 January 1954; W. R. Burgess, 'Memorandum to the Director of FOA', 25 January 1954: both in OIF-EUR, b. 28, EUR/3/12.

23 Memo from L. C. Boochever to Ben T. Moore, 'Position Paper for OEEC Meeting', 840.00/4-1654, RG 59.

24 Council on Foreign Economic Policy, *Report to the President and the Congress*, op. cit., and the memo by John H. Williams (of the Randall Commission), 15 December 1953, in FRUS, 1952–4, vol. I, pp. 340–8, which articulates the economic rationale for preserving EPU. It was the argument later publicized by R. Triffin, *Europe and the Money Muddle: from Bilateralism to Near-Convertibility 1947–1956* (New Haven, 1957).

25 See the documents of the National Advisory Council on International Monetary and Financial Policies, meetings of 3 February and 8 and 15 April 1954, in NA, Record Group 56, Records of the NAC (hereafter RG 56 NAC), b. 3.

26 National Security Council Directive no. 5433, 16 September 1954, in NA, Record Group 273. See the minutes of the Discussion Group on 'Western Europe' 1954–5, in the archives of the Council on Foreign Relations, vol. LVII, and particularly the meeting of 31 January 1955, Records of Meetings, vol. XX.

27 FRUS, 1955–7, vol. IV, pp. 290, 301–3, and 304–5. See also J. E. Helmreich, 'The United States and the formation of Euratom', *Diplomatic History*, XV, 3, 1991, pp. 387–410.

28 See 'US Economic Operations in Western Europe', 20 July 1955, in RG 469 ROS, b. 47, f. 'Economic Situation in WE'; 'Summary Record of the Conference of Senior Economic Officers', Paris 19–21 September 1955, in RG 469 ROS, b. 106, f. 'SPEC'. For a detailed discussion of the evolution of FOA-ICA's approach to European 'integration' as increasingly centred on the OEEC see Boccia, 'L'amministrazione', op. cit., ch. 4.

29 Memo by A. E. Lachman, 'Discussion with Dr. Emminger, German Executive IMF Director', 1 December 1955, in RG 469 ROS, b. 93, f. 'OEEC 1955'; see also 'Summary Record of the Conference of Senior Economic Officers', op. cit.

30 FRUS, 1955–7, vol. IV, pp. 348–9 for Eisenhower's remarks. For Dulles's see ibid., p. 363.

31 FRUS, 1955–7, vol. IV, pp. 388–9 and 400. On the role attributed to Euratom see also p. 355.

32 FRUS, 1955–7, vol. IV, pp. 374–6 and the undated (but December 1955) State Department position paper, 'Considerations Regarding the Proposed European Common Market', copy in RG 469 ROS, b. 59, f. 'CSC 15-general'.
33 FRUS, 1955–7, vol. IV, pp. 450–3; also the State–ICA–Treasury instruction to Paris, 840.00/7-1856, RG 59.
34 FRUS, 1955–7, vol. IX, pp. 24–5; ibid., vol. IV, p. 469 and also pp. 460–1.
35 See P. Melandri, *Les Etats-Unis et le 'Défi' européen 1955–1958* (Paris, 1975).
36 See the memorandum from G. Humphrey to Dr G. Hauge, 24 September 1956, in NA, RG 56 Office of the Secretary of the Treasury, Records of Sec. G. Humphrey, Subject Files (hereafter RG 56 Sec. Humphrey), b. 12, f. 'White House'; and FRUS, 1955–7, vol. IX, pp. 308–10. Available sources do not reveal why the Treasury, in spite of its hostility towards regional discrimination, did not request a harsher treatment for the common market. They make clear, though, that the department entertained a mistaken scepticism on the actual willingness of the Six to proceed to a substantial integration of their economies, and thus on the possibility that a real common market would come to life (see the memo 'Inflation as an Obstacle to European Integration', 6 November 1956, in OIF-EUR, b. 27, EUR/0/42).
37 FRUS, 1955–7, vol. IV, pp. 482–6.
38 See 'Summary of US Reply to the NATO Questionnaire', 30 November 1956 and J. C. Holmes to the Secretary, 'Atlantic Community Working Group Report', 3 August 1956, in NA, RG 59, State Department lot file 66 D 487, Policy Planning Staff records, b. 75.
39 Memo from Fields to Willis, 4 January 1957, in OIF-EUR, b. 27, EUR/0/42; 'State Department Bulletin', 4 February 1957, p. 182; 'Aide-mémoire', 31 January 1957, 840.05/2-157, RG 59; see also 840.05/1-857, 840.05/1-1957 and 840.00/12-1956.
40 See tel. 3786 from Paris Embassy to the State Department, 2 February 1957, copy in OIF-EUR, b. 27, EUR/0/42; memo from H. Kleine to Fitzgerald, 27 February 1957, in RG 469 ROS, b. 61, f. 'CM'; memorandum of conversation with Eric Wyndham White, 440.002/2-2857, RG 59.
41 FRUS, 1955–7, vol. IV, p. 535 and tel. from Dulles to Brussels, 440.002/3-757, RG 59.
42 FRUS, 1955–7, vol. IV, 11 April 1957; 'The Euratom and Common Market Treaties', in *Current Economic Developments*, April 1957, pp. 11–15; memo from M. J. Fields to Mr Willis, 21 February 1957, in OIF-EUR, b. 27, EUR/0/42.
43 See for instance the circular instruction 913, 840.00/3-3158, RG 59; the international consequences of the US attitude are analysed in G. and V. Curzon, 'The Management of Trade Relations in the GATT', in A. Shonfield (ed.), *International Economic Relations of the Western World 1959–1971* (London, 1976), vol. I, pp. 228–41.
44 FRUS, 1955–7, vol. IV, p. 556 and 440.002/5-2258, RG 59; see also Archives of the Council on Foreign Relations, Discussion Group on 'Western European Integration', vol. LXXIII, meeting of 5 June 1958; American Management Association, *The European Common Market: New Frontier for American Business* (New York, 1958).

45 O. R. Cook to D. Dillon, 440.002/7-2357, RG 59; S. R. Srole to I. Frank, 840.00/7-2658, RG 59; the Department of Agriculture position in the memo 'European Agriculture, the C.M. and the F.T.A.', 440.002/8-2157 RG 59.
46 See Kaufman, *Trade and Aid*, op. cit., pp. 113–32; for the internal debate R. Strausz-Hupé (ed.), *US Foreign Policy in Western Europe*, a study for the US Senate Committee on Foreign Relations, in 611.40/9-259, RG 59; Committee for Economic Development, *The European Common Market and its Meaning to the USA* (New York, 1959).
47 On US attitude towards the FTA and its lengthy negotiations see FRUS, 1955–7, vol. IV, pp. 564–5; 440.002/2-1358 and 440.002/3-2058, RG 59. A stimulating critique of American policy towards both Common Market and Free Trade Area in Melandri, *Les Etats-Unis*, op. cit., p. 200.
48 G. Humphrey to Eisenhower, 21 December 1956 in RG 56 Sec. Humphrey, b. 10, f. 'President'; see also the minutes of NAC Meeting no. 256, 19 February 1957 in RG 56 NAC.
49 FRUS, 1955–7, vol. IX, pp. 326–8; G. Humphrey to Eisenhower, 14 May 1957, in RG 56 Sec. Humphrey, b. 10, f. 'President'; R. Burgess to D. Dillon, Paris, 21 July 1957, 440.002/7-2157, RG 59; memo, 'Meeting of D. Dillon with L. Erhard', 611.62a/3-2458, RG 59.
50 Memo, 'US International Position re Development Financing Programs', 15 November 1958, in NA, RG 56 Records of the Office of the Secretary of the Treasury, Subject Files of Secretary Robert B. Anderson (hereafter RG 56 Sec. Anderson), b. 24, f. 'Foreign Aid'; see also S. Strange, 'International Monetary Relations', in Shonfield, *International Economic Relations*, op. cit., vol. II, pp. 26–64; Kaufman, *Trade and Aid*, op. cit., pp. 152–3 and 175–9; data are from OEEC, *Foreign Trade Statistics*.
51 Memorandum for the President, 30 December 1958, in RG 56 Sec. Anderson, b. 25, f. 'IMF'; circular tel. 942, in 840.00/1-359, RG 59.
52 Colux 130 from Butterworth to the Secretary of State, 840.00/1-659, and circular tel. 826, 440.002/1-659, both in RG 59.
53 F. A. Southard to Secretary Anderson and Acting Secretary Dillon, 18 May 1959, in RG 56 Sec. Anderson, b. 25, f. 'IMF'; circular instruction 893, 840.00/1-2359, RG 59; tel. 2764 from Houghton (Paris), colux 148 from Butterworth (Luxemburg), and also tel. 1602 from Bonn, all 840.00/1-2859, RG 59.
54 Telegrams 840.00/6-1359 and 840.00/9-1459, both RG 59. Also Kaufman, *Trade and Aid*, op. cit., pp. 176–82.
55 See tel. 10.644 from D. Dillon to London Embassy, 440.002/6-259 and circular tel. 476, 440.002/10-1359, both in RG 59.
56 'Proposal for US Membership in a Reorganized OEEC', 440.002/11-2459, RG 59.
57 Memo by P. Schafferer, 'US Full Membership in OEEC', 11 December 1959, in RG 56 Sec. Anderson, b. 24, f. 'OEEC'; memo from T. G. Upton to the Secretary of the Treasury, 'Major Policy Proposals of State Dept. re OEEC', undated but December 1959, in OIF-EUR, b. 27, EUR/0/42.
58 Memorandum of conversation at the Foreign Office, 440.002/12-859; tel. 3021 from London, 440.002/12-1059; also Polto 999 from Paris, 440.002/12-359: all in RG 59.
59 Tel. from D. Dillon to the President, 840.00/12-1659, RG 59.

60 See L. B. Krause, *European Economic Integration and the United States* (Washington DC, 1968) and R. Hinshaw, *The European Community and American Trade* (New York, 1964).

7 CONCLUSIONS: THE VALUE OF HISTORY
Alan S. Milward

1 H.-J. Küsters, *Die Gründung der europäischen Wirtschaftsgeneinschaft* (Baden-Baden, 1982); A. S. Milward, *The European Rescue of the Nation-State* (London, 1992); P. Weilemann, *Die Anfänge der Europäischen Atomgemeinschaft. Zur Gründungsgeschichte von Euratom 1955–1957* (Baden-Baden, 1983): these are all monographs. E. Serra (ed.), *Il Rilancio dell'Europa e i Trattati di Roma* (Brussels, 1989) is a collective volume of essays.

2 R. T. Griffiths, 'The Common Market', in R. T. Griffiths (ed.), *The Netherlands and the Integration of Europe 1945–1957* (Amsterdam, 1990).

3 R. Bullen, 'Britain and "Europe", 1950–1957', in Serra (ed.), *Il Rilancio*, op. cit.; S. Burgess and G. Edwards, 'The Six Plus One: British Policy-Making and the Question of European Economic Integration, 1955', *International Affairs*, LXIV, 3, 1988; J. W. Young, '"The Parting of the Ways"? Britain, the Messina Conference and the Spaak Committee, June–December 1955', in M. Dockrill and J. W. Young (eds), *British Foreign Policy 1945–56* (London, 1989).

4 Several works have used the papers of steel firms and manufacturers' associations to elucidate the Treaty of Paris, notably W. Bührer, *Ruhrstahl und Europa. Die Wirtschaftsvereinigung Eisen-und Stahlindustrie und die Anfänge der europäischen Integration 1945–1952* (Munich, 1986); J. Gillingham, *Coal, Steel, and the Rebirth of Europe, 1945–1955. The Germans and French from Ruhr Conflict to Economic Community* (Cambridge, 1991); P. Mioche, 'Le patronat de la sidérurgie française et le Plan Schuman en 1950–1952: les apparences d'un combat et la réalité d'une mutation', in K. Schwabe (ed.), *Die Anfänge des Schuman-Plans 1950/1* (Brussels, 1988); R. Ranieri, 'The Italian Steel Industry and the Schuman Plan Negotiations', in ibid. Some effort, with less reward, because most records remain inaccessible, has been made to use records of farmers' organizations, notably G. Noël, *Du Pool Vert à la Politique Agricole Commune. Les tentatives de communauté agricole européenne entre 1945 et 1955* (Paris, 1988) and L. Van Molle, 'Le milieu agricole belge face à la "concurrence européenne" 1944–1958', in M. Dumoulin (ed.), *La Belgique et les débuts de la construction européenne. De la guerre aux traités de Rome* (Louvain-la-Neuve, 1987).

5 This applies both to popular historical works like R. Mayne, *The Recovery of Europe* (London, 1970) and detailed works of research such as W. Lipgens, *A History of European Integration, 1945–1947*, vol. 1, *The Formation of the European Unity Movement* (Oxford, 1982).

6 For an analysis of Schuman's ideas based on historical evidence, R. Poidevin, *Robert Schuman, Homme d'état, 1886–1963* (Paris, 1986) and *Robert Schuman* (Paris, 1988). For a similar approach to Adenauer, H.-P. Schwarz, *Adenauer. Der Aufstieg 1876–1952* (Stuttgart, 1986). For an attempt to do something similar for the others, Milward, *European Rescue*, op. cit., ch. 6.

7 Küsters, *Die Gründung*, op. cit.
8 Recorded in Serra (ed.), *Il Rilancio*, op. cit., pp. 525 ff.
9 P. Guillen, 'La France et la négociation des Traités de Rome: L'Euratom', in Serra (ed.), *Il Rilancio*, op. cit.
10 E. Devos, *Le Patronat belge face au Plan Schuman (9 mai 1950–5 février 1952)* (Brussels, 1989); Milward, *The European Rescue*, op. cit., pp. 64 ff.
11 Noël, *Du Pool Vert*, op. cit.
12 M. J. Hogan, *The Marshall Plan. America, Britain and the Reconstruction of Western Europe, 1947–1952* (Cambridge, 1987).
13 Gillingham, *Coal, Steel*, op. cit., p. 363.

Index